THE PROMISE
OF PRESCHOOL

THE PROMISE OF PRESCHOOL

From Head Start to Universal Pre-Kindergarten

ELIZABETH ROSE

OXFORD

UNIVERSITY PRESS

2010

OXFORD

UNIVERSITY PRESS

Oxford University Press, Inc., publishes works that further
Oxford University's objective of excellence
in research, scholarship, and education.

Oxford   New York

Auckland   Cape Town   Dar es Salaam   Hong Kong   Karachi
Kuala Lumpur   Madrid   Melbourne   Mexico City   Nairobi
New Delhi   Shanghai   Taipei   Toronto

With offices in

Argentina   Austria   Brazil   Chile   Czech Republic   France   Greece
Guatemala   Hungary   Italy   Japan   Poland   Portugal   Singapore
South Korea   Switzerland   Thailand   Turkey   Ukraine   Vietnam

Copyright © 2010 by Elizabeth Rose

Published by Oxford University Press, Inc.
198 Madison Avenue, New York, NY 10016

www.oup.com

Oxford is a registered trademark of Oxford University Press

Library of Congress Cataloging-in-Publication Data
Rose, Elizabeth.
The promise of preschool: from Head Start to universal
pre-kindergarten / Elizabeth Rose.
p.   cm.
Includes bibliographical references and index.
ISBN 978-0-19-539507-5
1. Education, Preschool—United States.
2. Head Start programs—United States.
3. Educational equalization—United States.   I. Title.
LB1140.23.R67 2009
372.210973—dc22   2009023179

3 5 7 9 8 6 4

Printed in the United States of America
on acid-free paper

To my parents,
Ann and David Rose

And my children,
Eli
Eva
Maya

CONTENTS

ACKNOWLEDGMENTS

This book emerged from my desire to understand how history might help to inform policy discussions about early childhood. As a historian interested in families, I have an ongoing interest in how American society has chosen to provide for children, and how that has changed over time. After writing my first book (*A Mother's Job: The History of Day Care, 1890–1960*)—on the history of child care—I had the opportunity to participate in a study of the Schools of the Twenty-first Century program at Yale University, which spurred my interest in the emerging movement to expand publicly funded preschool. I was fortunate to have the chance to delve much deeper into this topic thanks to a postdoctoral Advanced Studies Fellowship at Brown University, funded by the Spencer Foundation and the William and Flora Hewlett Foundation. I would especially like to thank Carl Kaestle at Brown for his dedication and skilled leadership of the Advanced Studies Fellowship group, and my colleagues in the program for their encouragement and constructive criticism of my early efforts. Carl Kaestle and Kathryn McDermott read the entire manuscript, and I thank them especially for their helpful comments.

I would also like to thank the Zigler Center for Child Development and Social Policy at Yale University, where participation in the ongoing Social Policy Lecture Series connected me to larger discussions about the intersection of research and policymaking on children's issues. I also appreciate the center's help with administrative matters, which helped my work on the book proceed. Thanks also go to colleagues at Trinity College and at Central Connecticut State University, who helped me find time to work on this project amid other responsibilities. I would also like to thank the people who took time out from their work on preschool to allow me to interview them, and to all those working on this issue around the country for making important information about preschool programs and advocacy widely available.

My first explorations of the many worlds of preschool were with my three children, Eli, Eva, and Maya. My belief in both the promise and the perils of our existing system comes from our experiences with nonprofit and for-profit centers in four different states, as well as home-based and family day-care providers. The dedicated staff of the Vanderbilt University Child Care Center and Susan Gray School for Children in Nashville, and of the Knight Hall School and Child Care Center in West Hartford, have inevitably shaped my personal vision of what high-quality preschool can be. Now well beyond their preschool years, my children have only occasionally asked if I was "still working on that book" or suggested I write instead about a more exciting topic. I thank them for filling my life with distractions and the joy of watching them grow up.

I would never have undertaken this project at all without Jack Dougherty's encouragement and probably never would have finished it without his multifaceted advice and support. He has read more versions of my writing on this topic than either of us would prefer to remember, and was always my best critic. His belief that I had something to contribute often buoyed my spirits. More important, his love and partnership have been at the center of my world for the past twenty years, seeing me through professional ups and downs and the sometimes challenging joys of family life.

What follows is not a set of detailed policy prescriptions or an argument for a particular approach to preschool, but rather an effort to explain how we arrived at our current set of dilemmas about preschool and what questions need to be answered in moving forward. I hope it will be of value to people engaged with preschool policy and education reform, those working in the field of early education, and parents wondering how their own preschool choices fit into a larger picture.

West Hartford, Connecticut
May 2009

THE PROMISE
OF PRESCHOOL

Introduction

Hannah and Thomas were the parents of three children in a small rural area in San Diego County, California. Though they were barely making ends meet with an income of around $35,000 a year, they earned just a little bit too much to qualify for a child care subsidy for their youngest. Hannah explained, "it seemed like every program we went to, we just couldn't get help . . . so that's why we ended up just going on our own and trying to wing it." They ended up placing their son Seth with a family day-care provider who did not take good care of him; although he was unhappy there, Hannah explained, since "we couldn't afford to pay for a day care anywhere else in the world, it was pretty much we were stuck with it." Indeed, even the relatively modest fees they paid for this day care put a strain on the family. Later, Hannah took on a second job, and found a faith-based preschool where Seth was happy. The staff at this preschool had early childhood training, and they taught him the alphabet, numbers, and reading skills. Thomas noted, "Such a big difference between one child care facility and another one. It amazed me!" But this happy arrangement came to an end when the family moved to another community in the county. Seth soon entered kindergarten, but it was only a half-day program, so he spent his afternoons at an inadequately staffed private center where he was bullied by older children. Although there was a better center nearby, Hannah lamented, they could not afford its fees: "The quality of care we would like to see him in is not in our world!"[1]

In New York City, single mother Uma relied on the Head Start center her daughter attended. With no family to help her with child care (her own parents had died before her daughter's birth), she had visited more than a dozen Head Start centers until she found one with a program that would accept her daughter at the age of two. Uma put up with problems at the Head Start center, saying, "They know you have no choice, I mean, when the program is free, what can you do? The program is not that good, but what can you do? It's like when you begging or they think you beggin,' you can't be choosy . . . you should just be happy with what you got."[2]

Traci, a Brooklyn native, struggled to find good care for her two children so she could work, rather than depending on public assistance. She felt that life in New

York City was difficult, "unless you are rich or well off, where you have a nanny or somebody who's there for you." She brought her daughter to two different family day-care homes, but was dissatisfied with each one—one "lady's home was filthy, I couldn't leave my baby there," while another provider failed to report that the child had been injured while in her care. Traci then tried to enroll her daughter in Head Start, which Traci had attended herself as a child. The Head Start center "was better-quality, more activities, more professional people, people in the classrooms who are teachers…Also it was much less expensive." But when she went to make her application, she found that she was not eligible, because her earnings as a temporary office worker and customer service representative put her above the poverty line. "I make $10 an hour, and they say I am not eligible." Instead, Traci shifted her daughter to a different private child care center that would accept her subsidy voucher.[3]

Anita Singh and her husband earned enough to cover the tuition for their son at Challenger Preschool in Sunnyvale, California—but only if they watched their household budget carefully. "We don't spend on anything except education," she said. "We don't go to the movies or eat out. We've cut our budget to the bare minimum." The tuition at the private preschool—$6,320 a year for a half-day program in 2006—was almost twice the cost of a year at a California State University campus, though it was by no means the most expensive option in the area. Challenger's growing network of twenty private schools (in California, Idaho, Nevada, and Utah) featured a curriculum that stressed reading and math skills (four-year-olds were to read one- and two-vowel booklets, count to 100 and do basic arithmetic), as well as science, logic, and art. The slogan on the company's website—"Because You Know the Value of Education"—encouraged parents like Anita to see their tuition payments as a worthwhile investment in their children's future.[4]

Jack Grubman, a wealthy New York City financial analyst, could easily afford the cost of preschool. Yet he went to extreme lengths to get his twin two-year-old daughters into the sought-after preschool at the 92nd Street Y in Manhattan. Commenting that it was easier to get into Harvard than to get into this preschool, he wrote to his boss at Citigroup, "for someone who attended public schools, I do find this process a bit strange, but there are no bounds for what you do for your children." (In fact, one journalist noted that Grubman's claim was not far off; anyone could apply to Harvard's freshman class, but the preschool only permitted applications from the first three hundred people who called for tour appointments the day after Labor Day, and these slots were invariably taken within hours by savvy parents who lined up friends and relatives to "engage in a frenzy of speed-dialing and redialing.") Agreeing to help, Grubman's boss made some calls to members of the Y's board, and later arranged a $1 million contribution from Citigroup to the Y. Grubman, in turn, concocted a stock rating for A T & T that *boosted the fortunes of his boss. While his twins enrolled in the preschool soon afterward, Grubman's actions eventually helped lead to his criminal indictment. The preschool, which charged $14,000 for tuition in 2002, denied that the contribution was a factor in their admissions process.*[5]

These stories show families struggling privately with decisions about the problems they faced in providing care and education for their young children. Clearly different economic situations shaped these parents' child care choices; while all of them may have agreed with Jack Grubman that "there are no bounds for what you do for your children," most of them faced more constraints about what they *could* do for their children.

But these stories also show how public decisions influence private ones. Whether they sought to qualify for Head Start or to get their children into an expensive private school, all of these parents were living within a framework created by policymakers' past decisions about public policy for young children. The choices these parents were making were shaped by the choices made for four decades, by presidents from Lyndon Johnson to George W. Bush, and by members of Congress, governors, state legislators, educators, children's advocates, community activists, foundation leaders, and others. As they created Head Start for poor children, encouraged the growth of a private child care and preschool market, and provided limited subsidies and minimal regulation of child care, they established our nation's approach to policy for young children.

That approach has been a *fragmented* one, helping to create a patchwork of different public and private programs to serve children of different economic backgrounds, ages, and needs. Two-thirds of American four-year-olds now attend preschool, as do more than 40 percent of three-year-olds.[6] These children's first experiences of "school" may be called pre-kindergarten, Head Start, child care, or nursery school; may be sponsored by federal or state government, school districts, private for-profit providers, nonprofit agencies, or religious organizations; and may provide very different types of early education. Some parents pay no fees to enroll their children in preschool, while others spend a significant portion of their monthly income on tuition. Publicly funded programs like Head Start are targeted to the nation's poorest families, excluding parents like Traci, Hannah, and Thomas, who earned just a little too much to qualify. While the wealthy paid to send their children to the most sought-after private preschools, such as the 92nd Street Y, those in between scrambled to find the best solutions they could, often without much assurance about the quality of care they were providing for their children.

Our policy approach has also been *market-based*, relying on individual providers, for-profit chains, and nonprofit agencies such as churches and community centers to meet the needs of families with young children. This preschool market developed as policymakers embraced a largely private approach to child care, circumventing social conflicts over mothers' employment and controversy about the proper relationship between families and government. As mothers of young children entered the labor force in record numbers in the 1960s, 1970s, and 1980s, most families were left to find their own solutions to the child-rearing dilemmas they experienced. Public funds subsidized a portion of the expenses parents incurred, but only a fraction of the poorest working families received direct child care subsidies, and government regulation of the child care market was minimal. In this market, the amount parents could pay for their children's care dictated their options. Thus Hannah and Thomas struggled to find a place that they could afford to send their young son, knowing that the better programs were "not in our world," while Anita Singh and her husband stretched their budget to cover the tuition payments for their son to attend the Challenger preschool.

The choices American policymakers have made about preschool over the past four decades mean that American families face different choices from those of their counterparts in most other industrialized countries. In France, Belgium, and Italy, almost all young children attend publicly funded preschool offered as part of the public education system.[7] In Sweden, Denmark, France, and Belgium, support for preschool is embedded within a range of public policies designed to make it easier for parents to combine paid employment and child-rearing, such as paid parental leave, child allowances, and flexible work hours. In other countries (including western European nations as well as Japan, Singapore, South Korea, Hong Kong, Taiwan, Russia, and most of Latin America), preschool is simply offered as part of public education starting at age three or four. In responding to similar social needs, the United States has followed a different path, relying on market-based rather than government solutions. This reflects American policymakers' commitment to the idea of private responsibility for families and a preference for a limited welfare state, as well as the outcomes of particular policy struggles.

Yet at the same time that it embraced the idea of private responsibility for children's care, and market solutions to social needs, the United States also stood out for its commitment to public education. Historian Miriam Cohen notes that although the United States has little tradition of government spending for social welfare, no other country outmatches it in public expenditures on education. Rather than providing "floors" of social guarantees for a minimum standard of living, she observes, Americans have been willing to open "doors" of opportunity through education. While "Americans have never agreed that citizens have the right to jobs, to health care, or to homes," they have agreed that children have a right to education. Indeed, Americans' faith in education as a pathway to both individual success and the nation's collective advancement is legendary. In the decades following World War II, support for education often took the place of other efforts to ensure equality and address social needs, and in recent decades, liberals "have strategically fallen back on the traditional faith and commitment to schooling" in order to generate public support for social needs.[8]

Programs for preschool children in the United States straddle this crucial divide between education (which is seen as a public responsibility) and care (seen as a private one). While in reality most programs for young children combine care and education, it matters greatly whether a preschool program is understood as being primarily in one category or the other. Thus Head Start, which had many different aims, initially gained broad support because it was seen as an effort to prepare disadvantaged children for school. Public funding for child care, on the other hand, remained a political "hot potato" for years because it seemed to intrude on parents' responsibility for caring for children, as well as raising the controversial question of whether mothers should be employed at all.

Today's advocates cast preschool as part of education, and are pushing to make publicly funded pre-kindergarten as universally available as first grade. In the past decade, state-funded programs have grown dramatically, and now enroll more than a million children (primarily four-year-olds) in thirty-eight states. States are now the largest source of publicly funded preschool, enrolling 22 percent of the nation's four-year-olds, although the federal Head Start program also continues to play a crucial role, serving more than 900,000 children.[9] By expanding public programs to serve all children, advocates hope to improve the quality of children's preschool experiences across the board and build political support by serving middle-class families as well as the poor. Their efforts to achieve "universal pre-kindergarten" have already met with considerable success in some states, and promise to reshape the landscape of early childhood in significant ways. But questions remain about the best ways to shape policy that will endure, fulfilling the promise of preschool.

In recent years, advocates, policymakers, and experts have changed their answers to these central questions: Who needs preschool? What is preschool's purpose? Who should provide it? What is its connection to K–12 schooling? This book explores these changes, asking how past policy decisions have brought us to the current campaign for universal pre-kindergarten and how history can inform the questions that need to be answered in order to move ahead. As a historian examining the roots of current policy debates, I have been struck by the connections between past and current efforts to provide care and education for young children, as well as by how "lessons" from the past inform advocates' efforts to shape strategy for the future.

In *Thinking In Time: The Uses of History for Decision Makers*, Richard Neustadt and Ernest May urge political leaders to learn the habit of drawing on history to frame sharper questions about the decisions they must make, and to think of their decisions as part of a stream of history, originating in the past and having consequences for the future. One tool they offer is a simple lesson from former grocery store magnate Avram Goldberg. Goldberg said, "When a manager comes to me, I don't ask him, 'What's the problem?' I say, 'Tell me the story.' That way, I find out what the problem really is."[10] By "telling the story" of how preschool policy has developed over time, I hope this book illuminates the problems and choices we face today in shaping an effective approach to preschool.

One reason those who care about preschool today need to examine the issue's history is that past decisions help to shape our current options and strategies, both guiding and constraining us. Political scientists use the concept of "path dependence" to explain how key policy decisions create a path that subsequent policymakers follow, rejecting other alternatives because structures, funding streams, and constituencies have already developed around a particular approach. Just as early adoption of a certain technology (such as the QWERTY typewriter keyboard or the standard-gauge railroad track) shapes subsequent decisions, so do certain policy decisions.[11] In the case of policy for young children, key moments such as the creation of Head Start in 1965 and the failure of federal child care legislation in 1971 created pathways for future policy. These early decisions set a course for preschool that diverged from that of public K–12 education, assigning preschool largely to private providers and community-based agencies, and legitimating public support only for the poorest children.

The first part of this book takes a chronological approach, starting when the promise of preschool for poor children first drew widespread public attention—at the creation of Head Start in 1965. Chapter 1 explores the relationship between research and politics that shaped the program, as well as the significance of Head Start's multiple goals and its identity as part of the War on Poverty. While Head Start was limited to the nation's poorest children, its popularity brought increased attention to the promise of preschool, fueling pressure to expand programs for young children in general. Chapter 2 looks at efforts to build a national system of child care serving children from all backgrounds in the 1970s. This federal legislation, backed by civil rights, labor, and women's groups, gained broad support in Congress before Richard Nixon vetoed it in 1971, appealing to a growing conservative movement that opposed government involvement in family life. Nixon's veto was a watershed moment for policy; rather than creating a public child care program open to all children, federal policy instead helped give rise to a patchwork approach to child care, dominated by the private market. This not only appealed to those who wanted to limit the role of government but also allowed policymakers to avoid conflicts about whether or not public policy should encourage mothers' employment. By the mid-1970s, a policy "path" had been established that favored private provision of child care for all but the poorest Americans; as time went on, and more families found solutions in the private market, this policy choice would come to seem natural.[12]

But path dependency does not mean that policy cannot change, especially when activists adapt their strategy to new contexts. In the 1980s and 1990s, dissatisfied with the path policy was following, children's advocates shifted course by defining the issue in terms of preschool education rather than of child care. Pointing to compelling research that showed that high-quality preschool could improve the school lives of disadvantaged children, they argued that preschool programs were an important part of K–12 school reform. As "school readiness" became part of the education reform agenda, most states created public pre-kindergarten programs for at-risk children. Foundations and national organizations embraced preschool as a solution to educational and social problems, and pushed to make it available to all children. Chapter 3 explores how the education reform movement of the 1980s drew preschool closer to the world of public education, leading to the spread of public pre-kindergarten programs, and spurring reformers to urge bringing preschool "into the education tent," as an extension of the K–12 system. At the same time, advocates also pushed child care back onto the federal agenda, prompting unprecedented political debate over children's policy and securing a new federal commitment to supporting child care for low-income families. Chapter 4 describes how publicly supported pre-kindergarten grew during the 1990s, looking in depth at four states that dramatically expanded access to preschool. Georgia, New York, and Oklahoma made their pre-kindergarten programs universal, while New Jersey courts required the state to fund preschool only in its poorest school districts. The chapter examines the different paths these states followed to universal pre-kindergarten and how those paths shaped the programs each state created.

In creating a new movement for publicly supported preschool, advocates sought to learn from history, hoping to avoid the pitfalls that troubled earlier efforts to provide for young children. They developed a vision for preschool—

available to all children, taught by well-trained teachers, funded by states, and integrated with public education—and a strategy for achieving it that were shaped by an understanding of what had gone before. Rather than continuing to push for the expansion of targeted programs like Head Start, advocates shifted to a universal strategy, believing that a program that served middle-class families would build more enduring political support over time. Chapter 5 describes how, in the past decade, advocacy groups spurred a movement for universal pre-kindergarten that has had considerable success around the country.

The last three chapters take a thematic approach, exploring the central questions that face those who want to shape preschool policy today: which children should publicly funded preschool serve, how should it be delivered, and how can quality be assured? Chapter 6 looks at state experiences with enacting universal preschool and finds that the political promise of a universal approach has often been elusive. Attempts to enact universal pre-kindergarten in California and several other states ran into opposition precisely because the idea of providing "preschool for all" seemed a questionable use of public dollars. Nor were the universal programs that states designed necessarily of higher quality than targeted programs. While some efforts to create large-scale universal programs have been disappointing, the experience of other states points to an incremental strategy of building programs for disadvantaged children, and gradually opening them up to others. Chapter 7 looks at the question of how public preschool is being organized and delivered through a combination of private providers and public schools. The chapter examines how this approach, shaped by preschool's history outside the "education tent," offers both challenges and opportunities. Chapter 8 outlines key questions that policymakers today face as they seek to ensure that the preschool system they build will be of high quality: teacher training and compensation, curriculum, and parent involvement. Finally, the conclusion draws out the historical "lessons" that have shaped the current movement for pre-kindergarten, and explores additional ways history can inform our current thinking about how to achieve the promise of preschool.

The policy decisions explored in the following pages not only shaped the dilemmas and choices that families like Hannah and Thomas, Uma, Traci, Anita Singh, and Jack Grubman faced on behalf of their children. These policy decisions also influence the solutions policymakers and advocates consider today as they try to create effective policy to support young children's growth and prepare them for success in school. As Americans continue to seek ways of crafting sound policy in this area, it is essential that we look thoughtfully at the past and carefully weigh different approaches to fulfilling the promise of preschool.

PART I

How We Got Here

CHAPTER 1

Promises and Politics

Head Start Sets the Stage in the 1960s

In March 1967, a six-year-old boy named Pancho Rivera, son of a Mexican-American tractor driver in California's San Luis Obispo County, was a guest of honor at the White House. Scrubbed, combed, and dressed in a black suit with white buttons and short black cowboy boots, Rivera stood in the glare of photographers' floodlights as President Lyndon Johnson proclaimed him "Head Start Child of the Year." Attendees at the ceremony watched a short documentary film, *Pancho*, which showed the remarkable transformation the boy had experienced after a Head Start doctor treated the thyroid condition that had gravely limited his physical and mental growth. Lady Bird Johnson welcomed Pancho Rivera as a "movie star," and congratulated the many Head Start teachers and volunteers whom she called the "producers" of the show: the Head Start program that in two years had reached almost 1½ million children. Sargent Shriver, head of the federal Office of Economic Opportunity (OEO), celebrated Head Start's achievements, and urged his listeners to help get "Pancho's message" out to the wider public so that the program could be expanded.[1] While he was in Washington, Rivera was given a special tour of the White House, visited his congressman, and was introduced to the Speaker of the House.[2]

With the creation of the Head Start program in 1965, young children from poor families like Pancho Rivera suddenly appeared on the national stage, although their lines were almost always written by others. The federal government, which in the past had demonstrated only a passing interest in programs for young children, now created Head Start programs for disadvantaged preschoolers in every state in the nation. Furthermore, government officials promised great things for these new programs. Head Start was born in a time of enormous optimism, both about the impact early intervention could have on children's development and life trajectories and about the federal government's ability to solve deep-seated problems of poverty and inequality. The preschool years suddenly seemed to be of crucial importance not only to individual children, but also to society as a whole.

While the idea of attacking poverty by helping young children from poor families was very appealing, it was not always clear exactly how it was supposed to work. Head Start sought to combat poverty, and the harm it did to children, by providing health services and nutritious meals, job opportunities for poor parents and preschool education for children, and by encouraging community organizing and parent involvement. The endeavor echoed earlier federal efforts to provide nursery schools for the poor during the 1930s, as well as the philanthropic efforts of earlier generations of reformers who had sponsored charitable kindergartens and day nurseries in order to help families rise out of poverty.[3] But Head Start's "producers" did not spend much time looking to the past to assess the results of these earlier efforts. They cobbled the program together quickly out of different approaches, relying on a relatively thin new body of research about what would make a difference for children. Head Start's multiple goals—what Lois-ellin Datta has called its "glorious goalfulness"—and its autonomous, grassroots structure produced a rich array of programs, but no clarity about which of these goals was paramount or how they could best be achieved.

By the time Pancho Rivera was ten years old, the "show" in which he had briefly starred would be subject to mixed reviews; some would suggest changing producers, or even canceling it altogether. But with a growing constituency and a ready audience, Head Start went on, staking an enduring claim for young children in national policy. With its multiple goals, decentralized structure, and focus on poor children, Head Start set the stage for federal involvement with young children for decades to come.

FROM RESEARCH TO POLITICS

Head Start was created when an activist federal government picked up ideas psychologists were exploring about the malleable nature of intelligence in young children, and launched these ideas into policy, on a much larger scale than most had thought possible. The promise of early intervention as a way to improve the lives of the poor inspired federal action, while political considerations shaped decisions about the size, structure, and goals of the program. The intellectual foundations of the program were called into question within four years of its beginning. But the political judgment that led to launching it quickly and on a large scale was dead-on: the idea struck a responsive chord in communities across the country, and quickly produced strong grassroots support for the program that would ensure its survival over the course of decades.

Head Start was inspired by dramatic changes in how psychologists thought about intelligence. The mainstream view had long been that intelligence was fixed, determined largely through heredity, but in the 1950s and early 1960s researchers started to argue that it could be modified through experience. The work of J. McVicker Hunt and Benjamin Bloom promoted the idea that intelligence was plastic and that the child's environment was a critical factor in development. "With improved understanding of early experience," Bloom wrote in 1964, "we might counteract some of the worst effects of cultural deprivation and raise substantially the average level of intellectual capacity."[4] Several researchers launched small-scale experimental projects to explore the promise of preschool for helping poor children. In Tennessee, Susan Gray found that an intensive summer preschool program for poor African-American children, followed by a series of home visits, produced a modest increase in the children's IQ and verbal abilities. In New York, Martin and Cynthia Deutsch created carefully structured preschool activities for poor children designed to develop language skills and key concepts, emphasizing labeling of common items and using puppets and other objects to teach key concepts. In Ypsilanti, Michigan, school psychologist David Weikart was frustrated with his school district's acceptance of African-American students' dismal academic achievement. He turned to the idea of creating an enriched environment for poor children, and ultimately found that the program he developed (named the Perry Preschool program after the school where it began) had a striking short-term impact on children's IQ, and long-term impact on their school achievement.[5]

This emerging research entered federal policy as a way of bolstering political support for the Johnson administration's antipoverty efforts. In 1964, Sargent Shriver, newly appointed as director of the newly created OEO, was looking for a way to spend money on children. Not only had he recently learned that half of the nation's poor were children, but also his political instincts told him that programs for children would be much more popular than other parts of the War on Poverty. Much of the money Congress had allocated for the OEO was not being spent, because city and local government leaders were wary of initiating community action projects that might result in riots, protests, and threats to their political bases. The OEO was already under attack by some members of Congress, and Shriver wanted to offer a program that would build support for the War on Poverty both in Congress and in local communities. He later recalled thinking:

> In our society there is a bias against helping adults...but there is a contrary bias in favor of helping children. Even in the black belt of the deepest South, there's always been a prejudice in favor of little black children....I hoped that we could

overcome a lot of hostility in our society against the poor in general, and specifically against black people who are poor, by aiming for the children.[6]

Preschool was increasingly being seen as an innovative response to the challenges of poverty and schooling, and was part of antipoverty discussions within both the Kennedy and Johnson administrations. In the Senate, a committee report on the 1964 antipoverty legislation specifically mentioned the importance of preschools in that they could provide "an opportunity for a head start by canceling out deficiencies associated with poverty that are instrumental in school failure." Commissioner of Education Francis Keppel starting talking about the importance of early childhood education in mid-1964; one of his advisers called the expansion of such programs "inevitable." Vice President Hubert Humphrey noted the importance of early childhood education in breaking the cycle of poverty in his 1964 book *War on Poverty*, and Johnson's Education Task Force also included recommendations for preschool education. Shriver may have worried that other federal agencies would seize the issue if OEO did not.[7]

Shriver remembered, through his earlier involvement with the Joseph P. Kennedy Jr. Foundation, visiting Susan Gray's research project in Tennessee and being "dumbfounded" at Gray's results with poor children's IQs. He also recalled, from his time serving on the Chicago school board, the barriers poor children faced in adjusting to school. He now envisioned a program that would get poor children ready for the demands of school and get them used to the school environment. He recalled his goals:

> Let's get these youngsters *ahead* of time, bring them into school and culturally prepare them for school: for the buildings and teachers, desks, pencils and chalk, discipline, food, etc. . . . We'll find out where they stand in reading, and find out if they need 'shots.' . . . We'll help IQ problems and the malnutrition problem; we'll get these kids ready for school and into the environment of a school.[8]

Believing that an antipoverty project for young children would be "smart policy, and also smart politics," Shriver started asking doctors and psychologists for their opinions.[9] In the late fall of 1964, he asked his friend and family pediatrician, Robert Cooke of Johns Hopkins University, to organize a committee of experts to plan the program. Cooke's committee shifted the program away from Shriver's idea of getting poor children used to the school environment and toward a much more holistic child development effort that was to include health care, nutrition, and family involvement. The committee decided to create a comprehensive program of health, social services, and education services directed at children, families, and communities. Head Start would be about not only what happened in the preschool classroom but also medical and dental care, nutritious meals, home visits, parent participation, and community organizing.

Thinking like scientists and not realizing the scale the administration had in mind, the committee focused on designing a workable program for field trials. Shriver rejected respected psychologist Jerome Bruner's opinion that only a small pilot program serving about 2,500 children was possible, as there were not enough trained teachers to do more. Such a small program could not begin to address the reality that there were a million children living in poverty, nor would it do much to shore up the administration's antipoverty efforts. Instead, Shriver insisted on a big program with big publicity and big numbers. Cornell University psychologist Urie Bronfenbrenner, who was a member of the committee, remembered Shriver declaring, "We're going to write Head Start across the face of this nation so that no Congress and no president can ever destroy it." In fact, before the planning committee made any recommendations, the Johnson administration had already decided to launch a preschool initiative based in the OEO's Community Action Program, serving 100,000 children.[10] Ultimately, despite the reservations they shared about such a rapid expansion of an untested program, the committee went along with this plan, recommending that 300 programs be put in place to serve 100,000 children that summer. Shriver was thrilled, as he was eager to launch a program that would bolster OEO's efforts to fight poverty while avoiding the controversy that surrounded its other efforts. Indeed, OEO needed Head Start more than Head Start needed OEO. Shriver's biographer Scott Stossel writes: "Bruised by the mounting assaults on Community Action and the Job Corps, Shriver was desperate for the OEO to have a political triumph. Head Start seemed to fit the bill."[11] Within a day of receiving the committee's report, Shriver presented it to Johnson, who shared his enthusiasm and upped the ante, saying the program should be tripled to serve 300,000 children.

The kickoff event for the program—a White House tea for 250 women, hosted by Lady Bird Johnson—signaled that Head Start would have a very different reception from some of the administration's more controversial antipoverty efforts. As word of the social event spread, senators and representatives started to call, asking for invitations; even the wives of governors who were most resistant to Johnson's civil rights initiatives were eager to attend. A *New York Times* article described the tea as including "some of the most glamorous women in America today," including actress Donna Reed (who subsequently made television spots to promote Head Start). The first lady, serving as honorary chair of Head Start, asked her guests to help recruit thousands of women volunteers to help with the new program. Coverage of the event in the society pages cast the program in a very favorable light and spurred an outpouring of such volunteers. For instance, in covering the White House tea, the *Charleston Gazette* in West Virginia emphasized the need for volunteers: "Every West Virginia woman will be given an opportunity this summer to work for a just cause."[12]

The work of many volunteers, as well as creative thinking by program administrators, made it possible to get the program off the ground only twelve weeks after it was announced—an administrative miracle that earned Head Start the nickname "Project Rush-Rush." A group of wives of cabinet members and members of Congress spent hours on the telephone finding people in the country's 300 poorest counties who would be willing to sponsor Head Start programs, and 125 interns from different federal agencies spent their weekends traveling to these communities to help them draw up applications. Other applications also came pouring in, and soon filled the bathtubs at the old hotel that served as Head Start headquarters in Washington. A colleague of Shriver's who saw the application processing line said he had not seen anything like it since his days as a Marine during World War II: the only sound was a repetitious thumping of rubber stamps as the reviewers (substitute teachers from the D.C.

Figure 1.1 Lady Bird Johnson, who served as honorary chair of Head Start, visits a Head Start classroom at the Kemper School in Washington, D.C., in March 1968. *Lyndon Baines Johnson Library, Austin, Texas*

public schools) scanned each application, checked five boxes, and sent it on for funding. The goal was not to find the highest quality proposals but to fund as many programs as possible, especially in the poorest communities.[13] Shriver was eager to spend money from his OEO budget, so as more applications for Head Start programs came in, they were approved. Shriver recalled: "It was like wildcatting for oil in your own backyard and suddenly hitting a gusher....I pumped in the money as fast as we could intelligently use it. It was really quite spectacular." Eventually the budget for that first summer mushroomed from $10 million to $70 million.[14] The program began that summer in over 3,000 communities, with 560,000 children, surpassing even President Johnson's initial target.

In the rush to launch programs, elements of Head Start that had seemed important to its planners were often set aside. One OEO staffer, Polly Greenberg, was concerned that only a few of the hundreds of proposals she was getting from communities in the South "bore close resemblance to Head Start as it had originally been conceived," with meaningful parent and community participation in running local programs and creative teaching techniques geared to young children. Nevertheless, proposals were accepted "because the President wanted thousands of Head Starts to announce in the Rose Garden on Thursday."[15] Similarly, project leaders were not daunted by the fact that the country did not have anywhere nearly enough trained nursery school educators to provide teachers for a half a million children. David Weikart remembered attending a meeting in Michigan in the spring of 1965 with more than 300 teachers and administrators who were to be involved in operating Head Start programs. "They asked how many of us worked with or had experience with preschool children. About 15 people raised their hands. A very slender reed for a national program, indeed."[16] In late March, the government contracted with 140 universities to provide six-day training programs for about 42,000 Head Start teachers (many of them elementary school teachers who were willing to staff Head Start during the summer). Some of the program's planners had worried that teachers accustomed to teaching older children in public schools would not be ideal for Head Start's more holistic and creative classrooms, but immediate staffing needs took precedence over such concerns.

Committed to getting the program off the ground quickly, Shriver and other administrators made important decisions in a somewhat haphazard fashion. Before announcing the program, Shriver needed a quick estimate of cost per student; he gave administrator Jule Sugarman an hour to provide the answer. Over lunch at the Madison Hotel, Sugarman came up with a figure of $180 per child, based on assumptions about using inexpensive teachers with little special training.[17] Martin Deutsch, whose model preschool program for poor children in New York City was one of the few operating in the country before Head Start was created, felt the expenditure should be much higher, at least $1,000 per child. He had opposed the plans for a summer Head Start program in 1965 on the grounds that there was not enough time or funding to provide a quality program. Others with experience in running preschools, like Frances Degen Horowitz at the University of Kansas, also found the government's figure inadequate. She submitted an application to establish a Head Start program in 1965, creating a budget based on her years of experience running quality preschool programs. The response from Head Start officials, Horowitz remembered, was "This is not supposed to be a quality preschool program; this is Head Start."[18]

The official launching of the program took place in the White House Rose Garden; President Johnson had been encouraged by his aides to take part, for they saw it as "a whopping big announcement and a terrific story" that would gain lots of positive media coverage, especially as it came close to Mother's Day.[19] At that ceremony, Johnson made some big promises for this fledging program:

> All this means that nearly half the preschoolers now stagnating in poverty will be given head starts on their future.... It means that thirty million man-years—the combined life spans of these youngsters—may be spent productively and rewardingly rather than wasted in tax-supported institutions or in welfare-supported lethargy.

He declared: "Five- and six-year-old children are inheritors of poverty's curse and not its creators. Unless we act, these children will pass it on to the next generation like a family birthmark."[20]

DIFFERENT PROMISES: CHILD DEVELOPMENT AND COMMUNITY ACTION

Head Start promised not only to improve poor children's school performance but also to provide health care, nutrition, parent education, and cultural enrichment; to open up opportunities for poor parents; and to spur community organizing. It was successful in its first years of operation in part because different constituencies—psychologists, pediatricians, politicians, antipoverty warriors in OEO, community activists, teachers, parents, and middle-class volunteers— all found something appealing in it. The different promises the program made brought political and material support from many quarters—but also led to confusion and conflict, as over time some goals became more important than others.

When the experts on the planning committee first recommended the program to Sargent Shriver in 1965, they listed seven general goals. These included improving poor children's physical, cognitive, and social-emotional development; strengthening the bonds between the child and the family; increasing a sense of dignity and self-worth within the child and the child's family; and developing in both child and family "a responsible attitude toward society." At the same time, the committee said the program should provide "opportunities for society to work together with the poor in solving their problems."[21] These relatively vague goals left open many possibilities for actual programs, making clear only that Head Start was to take a comprehensive approach to the challenges poor children faced, and that families were part of the equation.

It was up to antipoverty staff in the OEO to develop and administer the program, and their commitment to local autonomy and organizing the poor shaped the way they approached and structured the program. Believing that only grassroots efforts could mobilize poor people and create change, the OEO channeled federal aid directly to local community action agencies, bypassing the usual structures of state and local government. These community agencies were meant to be run with "maximum feasible participation" by the poor themselves. For the OEO, then, empowering poor parents and transforming communities was an important part of Head Start's promise. Staffers like Polly Greenberg hoped that parents, once empowered and brought together within Head Start, would also start to demand changes in the public schools, the local health care system, welfare agencies, and local government. Greenberg explained later that she saw Head Start affecting poverty not by changing individual children but by changing "the political equation," maximizing poor parents' and poor communities' involvement in the decisions that affected their lives.[22]

In order to involve parents and create opportunities for them, Head Start policy emphasized employing parents and community residents as teachers, aides, cooks, and drivers. An explanation of Head Start hiring policy in 1970 reiterated that along with quality programs, "employment opportunity and career development of economically disadvantaged persons (particularly the parents of enrolled children) are major purposes of Head Start programs."[23] Teachers did not need to have college degrees or certification; Head Start training courses, lasting from six days to eight weeks in the 1960s, taught both new and experienced teachers about the goals of the program and techniques for working with young children. In addition, staff could take college courses leading to a degree through the Supplementary Training program, a particularly welcome opportunity for poor parents with children in Head Start.

Hiring poor parents and community residents helped Head Start programs provide opportunity and link the preschool program to the community, but did not always result in having well-trained teachers. In some communities, the desire to provide jobs outweighed the desire to operate a high-quality educational program; some community action agencies dictated the choice of Head Start staff and drove away teachers with more experience in early childhood education. By 1967, early childhood educator Eveline Omwake worried that "the employment function of the project was taking precedence over the educative function," leading to a program that had better outcomes for parents than for their children.[24] Head Start planner James Hymes reflected later: "We never did face up to the disadvantaged young child's need for skilled and trained teachers; we never did face up to the need for top-flight educational leadership in what was to be a massive educational program." Operating from the mistaken assumption that "anyone can teach young kids," he argued, "Head Start was never staffed to produce consistently good educational programs."[25] Tension between the program's goals for children (promoting physical, cognitive, and socio-emotional development) and its goals for adults (creating new job opportunities, empowerment, and community action) was thus built into the way the program was implemented.

In accordance with the OEO's emphasis on grassroots change, control over Head Start resided largely outside the structures of public schools. Administrator Jule Sugarman recalled that the Head Start planning committee was "deeply skeptical about the public schools," an attitude that was "perfectly compatible with the prevailing view of OEO staff that existing educational institutions had failed."[26] Planners hoped that in the more nurturing soil of community agencies, the holistic child development and parent involvement program they envisioned would grow, and in turn inspire local schools to change. Similarly, OEO staffers feared that minority parents and staff would have no voice in a Head Start program run by white-dominated school systems, and believed that setting up a parallel structure outside the schools was the only way to compel change. (In fact, during Head Start's initial "Project Rush-Rush" startup phase, school districts played a large role, sponsoring over 80 percent of the first summer Head Start programs and providing most of the teachers. Once the main format shifted to year-long programs, however, two-thirds of the programs were shifted to community agencies, while school districts operated about one-third, often as subcontractors of those agencies.)[27]

Poor parents and their advocates often had very good reason to mistrust the local schools, and Head Start's independent structure enabled it to offer a federally sponsored alternative. In many places, there would have been no Head Start program had it been up to local school authorities. In other places, school-sponsored programs would have been less likely to focus on poor children or to provide the range of health and social services Head Start did. (This was true, for instance, of preschool programs funded by Title I of the Elementary and Secondary Education Act during this period.)[28] In Lee County, Alabama, in the early 1970s, Head Start parents requested permission from the county to use a school building that was being shut down (largely because it housed an all-black school to which white parents, unwilling to comply with school integration, were refusing to send their children). The school board not only rejected the Head Start parents' request but also announced that instead it would sell the building for a dollar to a man who was starting a segregated white academy. Only under threat of a lawsuit by the local Head Start director did the board reverse itself and allow Head Start to have the building.[29] In an era of struggle over school segregation across the country, OEO officials were proud that federal Head Start programs were required to open their programs to families of all backgrounds. In a 1966 memo (marked "for the president's night reading"), aide Bill Crook wrote: "When I left the Nacogdoches area in 1960, school officials were pledging to 'die on the door step' before they would permit the integration of the races. The President might be interested in seeing the attached pictures"—showing black and white children and teachers playing together at the Chireno, Texas, Head Start site. Crook noted, "Deep East Texas will never be the same again thanks to the Head Start Program."[30]

Indeed, Head Start's location outside the structure of the public schools gave it freedom to innovate in many of the ways its planners had hoped. Programs combined preschool education with health, social services, and parent involvement in new ways, benefited from an enormous outpouring of volunteer labor and donations, hired and trained poor parents to serve as teachers and aides, gave parents a role in governing programs, and adapted Head Start ideas to local conditions, producing a wide variety of program approaches. It is difficult to imagine any of this happening within the ordinary structures of state departments of education and local school districts in this time period. Yet the decision to separate Head Start from the public schools also had a serious risk: the lack of ongoing institutional support in a politically charged environment. Jacqueline Wexler, one of the original Head Start planners, feared the rigidity of public school bureaucracies, but she also feared that unless Head Start programs "became first-class citizens of the established school systems, they were doomed to an ephemeral success." Planner James Hymes also observed in 1979:

> I found it hard in the planning days to visualize a continuing, growing service to young children cut off from the public school....I find it hard to visualize this

today. I am afraid that Head Start did not help us find a proper and permanent place for early childhood education in our governmental array.[31]

Head Start's structure of making direct federal grants to community agencies made it possible for local communities to shape their Head Start programs as they wished, resulting in a rich diversity of approaches. Individual Head Start programs had enormous flexibility about how to shape their offerings, leaving open room for struggle over which of a program's many goals was paramount. Local programs took different approaches to helping young children prepare to enter school. Some focused on teaching pre-academic skills such as letter and number recognition; some depended on children's exploration and discovery of materials to enhance their overall development; and others followed no specific curriculum at all. June Solnit Sale described the eleven agencies running Head Start programs in Los Angeles County in 1966 as a mix of grassroots organizations, community action groups, religious organizations, school districts, and philanthropic agencies. None of them had much previous experience operating early childhood education programs, and each interpreted the program's educational goals differently. Programs offered a range of approaches, from "'warmed-over' kindergarten" to a "summer camp" approach with lots of field trips, to programs based on ideas about creative play, Montessori philosophy, or behavior modification. At one site, where a reading lesson was taught via television monitor, children spent thirty minutes repeating the words "I see Sam"; they were also taught colors, shapes, and forms by rote repetition. At another site, children were busy playing in different areas with blocks, housekeeping toys, painting, and dough; there was a lot of peer interaction and warmth shown between teachers and children. Some programs were exemplary, and a few, Sale felt, should have been closed down.[32]

Some programs saw their mission in terms of community building rather than the education of preschoolers. In answering the question "What Is Head Start?" the director of the program in a rural Indiana community wrote about linking Mexican migrant working families to the public school; giving a local girl employment in the kitchen and encouraging her to pursue more education; training a teenage mother to be a classroom aide; and educating parents about the need for preventive medicine, dental care and vaccination. This director also described Head Start as an outpouring of volunteer effort from all sectors of the community: a teacher taking care of a hospitalized child, a dentist spending his day off treating Head Start children, a group of young men creating a wonderful playground from discarded equipment, sorority members volunteering in the classroom, and civic clubs and churches providing a graduation party, a Santa Claus visit, shoes, tricycles, and a trip to the zoo or farm.[33] Indeed,

Head Start attracted thousands of volunteers, from doctors and other health care professionals to churches, youth organizations, YMCAs, and local businesses. (The award for the most unusual contribution to a Head Start program might have gone to Pacific Southwest Airlines, which in 1968 was flying fifteen Head Start children from San Diego to Los Angeles and back again every Saturday. After the twenty-minute flight, the children toured the Los Angeles airport and were given a snack while watching planes land and take off. This adventure "was arranged as one way of providing new experiences for the Head Start children.")[34] The OEO reported that 250,000 people—half of them Head Start parents—volunteered in classrooms that first summer. Recognizing the public support generated by volunteers as well as their contributions to the program, the OEO used every opportunity to recruit volunteers for Head Start, producing TV spots featuring the first lady in 1968, and a poster that read "Head Start Wants YOU," which was plastered on 68,300 U.S. mail trucks in June 1969.[35]

Just as they varied in their approaches to helping children develop, Head Start programs also took very different approaches to "parent involvement." Some saw parent empowerment and control of programs as the key to improving the conditions of poor families; others had a much more limited idea of parent involvement, consisting largely of efforts to improve parenting and housekeeping skills. At the far end of the continuum was the Child Development Group of Mississippi (CDGM), a highly effective network of Head Start programs that placed a premium on empowering poor parents. The CDGM, which received the largest Head Start grant in the country in 1965, grew directly out of the civil rights organizing of Freedom Summer in Mississippi in 1964. Polly Greenberg, who left the OEO in order to work for the CDGM in the spring of 1965, described the effort as creating "Freedom Schools at the nursery level"— programs planned, staffed, and controlled by the poor. (Asking directions to one hard-to-find rural Head Start site, Greenberg had no luck until she asked for "the school Negroes are making for themselves.")[36] Each of the eighty-four communities in the CDGM ran its own program, found its own building, hired its own staff, and decided what it wanted Head Start to be, while the central staff provided resources, ideas, and training. The CDGM staff saw their work as an integral part of the broader civil rights struggle: they strongly emphasized empowering poor communities and individuals to make their own decisions, even at the risk of creating administrative chaos and uneven programs for children. Indeed, Greenberg found great variety among the local CDGM programs, ranging from one where children spent their time "creating, pretending, playing, singing, looking, listening, and wondering" in a playground in the woods to those that stressed rote learning and etiquette, punishing children if they did

Figure 1.2 "Head Start Wants You." Office of Economic Opportunity poster. *Still Picture Division, National Archives, College Park, Maryland*

not address adults with the correct manners. Parents were involved in nearly every aspect of the CDGM programs, working to construct and repair buildings, cook meals, find classroom supplies, recruit and transport children, staff classrooms, and other tasks that in most other Head Start programs were done for pay or by outside volunteers. After visiting the CDGM, Head Start's national training director said "that now he really understood for the first time what participation of the poor really means."[37]

Not everyone was so enthusiastic about empowering poor black parents. Both whites and blacks in Mississippi recognized that the CDGM represented a new phase of the civil rights movement in the state, strengthened because it was pouring millions of federal dollars into black communities.[38] While local segregationists harassed CDGM workers and burned some Head Start sites, Senator John Stennis of Mississippi sought to cut off its funding, claiming the group was misusing Head Start funds for civil rights activities. Following several rounds of investigations, protests, and negotiations, Shriver decided in October 1966 to cut off funding to the CDGM and grant the funds instead to a group less threatening to Mississippi's power structure. This decision came right in the midst of an uncertain congressional vote on OEO appropriations, and was influenced by the fear that Stennis, who was chair of the Appropriations Committee, would eliminate funding for the OEO altogether.[39] The CDGM became a cause célèbre among northern liberals and others who saw Shriver's move as a betrayal, sacrificing Head Start and civil rights to appease a powerful segregationist. Protests came from liberal senators, the National Council of Churches, and other respected voices; Martin Luther King met with Shriver, and Hubert Humphrey offered to mediate. Shriver was crushed when a group of 160 religious, educational, labor, and civil rights leaders signed a full-page ad in the *New York Times* denouncing his capitulation to political pressure; in large, bold type, the headline read, "Say It Isn't So, Sargent Shriver."[40] Debate raged, and morale sank within OEO, where employees circulated a petition of support and crowded a large in-house meeting to protest the decision.[41] Ultimately, a reorganized, much smaller, and somewhat subdued CDGM was refunded, and it operated Head Start programs in the state alongside the other group that had been created to replace it.

Other Head Start programs also encouraged parents to become community activists. A 1970 report found examples of Head Start parents organizing to desegregate health facilities, establish a community food cooperative or a visiting nurse program, or pressure the public schools to provide tutoring, after-school programs, social workers, and a multicultural curriculum. In one (unnamed) western city, Head Start parents "allied themselves with local black activist groups to bring about specific changes they wanted in the school system.

Head Start staff and delegate agency people organized parents and encouraged them to press for changes such as hiring Negro teacher aides and providing free hot lunches for needy children."[42] In the mountains of central Pennsylvania, Head Start parents worked together to get television service for their community, and "got excited when they began to see that they could make an impact on their environment." In New York City, Head Start fathers studied together to pass the employment examination to get public jobs as apartment building custodians.[43] In Clark County, Washington, Head Start sponsored a Public Assistance Club, whose members studied public assistance laws, raised money to hire a bus, and traveled to the capitol to talk with legislators, the state public assistance director, and the state attorney general about their proposals for improving welfare and child support.[44]

At the other end of the spectrum, parent involvement was much more limited. For many Head Start programs, parent involvement meant encouraging parents to volunteer in classrooms, hiring some of them as staff, and offering "parent education" classes that focused mostly on becoming better parents and household managers. Such classes featured topics such as child development, speech, health education, purchasing nutritious food at low cost, discipline, weight reduction, home beautification, and money management. The tone of reports on these programs was sometimes condescending, as in the description of a Phoenix Head Start program called "Mothers Learn to Cook," which told how

> 300 mothers… accustomed to a traditional diet, were shown ways to prepare balanced meals from canned meat, dry milk, flour, cornmeal, split peas.…The women, whose cultural differences have made it difficult to prepare dishes using some of the staples, have been eager to learn ways to improve their families' diets.[45]

Surveys of local Head Start programs conducted in the 1960s suggest that parents found such instructional programs of limited value. In New Haven, Connecticut, only half of the Head Start parents reported attending parent education seminars, while in Los Angeles, they were rated the least helpful aspect of the program.[46]

Involving poor parents in running Head Start programs was more challenging than offering cooking classes. In 1967, OEO reported that half of the programs lacked parent involvement, in part because of the attitudes of directors, like one in Massachusetts who thought "too many cooks spoil the brew" or the head nun in a Louisiana program who called parent participation "touching but irrelevant."[47] Furthermore, empowering parents risked alienating school boards and other local officials. When OEO's initial 1966 guidelines gave parents veto power over Head Start hiring decisions and urged their involvement in budgetary decisions, some local school boards immediately protested, and fights ensued in several large cities where school boards were already facing increasing demands for "community control" of public schools. The OEO backed off, but maintained a commitment to parent empowerment and involvement in governing local Head Start programs. Head Start's 1967 manual cautioned that real parent involvement meant that staff "must learn to ask parents for their ideas" and "take care to avoid dominating meetings."[48] A staff position of parent coordinator was created to focus on encouraging and organizing parent involvement in local programs, and many programs had parent rooms to encourage both involvement in the classroom and networking among parents.

In the first four to five years of Head Start's existence, the program tried to fulfill its promises to provide education and services to poor children as well as jobs and political empowerment to poor parents. Programs varied widely in how they combined these two types of goals and in what priority they assigned to each. The "glorious goalfulness" of Head Start—produced by the planning committee, OEO staff, and others—left room for many different understandings of the program's purpose. As time went on, however, Head Start supporters would be pressed to decide which of its goals was most important.

SURVIVING THE NIXON YEARS

In the late 1960s and early 1970s, both the political context and the intellectual foundations that had supported Head Start were shaken up. Johnson's War on Poverty came to an end with the election of Richard Nixon in 1968. While the new Nixon administration was deciding what to do with Head Start, evaluation studies were released that cast doubt on the program's effectiveness at improving children's performance in school, and psychologists again debated whether early education programs could affect children's intelligence and school performance. The promises of researchers—that children's IQs, school careers, and life chances could be altered through brief preschool interventions—now came into doubt. But the political judgment that Shriver and Johnson had made in 1965 paid off. Creating Head Start on a massive scale had helped produce a broad base of political support, overriding questions about whether its intellectual foundations or founding assumptions were strong enough.

Recognizing the strong political support that Head Start enjoyed, Nixon created a new home for it within the Department of Health, Education, and

Welfare (HEW). He also placed the program in sympathetic hands, appointing Yale psychologist Edward Zigler, who had served on the original Head Start planning committee, to direct HEW's new Office of Child Development (OCD). Zigler believed he could use his scientific background to improve policy in Washington, and was encouraged by a speech Nixon had made in April 1969 affirming the nation's commitment to "providing all American children an opportunity for healthful and stimulating development during the first five years of life." Zigler was skeptical of efforts to raise IQ through Head Start and eager to defend the program for its other contributions to the development of poor children. He launched the new office with a commitment to strengthen Head Start and other children's programs and a pragmatic approach to politics. A profile in the *New York Times* described him as having "the zest and self-assurance of one who has a broad mandate."[49]

Zigler's task, however, was a complicated one. In the same speech in which Nixon announced Head Start's transfer to HEW, he referred to a "major national evaluation" that would confirm "what many have feared: the long-term effect of Head Start appears to be extremely weak."[50] This was the national evaluation of Head Start being conducted by the Westinghouse Learning Corporation and Ohio State University, which had been commissioned by the OEO two years earlier. As the first national evaluation of any of the War on Poverty programs, released at a time of political transition with significant attention from the White House, it gained much attention in Washington circles and controversy among researchers.

In order to determine whether or not Head Start had long-term effects on children's academic achievement, the Westinghouse researchers compared cognitive test scores of first-, second-, and third-grade children who had attended Head Start with those of children who had not. (The study contained no information on the characteristics of the Head Start programs the children attended, or of the public schools they went to afterward.) They found no effect for the six-week summer program, but a limited effect of the full-year program among both first- and second-grade children, with greater effects among certain subgroups such as black children in large southeastern cities. These negative findings were not surprising to those who had been following smaller evaluation reports that showed that cognitive gains in Head Start tended to "fade" (or more accurately, that non–Head Start children tended to "catch up") as children progressed through elementary school. But the conclusions the Westinghouse researchers drew were damning: "Head Start as it is presently constituted has not provided widespread cognitive and affective gains," and "its benefits cannot be described as satisfactory."[51] This, of course, was ammunition for those in the Nixon administration who were eager to criticize Johnson-era social programs.

This first large, national evaluation of Head Start aroused considerable controversy. When plans for the evaluation were first announced in 1967, experts—including Edward Zigler and Urie Bronfenbrenner—pointed out problems with the study's design, and tried to dissuade OEO officials from sponsoring it. But they stuck by their plans, arguing that there was not enough time for a more methodologically desirable study; Congress was going to be asking for data about Head Start's effects and they needed to have something to show.[52] Once the study was released, other researchers raised the same criticisms of the study's design and questioned its conclusions; several reanalyzed the data with different results. Of particular concern was the fact that the control group children came from families of higher socioeconomic status than the families of the Head Start children; researchers disagreed about whether any statistical corrections could adjust for this. Others raised questions about the sample size and whether it was representative. Stanford statistician William Madow, who had been a consultant to the study, resigned and asked to have his name stricken from the report. Sheldon White of Harvard, who also served as a consultant, defended the study, as did its authors and sponsors in OEO's Planning and Evaluation office.

Beyond these methodological issues lay broader questions about what grounds could be used to judge the program's effectiveness. Both Head Start's grassroots structure and its multiple goals made it particularly difficult to assess. There was never really one "Head Start program" that could be evaluated, but thousands of different variations, shaped by local community needs and dynamics. Researchers also had to decide which of the program's multiple goals—improving children's health, empowering parents, providing employment, promoting cognitive development—to focus on. Zigler wrote years later that the main problem

> was that we did not know what to measure. Public health researchers might have assessed the number of measles cases prevented, or the reduction in hearing or speech problems. Sociologists might have looked at the number of low-income parents who obtained jobs through Head Start. But the only people evaluating Head Start were psychologists, and, for a time, that greatly limited the focus of the research....Head Start had been designed to de-emphasize cognitive development, yet it was being evaluated primarily on the most cognitive measure of all.[53]

Indeed, one unintended consequence of the Westinghouse report was to define for the public what the primary goal of Head Start was: raising children's scores on cognitive tests. Zigler noted:

> To the public Head Start appeared to be a quick, two-month program to make poor children smart, while to the planners, and those in the program, it was but

the beginning of a long cooperative effort of teachers, health-care professionals, and parents to make children physically healthy and socially competent.[54]

Although the program's planners and administrators had seen Head Start as a "comprehensive child development program" tied to community action, these concepts were not easy to communicate. Johnson, Shriver, and others charged with "selling" Head Start had found it easier and more effective to simply talk about IQ scores, even though expecting change in IQ (a very stable measure) created unrealistic expectations. For example, during Shriver's testimony before Congress on the Equal Opportunity Act amendments of 1966, he was asked to identify the War on Poverty's greatest measurable success, and he named Head Start, pointing to initial research that had found that the summer program produced an IQ gain of ten points. This also fit in with Shriver and Johnson's initial conception of Head Start as primarily an effort to improve children's success in school. This academic emphasis made sense to OEO evaluation director Robert Levine, who wrote in 1970:

> Head Start may be a fine Community Action program, and the indicators are that it is. It may improve the health of kids. But it is *primarily* a program to improve children's learning abilities, and on this criterion it must finally stand or fall. If the program does not bring about educational improvement, then the other favorable effects may be brought in much more cheaply.[55]

Indeed, it is not surprising that public discussion of the program focused on modifying IQ. Head Start had been inspired by experimental studies that showed improvement in IQ scores and work by J. McVicker Hunt and Benjamin Bloom that suggested that manipulating the environment of young children could make them "smarter." Furthermore, IQ and achievement measures were available and their validity widely accepted, while nothing comparable existed for assessing children's social and emotional growth. Promoting children's success in school was the most popular of Head Start's objectives, and the Westinghouse evaluation seemed to prove that it was not being met.

The Westinghouse study was one of a string of evaluations that cast doubt on the effectiveness of educational interventions for changing poor children's school performance. The Coleman Report, published by HEW in 1966, had already called into question the utility of separate compensatory programs. Evaluations of the Title I program of aid to schools serving disadvantaged children also found little effect. Around the same time the Westinghouse study was released, the *Harvard Education Review* published an article by psychologist Arthur Jensen on the nature of intelligence that opened by saying "Compensatory education has been tried and it apparently has failed," and went on to argue for a genetically deterministic explanation of IQ and achievement. Taken together, these reports had a strong cumulative effect. Lois-ellin Datta characterizes this period as a long "winter of disillusion and some despair about education and the Great Society in general" among researchers. As one put it, "sooner or later since Head Start was oversold, the balloon would have had to deflate. But the Westinghouse Report was like a pinprick to the balloon. It exploded."[56]

While these negative evaluations had a large impact on researchers, they seem to have made only a small dent in Head Start's political support. Head Start's appeal to legislators and its broad base of political support would continue to be at least as important as any research findings. Almost no mention was made of the Westinghouse study in the *Congressional Record* when it was released, or the following year. Researcher Jeanne Ellsworth noted that the study was not covered by the national newsmagazines at all and was dismissed by some in congressional hearings, where increasing amounts of time were given over to testimonials from parents or graduates.[57] For instance, during hearings on a bill he introduced shortly after the Westinghouse report was released, Senator Walter Mondale commented:

> One of the things that always strikes me about Westinghouse type studies is that their results so often conflict with the judgment of people experienced in the program. I have rarely talked to educators or Headstart teachers or parents of children in Headstart who weren't delighted. They think it is working, they think it is helpful.... Wherever you go you get the same reaction except from reports like Westinghouse.[58]

Nor did the Westinghouse report lead Nixon to cancel Head Start. Calculating that the political costs of eliminating the popular program were too high, his administration continued it with level funding. The report helped bolster the decision to move Head Start out of the OEO and to shift funding from summer programs to full-year programs, which was politically difficult because it meant cutting the size of the program by about half. The report also provided a reason to hold back from expanding the program. In his notes from a meeting with Nixon in May 1969, domestic adviser John Erlichman noted that it "may be too late to abolish" Head Start, which was supported by powerful members of Congress, but that no increases should be considered.[59] Since Head Start was only serving about 10 percent of the children who were eligible, this was a serious problem. Jude Wanniski wrote in his newspaper column: "educators and social scientists who had envisioned Head Start doubling in size and ultimately solving all the preschool deficiencies of the poor will now have to wait until

HEW finds a formula that it believes will work."[60] Head Start would remain an "experimental" program, albeit a very large one.

Even keeping funding level was not assured when Zigler took his post in 1970. The influential Office of Management and Budget proposed cutting Head Start's budget that year and developed a plan to phase it out in three years. A staff member in HEW secretary Elliot Richardson's office recalled a "great deal of talk about Head Start being dead, cut out of the budget, over."[61] The president himself seemed uninterested, refusing to engage in discussion of the pledge he had made to address the needs of children during the "first five years of life." Zigler and Richardson were frequently confronted with demonstrations by Head Start parents worried about funding cuts. Richardson did fight for the program, but its long-term future did not seem very secure. Zigler believed that in this period, "we were at best in a holding pattern." He undertook a "whistle-stop tour" to publicize Head Start, stressing that the Westinghouse report was flawed, and that the program should not be expected to perform miracles, especially with IQ scores. Instead of trying to expand, "I tried to dazzle people with all types of new demonstration projects.... I wanted Congress and the public to associate both Head Start and OCD with such a blur of useful activity that the administration would not dare close them down."[62] Zigler introduced new formats for delivering Head Start services, such as Home Start, Health Start, and the Child and Family Resource Program, both to put a Nixon stamp on a Johnson-era program and to provide more flexibility in the program.

Improving the program's quality and administration was also a high priority. Head Start had been designed to circumvent state and local government in favor of grassroots community agencies, but it had never really implemented an alternative system of managing and supporting local programs. Thus, Zigler later recalled, at the end of almost five years of operation, "Head Start administrators really had no accurate data as to how many children were served, or even what services were *actually* provided at what cost or benefit to those reported as enrolled."[63] To answer the need for a system of accountability and management control, Zigler's office worked to develop performance standards and procedures for assessment, monitoring programs, and offering technical assistance.

Zigler also moved to protect Head Start by eliminating anything that raised hackles in Congress, notably the emphasis on community action. Coming on the heels of the negative conclusions drawn from the Westinghouse report about the program's effectiveness, "any notion in Congress that Head Start money was being spent on inappropriate forms of activism was simply a perception the program could not afford." Of course, Zigler's own ideas about the program—based on his expertise as a psychologist and his experience in planning Head Start—also shaped his commitment to stress services to children rather than community action for adults. He worked to develop a stronger policy on parent involvement, giving parents a significant role in setting policy for Head Start programs, while also limiting involvement in broader efforts for community change. Activists who wanted to make Head Start a catalyst for community organizing objected to this move. At a meeting with a group of local community action leaders who were upset by his decision to prohibit the use of parent involvement funds for "disruptive tactics" such as sit-ins, Zigler recounts, one man became frustrated and said

> "Dr. Zigler, you don't understand. We are interested in systemic change. We are willing to give up a whole generation of our children in order to get it." I stood up at the other end of the table, and said that he might be willing to give up a genera- tion of children, but that I was not, and that was not my mission in OCD.[64]

Zigler's leadership through the early 1970s made this a period of consolidat- ing and institutionalizing the program, making improvements in program quality and administration that would help it weather a period of uncertainty. With its intellectual underpinnings questioned and its political support in the Nixon administration shaky, it seemed wise to focus the program in ways that would help it survive. Through most of the 1970s, Head Start remained an embattled and inadequately funded program. The promise Lyndon Johnson made at the end of Head Start's first summer—that soon all poor children would be getting two years of Head Start—remained very far from realization.

PRESCHOOL FOR THE POOR OR PRESCHOOL FOR ALL?

Head Start drew national attention to the promise of preschool for poor chil- dren, and in so doing raised questions about whether early education might benefit all children. The program was restricted to serving the poorest of the poor, those who fell below the federal poverty line and most clearly needed a "head start" in order to succeed in school and life. Yet as other parents read about the benefits of preschool education, they began to ask why this new gov- ernment program was available only to the poor. Some—including public school educators and the creators of *Sesame Street*—even proposed that pre- school should be extended to everyone.

Neither kindergarten nor preschool were available to all children in the 1960s. At the time of Head Start's creation, kindergarten had been a part of many public school systems for fifty years or more. Yet in 1965, only about half of the nation's five-year-old children attended kindergarten; eighteen states offered no funding for it, and only a handful of states mandated that school districts offer it. In the southern states, the kindergarten attendance rate in 1965 was only 10 percent. Nor was nursery school widespread; private nursery schools only enrolled about 10 percent of the nation's three- and four-year-olds.[65]

Given that so many children did not have access to preschool or kindergarten, some resented the fact that Head Start was restricted to the very poor. In a 1966 article in OEO's *Head Start Newsletter*, staffer Jack Gonzales wrote of "the outrage vented on OEO for enforcement of its income guidelines." Protests came from "articulate, lower middle class parents, backed by educators who thought they were 'poor.'" Although local Head Start administrators often wanted to admit children whose families were above the income cutoff, Gonzales declared: "the poorest must be served first." Yet it was not always easy to find the "hard-core poor" or to convince them to send their children to the program. To find "the right kids," Gonzalez wrote, a door-to-door campaign was necessary. He recommended using "neighborhood knowledge" of where the truly poor children were, drawing on social workers, policemen, clergymen, mailmen, local grocers, and real estate collection agencies. In one Cincinnati school, thirty vacancies were filled after a parent aide "scoured back alleys and made home visits to parents she knew had eligible children."[66]

In 1970, Edward Zigler proposed opening up Head Start to children from nonpoor families, arguing that segregation by economic status was no better than by race. He believed that many children whose families were just above the federal poverty line needed Head Start as much as those who fell just beneath it, and he was also concerned about political "backlash" from middle-class families whose children were excluded from the program. Furthermore, there was evidence that poor children would benefit from being in a classroom with children from other socioeconomic backgrounds. But Zigler's proposal did not catch on. The *New York Times* editorialized that his plan to open up Head Start to nonpoor children was "akin to demanding the same medical treatment for the healthy that is provided for the sick."[67] In this view, it was only poor children, suffering from various disadvantages, who needed the "treatment" of early education.

The spotlight Head Start focused on young children's learning, however, led to an increase in other early childhood programs. Public school kindergarten grew dramatically, especially in the southern states: between 1965 and 1980, kindergarten attendance in these states leaped from 10 percent to 89 percent. (Federal aid through Title I of the Elementary and Secondary Education Act helped spur this change, as many school districts used this money to offer kindergarten to disadvantaged children, before states started providing kindergarten funding.)[68] From 1965 to 1970, nearly a quarter of the states began funding kindergarten, and forty-four laws relating to kindergarten were passed, compared with only five laws in the first half of the decade. Laurel and Daniel Tanner argue that "kindergarten became a part of the public schools in these states because middle-class people, the taxpayers, wanted for their own children the advantages they were providing for the children of the poor" through Head Start.[69] Enrollment in private nursery school programs also increased dramatically in the late 1960s. A 1972 study of day care in southern California noted that publicity about Head Start "has been good for business in the proprietary sector. Increasingly, families seem to feel that nursery school is an advantage which they must provide." A 1966 *Newsweek* article noted that preschool enrollment was at an all-time high; while wealthy families were eager to get their children into the preschools linked to exclusive private schools, middle-class parents were inspired by Head Start to enroll their children in nursery schools. The chief of day care for the New York City Department of Health explained: "The middle-class parents read about Head Start, and figure 'if it's good for children from the other side of the tracks, it must be good for my children too.'" Following this trend, the article continued, "Many educators feel it is only a matter of time—and a considerable amount of money—before every 3-, 4-, and 5-year-old can toddle off to preschool."[70]

Indeed, at the same time Head Start was being launched, some public school educators were calling for preschool education to be made available to all children. In 1966, the National Education Association and the American Association of School Administrators called for public schools to serve four-year-olds as part

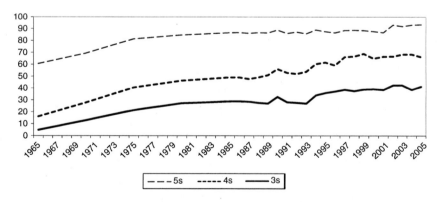

Figure 1.3 Kindergarten and Preschool Education Participation by Age: 1965–2005
Source: Reprinted with permission from the National Institute for Early Education Research, Rutgers University, New Brunswick, NJ. Data are from the October Current Population Survey, 1965–2005, and reflect parents' reports of children who are "enrolled in school."

of universal public education. Citing research about the early development of children's intellectual capacity, they asserted that all children, not just the "disadvantaged," could be helped by early education.[71] At its national meeting in 1966, the American Association of School Administrators adopted without debate a resolution calling for "free public prekindergarten and kindergarten of the best quality" to be made available to every child.[72] Similarly, in 1967, the New York Board of Regents announced a plan for extending free public education to all three- and four-year-olds whose parents wished it. This bold proposal was based on New York's year-old Experimental Pre-kindergarten program for disadvantaged children, which operated in the schools with certified teachers. The Regents cast preschool as the next logical step in the growth of public education: "In the two decades since World War II, American education has had tremendous expansion at the secondary and higher levels. We now realize formal education must be extended in the other direction as well, so that children may have the advantage of carefully planned schooling at earlier ages."[73] The Regents' plan was built on the assumption that all children could benefit from early education—and that taxpaying parents would support it if their children were included. Gordon Ambach, who helped write the Regents' statement in 1967, recalls:

> It was a very strong belief...that we should be striving for a genuinely universal opportunity. For two reasons: one of them is that it was an important enough level of education to make that public commitment, but secondly...it's very, very unlikely that you can generate a service which you provide universally for low-income families and children unless you can get political support from middle-level families, income families, and upper-level income families that they can have the same opportunity.

Setting income restrictions on such a program, he believed, would make it politically a "nonstarter."[74] The proposal laid out a three-phase plan, extending the program first to all four-year-olds as part of the state aid formula and then to all three-year-olds, with accompanying funding for facilities and for teacher training programs. However, the Regents' interest in providing preschool for all was quickly swallowed up by more urgent policy priorities in New York state, so this proposal was not acted on.

A more successful effort to provide early education for all children was the television show *Sesame Street*, which had its origins in the same concern about poor children and early education that gave rise to Head Start. With the encouragement of Lloyd Morrisett at the Carnegie Corporation, producer Joan Ganz Cooney proposed in 1967 to test television's usefulness in teaching young children, and combat what she considered the "educational wasteland" of preschool education.[75] *Sesame Street* was based on the idea that all young children would benefit from a high-quality program of early learning, and sought to attract as large a viewing audience as possible. But it was particularly intended to benefit poor, inner-city children. Its setting on a city street and its diverse cast were designed to appeal to urban children. Knowing that low-income parents were eager to have their children learn skills in reading, writing, and arithmetic influenced the show's designers to emphasize letters and numbers, even though the idea of using television to teach children to recite the alphabet produced "howls of repugnance" from some learning experts.[76]

Publicity efforts for *Sesame Street* also targeted poor, inner-city audiences. Failing to get inner-city children to watch the show was "perhaps... our greatest fear as *Sesame Street* was designed," adviser Gerry Lesser writes. Given public television's poor track record of attracting large inner-city audiences, the local stations could not be relied on to drum up interest in the show. Children's Television Workshop staff thus worked directly to encourage children to watch, sponsoring viewing groups in day-care and neighborhood centers and in homes, visiting homes in selected areas and telephoning regularly to encourage parents to view the show, and using newsletters and community newspapers, local merchants, parades and street fairs, sound trucks, library story corners, poster contests, and giveaways.[77] This extensive outreach seems to have paid off: the early shows drew a remarkably large audience of about half of the potential viewers in the country, including high percentages (from 78 to 91 percent) in selected city neighborhoods.[78] Audiences remained loyal and continued to grow through the early 1970s as the reach of public broadcasting increased.

Sesame Street's debut brought extremely favorable press coverage, applauding its originality and imagination; over time the show won numerous awards (including more Emmy awards than any other series in the history of television).[79] *Sesame Street* succeeded in using the techniques of commercial television—rapid pacing, repetition, music, humor, and short segments with appealing characters and celebrities—to attract children. Furthermore, evaluations of the show's impact by researchers from the Educational Testing Service said that children did in fact learn from watching. They found that the children who watched *Sesame Street* the most learned the most; this held true across lines of age, sex, geography, income, and IQ. A second-year study also found that teachers independently rated their students who were regular *Sesame Street* watchers higher in readiness for school, attitudes toward school, and relationships with their peers.[80] These findings were reported in the national press in uniformly glowing terms; for instance, *Time* reported: "Sesame Street has earned straight As."[81] Press coverage noted especially the researchers' initial conclusion that *Sesame Street* might be a way to reduce the educational gap

Figure 1.4 New York City children in a preschool day camp watch the new television program *Sesame Street* as part of an experiment to prepare them for public school, 1970. *Bettmann/ CORBIS*

between poor and affluent children.[82] This claim, however, raised questions about *Sesame Street*'s overall goal. Was it to teach all children or to reduce the gap between advantaged and disadvantaged children? Joan Ganz Cooney's original proposal had suggested it could do both. But given that the show was available to all children, it could not expect to reduce this gap, unless disadvantaged children either watched more or learned much more from watching than advantaged children.

Sesame Street's success also raised troubling questions about the cost-effectiveness of Head Start. Although the show's designers never suggested that it should be a substitute for actual preschool programs, policymakers were quick to notice that *Sesame Street* was an inexpensive way to promote preschool education. About half of the money used to establish the Children's Television Workshop came from federal sources, especially from the Office of Education, where commissioner Harold Howe was an enthusiastic proponent of using television to reach more preschoolers. Head Start had contributed some funds for the show's development, but Ed Zigler had to resist pressure to shift even more funds. At one HEW meeting, proponents argued, "'We can get *Sesame Street* to reach poor kids by spending sixty-five cents per child....Why should we spend over a thousand dollars per child on Head Start?'" Zigler responded, "How long would a poor child have to watch 'Sesame Street' to get his or her teeth filled?"[83]

The broader question of whether preschool education was for all children or only for the particularly "needy" went beyond *Sesame Street.* Compensatory programs like Head Start were based on the idea that poor children needed extra services before they started school in order to "catch up" with middle-class children once school started. But middle-class families were not standing still while poor children sought to catch up to them. They were inspired by Head Start and by media coverage about the importance of early learning in general to seek more preschool opportunities for their children. This led educator Robert Fischer to suggest, in a tongue-in-cheek essay, that what was needed was not Project Head Start for the poor, but rather "Project Slow Down" for the overachieving middle class. If infusing the suburban water supply with tranquilizers was not practical, he wrote, perhaps a system of "Slow Down nursery schools," where children were encouraged to play and to reject the achievement-oriented values of their parents, would have the desired effect.[84]

To those who advocated providing preschool to all children, it was not an "extra" needed only by the most disadvantaged but a fundamental part of every child's education. Differences on this question were strategic as well as philosophical: was more support for early childhood education to be gained from focusing on the particular needs of poor children or by widening the base, making early education available to all children? By drawing attention to the promise of preschool, and by showing that fulfilling this promise was a complicated endeavor, Head Start had opened up important questions about how the country would go about defining and meeting children's needs.

CONCLUSION

Head Start put poor children like Pancho Rivera on the national stage. The "producers" of the show (as Lady Bird Johnson called all those who worked to make Head Start a reality), however, sometimes had differing ideas about its purpose. Was it to provide medical care and nutritious food? To raise children's IQs? To improve their self-esteem and attitudes about learning? To organize poor communities and provide jobs? To empower parents to press for broader social change? To help gain support for the War on Poverty? Head Start gained broad support both because the idea of helping poor children succeed in school was widely appealing and because these different goals brought together different constituencies—academic researchers, community activists, public school teachers and administrators, poor parents, OEO staffers, and early childhood educators—who had somewhat different ideas about its purpose.

Head Start was also popular because it seemed to offer a simple, inexpensive and appealing solution to the problem of poverty in America. As Edward Zigler, Jeanette Valentine, and Deborah Stipek wrote in 1979, many of the key assumptions on which Head Start was based—that preschool intervention could eliminate poverty by preparing poor children for school, that education itself was a solution to poverty, that poor children were intellectually inadequate, and that the third and fourth years of life represented a "critical period" for intervention—had all been called into question: "We now understand that Head Start can have positive effects but cannot be an antidote to poverty."[85] Researcher Susan Gray observed in 1982 that Head Start was not only oversold but also eagerly bought by those concerned about educational discrimination: "How splendid it would be if one could take care of the pervasive problems of poverty, as experienced by young children, by something so simple as a relatively limited preschool program."[86]

Head Start was inspired both by the promise of early intervention and by the politics of Lyndon Johnson's War on Poverty. It was shaped by the OEO, with its creative, energetic, and often haphazard style, its determination to do things quickly and on a grand scale, its commitment to mobilizing the poor and circumventing state and local government. Head Start also went beyond OEO, securing the loyalty of academic experts, parents, educators, and volunteers across the country. This support helped Head Start secure a place in federal policy, and in national consciousness, that outlasted both the ideas and the politics that had given rise to it. Young children's place onstage was not secure in 1970, but in the years ahead it would be tenaciously protected by advocates, congressional allies, and Head Start parents themselves. Head Start's very popularity spurred the spread of preschool education far beyond the ranks of the poor, widening the audience and raising more questions about how to fulfill the promises that had been made for preschool.

CHAPTER 2

Creating a Patchwork Approach to Child Care
in the 1970s

As Head Start's future was being debated, members of Congress were also looking at early childhood programs from a different angle: the growing need for
child care among a wide range of families. As more mothers entered the paid
workforce, and as the women's movement mobilized, members of Congress
proposed building a nationwide system of universally available child care services. This represented an abrupt departure from previous government policy
on child care. In the past, child care had been understood as a custodial service
needed by poor, often dysfunctional, families where mothers had no choice but
to go out to work. It had been supported largely by local philanthropy, with
federal dollars only coming when the government had needed women workers
during wartime. Now Congress proposed funding child care centers to promote the development of children from families across the socioeconomic
spectrum, recasting child care as a universal entitlement akin to public
education.

Because of its universal approach, the Child Development Act of 1971 had a
broad appeal that at first "made it seem like a political sure bet," as political
scientist Kimberly Morgan writes.[1] Backed by members of both parties in
Congress and by a well-organized coalition of interest groups, the child care bill
also appeared to have support within the Nixon administration, which needed
a child care system to support its welfare reform plans. But as the bill moved
through Congress in 1971, proponents battled over who would control child
care programs, and conservative opposition to the idea of government-funded
child care centers mounted. Ultimately, despite its passage by both the House
and Senate, President Nixon vetoed the bill, slamming shut the window of
opportunity for creating a unified public system for child care and early
education.

The consequences of this bill's failure would be far-reaching, making it
politically difficult to act on the issue for years to come. As the demand for child
care grew through the 1970s, therefore, it was met largely through the private

market. Child care continued to be seen as a responsibility of individual families, not of society as a whole. While policymakers did not completely ignore the issue after 1971, they developed policies stratified along lines of social class rather than creating a single system. The result was a rather threadbare "patchwork" of child care programs, stitched together from scattered pieces.

A UNIVERSAL APPROACH TO CHILD CARE

While child care was not a new issue in 1971, approaching it as a universal entitlement was a bold, innovative idea. Since the late nineteenth century, charitable day nurseries had offered day care to poor working mothers in many urban areas and factory towns, but their backers had never imagined that their services would be widely needed. Day nursery leaders remained deeply ambivalent about mothers' wage work, and were often anxious to ensure that day care be seen as a last resort for poor families. This definition of day care as a charity that offered custodial care to poor children had lasting impact. Supporters of day nurseries were conflicted about the social value of the service they provided, and legislators opted to provide "welfare" in the form of pensions for mothers to care for their own children rather than providing day care for working mothers. The association between day care and charity was so strong that during World War II, even when the federal government temporarily funded child care centers in order to attract women workers to defense plants, some women were reluctant to enroll their children. One commented: "Child care centers are all right for charity cases, but my children belong at home." Even at the exemplary child care centers at the Kaiser shipyards in Portland, Oregon, women were leery until they became convinced that "it was not a 'charity thing.'"[2]

Attitudes toward day care began to change in the decades after World War II, as more women combined paid work with mothering, and as more families of all social classes came to believe that day-care programs could be beneficial for their children. Protesting the cutoff of federal funding for child care centers after the war's end, some mothers argued for day care as an ongoing public service, akin to public education. In most communities these campaigns were not successful, and publicly funded child care dried up not long after the war's end, as working mothers were generally unable to convince legislators that child care should be provided as a widespread public service. (California, where public "Children's Centers" continued after the war and became permanent in 1957, was an important exception.)[3] In 1954, Congress addressed child care in a different way, approving the first measure to make child care expenses tax deductible. The measure was limited: eligibility for the tax deduction was restricted to low-income couples and single parents, and the amount that could be deducted was capped at a low level. But the precedent of subsidizing private child care arrangements through the tax code rather than providing public services would have lasting influence.

Private child care arrangements—in for-profit centers, nonprofit centers, or private homes—were becoming more widespread, as the number of working mothers with young children grew dramatically, from 1.2 million in 1948 to 3.1 million in 1965. By the early 1970s, it was estimated that about two-thirds of available child care centers were proprietary, and the rest were sponsored by churches and other nonprofit agencies. A majority of centers served three- and four-year-olds only, and often chose names like "preschool" or "nursery school," appealing to mothers looking for educationally oriented care. Proprietors created new organizations to advance their interests; in California, the Pre-School Association lobbied for favorable legislation and played a watchdog role with its members, seeking to "maintain the image of private schools." In debates over the state's funding of public centers, private center directors claimed paying customers for themselves, arguing that families who could afford a fee should not be served by the public centers.[4]

Day care gradually moved onto the national agenda during the 1960s. New York City activist Elinor Guggenheimer had formed a new organization devoted to expanding and improving day care in 1958, and worked with federal agencies and members of Congress to organize a national conference on day care in 1960. The federal Children's Bureau and Women's Bureau sponsored several studies of child care arrangements, which revealed a significant increase in the proportion of mothers who were working and emphasized the inadequacy of existing day-care provision. President Kennedy's Commission on the Status of Women called for day care aimed at families of all economic levels in its 1963 report on removing barriers to women's participation in the workforce, and several state commissions on women echoed this call. But gaining public support for government-funded day care was not easy. Because the issues it raised about motherhood were volatile, day care remained a "poor cousin" in public policy, an issue that no one fully embraced or took responsibility for. Indeed, proponents of day care themselves still expressed ambivalence about whether or not mothers should work outside the home, and were hesitant to call for significant federal funding.[5]

The threat of expanding welfare costs in the 1960s forced policymakers to consider day care as a money-saving measure that would help move women out of welfare offices and into the workforce. Abraham Ribicoff, President John

F. Kennedy's secretary of HEW, saw day care in these terms as support for welfare reform. In 1962, he worked to incorporate funding for day care into amendments to the Social Security Act, which guaranteed federal matching funds for state services to welfare recipients. One California official referred to this funding as "a pot of gold," and welfare and education administrators in other states also took advantage of it.[6] As welfare rolls continued to rise, Congress amended the Social Security Act again in 1967, creating the Work Incentive Program (WIN), which gave states the option of requiring mothers of young children to get jobs or training, as long as child care was provided. This was a reversal of fifty years of state and federal welfare policy that had focused on keeping poor mothers at home with their children. WIN did not prove to be a winner, as most states did not set up the necessary training and child care programs, but the link between compulsory use of child care and welfare reform was firmly established.[7]

By 1969, when both houses of Congress started to debate bills on day care, the potential for building a cross-class constituency for day-care services seemed strong. A June 1969 Gallup poll indicated that 64 percent of Americans favored providing federal funds for day care "in most communities," and Congress was eager to pass legislation attractive to newly mobilized women voters.[8] Indeed, in the first eight months of the Ninety-second Congress,

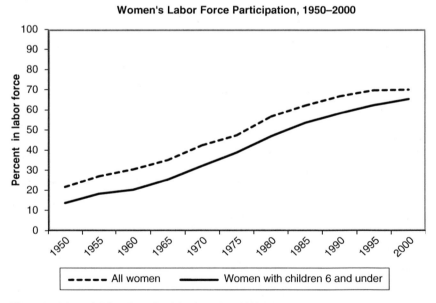

Figure 2.1 Women's Labor Force Participation, 1950–2000
Source: U.S. House of Representatives, *Green Book: 108th Congress* (Washington, D.C.: 2004), 9–3.

legislators introduced ten different child care bills, as part of a "bumper crop of women's rights legislation."[9] The labor force participation rates of women with children under six had nearly tripled since 1950. The nation had nowhere nearly enough organized child care to meet the demand; many communities had no child care programs at all, and those that existed were often too expensive for most families. As a result, only 1 percent of all children with working mothers were in organized child care, while the others were cared for by relatives, by neighbors, or in other arrangements.[10] Working mothers were coming increasingly from middle- and lower-middle-income families, representing a broader cross-section of American society. Union women had built support within the labor movement for the idea of government-funded child care, and could offer significant political support. New women's organizations—the National Organization for Women as well as grassroots women's liberation groups—identified child care as a feminist issue. Even the Nixon White House was interested in child care, as part of its broader welfare reform initiative. Supporting children's programs brought Nixon strong bipartisan support, and reassured some of his liberal critics that he was not planning to dismantle completely the Great Society.

Believing that there would be significant opportunities to expand and improve child care, OCD director Edward Zigler convened a conference on day care in 1970 that attracted 1,000 participants. Attendees believed that a major federal initiative in child care was in the cards, and wanted to help shape it. The main goal was to establish principles of quality care for children of different ages that would guide revision of federal child care regulations. Zigler worked to find a middle path between those who wanted high standards of care and those who sought a more inexpensive approach, and he created a set of standards to govern the federal programs he expected to administer.[11] Expecting a major expansion in staffing needs for both child care and Head Start programs, he also helped to create the Child Development Associate (CDA) credential to provide paraprofessionals with basic training in child development.

The 1970 White House Conference on Children provided another source of support for the idea of a federal program for young children. When the 4,000 conference delegates were asked to choose the most important children's policy issues from a list of hundreds of proposals, the very top vote-getter was establishing "comprehensive family-oriented child development programs including health services, day care and early childhood education." Indeed, the need for quality day care had been one of the common themes to emerge from the chaos of the conference. Sessions dealing with day care attracted overflow crowds, who heard "horror stories" of terrible conditions in day-care centers.

The delegates called for federal funding to increase substantially every year "until it reaches all families who seek it and all children who need it."[12]

For supporters of Head Start, this growing momentum for child care seemed like an ideal opportunity to protect the vulnerable program by linking it to the broader demand for publicly supported child care. Marian Wright Edelman, a veteran of civil rights organizing in Mississippi and advocate for poor children, explained later her conviction that "Headstart's survival depended on broadening the base of its constituency. This meant identifying the need for child care services in the larger population." Although her main concern was for poor children, she thought that addressing the needs of all children was the best approach. She recalled: "The 1971 bill tried to address the entitlement of *all* children and sought not to make child care a class issue. We don't need any more singling out of poor kids."[13] She led the Ad Hoc Coalition for Child Development, a broad alliance of more than twenty labor, civil rights, education, welfare, and women's organizations, in pushing for a child care initiative that would continue Head Start's emphasis on parental and community involvement but go beyond its focus on the poorest children. Indeed, the Coalition urged Congress to create a system of

Figure 2.2 (From right to left): Edward Zigler, director of the Office of Child Development, White House aide Stephen Hess, and President Richard Nixon, holding the report of the 1970 White House Conference on Children and Youth, which called for federal funding for child development and child care programs. *Courtesy of Edward Zigler*

publicly funded child care centers that would ultimately be available to all families.

Making child care universal was especially appealing to labor groups within the Coalition. Observers noted that the support of organized labor gave the Coalition its real strength. (Members of Congress would remember the link between labor and child care, for the Coalition's primary lobbyist was also a lobbyist for the influential United Auto Workers.[14]) Labor union women had been "among the most forceful and persistent proponents of child care programs" since the end of World War II, when they fought to maintain child care funding. During the 1950s and 1960s, they pushed their unions to take up the issue, both by influencing public policy and by establishing union child care centers. Unions representing the female-dominated garment industry (the International Ladies' Garment Workers Union and the Amalgamated Clothing Workers of America) were especially active on the child care issue, bringing with them the endorsement and political muscle of the AFL-CIO. The Amalgamated Clothing Workers had sponsored child care centers in five states, and staff members hoped, they said, that "our program will be the forerunner of heavy government involvement in day care." [15] Union leaders were eager to ensure that federally funded child care be open to working women, whose incomes typically put their families above the poverty line; these leaders therefore argued strongly for making such programs universal. Advocates like former AFL-CIO lobbyist and Women's Bureau director Esther Peterson called for public support for child care for all mothers, in order to erase child care's charitable stigma and ease working women's domestic burdens.[16]

Feminist organizations also wanted programs open to all. The National Organization for Women's 1967 Bill of Rights called for free, twenty-four-hour child care, established "on the same basis as parks, libraries, and public schools...as a community resource to be used by citizens from all income levels." Local feminist organizations also saw child care as a key concern, setting up their own cooperative day-care centers across the country; a coalition in New York secured city funding for these parent-run centers, and a group in Cambridge, Massachusetts, succeeded in passing a voters' referendum for twenty-four-hour, community-controlled child care in 1971.[17] New York state education officials noted:

> Day Care, once synonymous with poverty and welfare programs, is receiving much interest and a new status from middle-class professional parents who have been made aware of the importance of early learning and from Women's Liberation enthusiasts who are seeking personal freedom from household chores and satisfactions from personal pursuits.[18]

Absorbed with other issues, the National Organization for Women was not a central player in the child development coalition, and its leaders never testified in hearings on the legislation. But congresswomen Bella Abzug and Shirley Chisholm, both closely associated with the women's movement, not only testified on behalf of the bill but also introduced their own more generously funded version of the legislation. Abzug (who had donated space in her campaign headquarters in New York City to house a small day-care center) argued during her testimony that the federal legislation should be seen as a "women's bill" as well as a children's bill. Her version sought to meet more women's needs by allowing child care programs for those who worked at night, and by including a mechanism to expand coverage to greater numbers of women over time.[19] To be sure, some advocates for poor children, like Marian Edelman, were somewhat contemptuous of the claims of "middle-class liberationists who thought they should have access to day care if they wanted time to go to an art gallery."[20] But universality was a way of linking demands for child care from across the

Figure 2.3 Marian Wright Edelman played a key role in pushing for federal child care legislation in 1971, and, as head of the Children's Defense Fund, continued to lobby for child care and Head Start funding. She is pictured here at a press conference in Washington, 1983. *AP/Wide World Photos, photographer Dennis Cook*

socioeconomic spectrum to support for Head Start and other programs designed to serve the poorest children.

SHAPING LEGISLATION IN CONGRESS

Edelman's Coalition found strong allies in both houses of Congress who championed broad federal child care legislation. The Coalition worked with Minnesota Democratic senator Walter Mondale, who had become increasingly involved with the problems of the disadvantaged following the 1968 election. Expanding federal programs for child development, especially for poor children, fit Mondale's commitment to provide opportunity to those on the margins of American society. Speaking to a Senate subcommittee in 1970, he described his sense of profound frustration that such a "powerful and wealthy society" could "so tragically fail thousands and millions of our children."[21] Mondale's 1971 child development bill gave priority to poor children, but also included those from families above the poverty level, and provided a framework for eventually making the program available to all who wanted it. Indeed, the bill's preamble stated that "comprehensive child development programs should be available as a matter of right to all children," although priority should go to those with greatest economic and social need. Building on the experience of Head Start, Mondale's bill placed a high priority on parent and community participation.[22] In the House, Indiana Democratic congressman John Brademas viewed the issue primarily in the context of education, and shared Mondale's universal approach. Child care seemed to be a natural component of education policy; following Congress's enactment of the Elementary and Secondary Education Act and the Higher Education Act, turning to child care seemed the next logical step.[23] Recognizing the importance of securing bipartisan support, Brademas had lined up fifty Democratic and fifty Republican cosponsors. Moderate Republicans including Albert Quie of Minnesota, John Dellenback of Oregon, and Orval Hansen of Idaho were influential supporters of the child care legislation.

In the versions advanced by Mondale and Brademas, the 1971 child development legislation offered substantial federal funding ($2.5 billion) for universally accessible child care services, free to poor parents and with fees set on a sliding scale for others. Child care was presented as a right for all children regardless of income, though a majority of the funds were reserved for poor children. Programs were to be "comprehensive" like Head Start, offering health, nutrition, and social services as well as care and education. The legislation also provided funding for constructing new facilities and training staff, consolidated different federal programs under its umbrella, and established federal standards and monitoring. Political scientist Kimberly Morgan describes the child care legislation as "a child of the 1960s": its scope and ambition, as well as the strong role it envisioned for the federal government, reflect that era's confidence in government's ability to address social problems, and the era's willingness to invest significant public funds in order to do so. The way the legislation linked child care, child development, and community empowerment reflected the influence of the Head Start and community action programs of the War on Poverty.

Head Start's high visibility clearly helped draw attention to the issue of early childhood development. Brademas noted during the 1969 hearings: "If we hadn't had Project Head Start, I dare say we wouldn't be having these hearings this morning, and nobody would give a tinker's damn about preschool programs anyway."[24] Just as Head Start supporters felt they would benefit from allying themselves with the broader constituency for child care, child care supporters recognized that they benefited from an association with Head Start. Hawaii congresswoman Patsy Mink, who cosponsored the bill, explained during hearings in 1970:

> I took courage from the success of the Headstart program for what it meant for these youngsters who came from disadvantaged families; and more or less leaning on their success, felt that we could establish a program for working mothers who do not fall into the poverty level. These mothers deserve the concern of the Nation as well.

Later in the hearings, Brademas added: "Middle-class America has seen the advantages of Headstart to poor children. They want these opportunities for their children."[25]

Despite the precedent of Head Start, the idea of a "child development program" was relatively new and somewhat vague when this legislation was being debated. Supporters struggled to find the right term to convey what they were trying to provide: high-quality programs that offered comprehensive services, met child care needs, and were educational, not just custodial. Brademas's original 1969 version was a mouthful—the "Comprehensive Preschool Education and Child Day Care Act"—that tried to cover all bases. Testifying before Brademas's subcommittee in 1969, Milton Akers of the National Association for the Education of Young Children said he was "alarmed about perpetuating the term 'day care,'" "which evoked images of programs with no educational value. He suggested the term "childhood development" as a more meaningful one. Nancy Rambusch, the founder of American Montessori Society, commented: "The image evoked by day care is one of broken and disrupted families, inept mothers and imperiled children," an image that was no longer tenable. "Today's young mothers refuse to see themselves as the inert clay upon which a social worker's itchy fingers will make an impress." A new program needed a new name, perhaps something like "educare," in order to overcome this association. Later in the hearings, Brademas asked for comments about what to call the bill, feeling that both "day care" and "preschool" were too narrow. Psychologist Jerome Bruner suggested "aid to early growth," but the subcommittee eventually settled on "Comprehensive Child Development Act."[26]

The bills introduced by Brademas and Mondale proceeded fairly smoothly through both houses of Congress in 1971. A *Washington Post* editorial noted that Congress sometimes takes a "whole generation of pressure, debate and publicity" to come up with major social legislation, while other times "the wheels of change turn quickly and almost silently." Despite the absence of publicity, the *Post* argued, the child development bill could be "as important a breakthrough for the young as Medicare was for the old."[27] A *New York Times* article also noted that the legislation could have major implications; Walter Mondale commented: "This is social legislation in a class with Medicare, yet it is happening without any initiatives from the executive branch and without much public notice."[28]

Indeed, the idea of a strong federal role in early childhood programs was not controversial as these bills were going through Congress. Even owners of child care centers and employers who had developed centers for their workers favored public funding, recognizing that the private sector could not meet the existing needs on its own. For instance, Edward Breathitt (former governor of Kentucky) and his colleagues, who had developed the for-profit American Child Centers, Inc., testified in favor of the bill. Congressman Edward Koch spoke of his own efforts to encourage large companies in New York City to sponsor on-site day care for employees, and urged Congress to move quickly to fund preschool programs on a broader basis. William English of the pioneering computer firm Control Data Corporation testified that the federal government needed to subsidize child care costs if it expected private industry to provide jobs for the unemployed, while Kate LaFayette, director of a child care center sponsored by the audio company KLH in Cambridge, Massachusetts, suggested that government should split the costs of child care equally with employers and parents.[29]

The bill's central purpose—building a system of federally funded child care that would ultimately be available to all children—received a mostly favorable response. Legislators and others pointed to the large need for child care and education programs among working families, from those just above the poverty line to the middle class. Some saw the bill as a promising means of addressing the needs of working mothers across the socioeconomic spectrum. They also noted the potential value to the poorest children of being in mixed socioeconomic groups, pointing to the findings of the Coleman Report that testified to the value of such mixing in public school classrooms.[30] Congresswoman Shirley Chisholm spoke most explicitly about the political advantages of making the program universal. "Not only are increased services for women needed," she testified in 1969, "they are politically expedient." Later she warned:

> If we limit day care only to those at the lower end of the economic scale this bill is going to be labeled a poverty or welfare bill and will be a much more difficult task to secure the appropriations which are necessary. You will recall that this Congress was able to override a Presidential veto of education appropriations. This was because everybody had a stake in those education programs. Day care legislation has a similar constituency. Every woman, almost without exceptions, will support universal day care.[31]

Some did question whether federal funding should be used to serve non-poor children. The strongest words on this issue came from Harry Hallsted, speaking for an association representing directors of proprietary and nonprofit private school day care centers in Maryland. He contended that the need was not for a blanket, universal program but rather for special help for low-income parents and those with handicapped children. He warned that under this bill, one of the country's wealthiest counties could set up a comprehensive program of universal, free child care that would be open to thousands of upper-income-bracket families.[32]

The cost of a broad-based, universal program was significant. Cost estimates given during hearings ranged from around $1,000 to $3,000 per child per year. The OCD had estimated that it would cost about $2,000 to provide "adequate" care and $2,350 to provide "high-quality" care. The $2 billion Mondale sought as an initial appropriation would not go far in offering programs to all children; Zigler testified that it would take $1.5 billion just to include all the three- to five-year-old children eligible for Head Start (which had a stricter eligibility cutoff than the Senate bill). Marian Wright Edelman wrote in her statement of support for the House bill:

> No one expects that we will meet the full costs of universally available child development programs today. But that should not deter us from making a real start. A $2 billion authorization would be a realistic beginning, and we should be prepared to go beyond that to reach a level of at least $10 billion as rapidly as possible.[33]

Everyone knew that the amount of money that would actually be appropriated would be much less than what the legislation authorized, but assumed that funding would grow over time.

CONFUSION IN THE NIXON ADMINISTRATION

But would the Nixon administration support a child care bill championed by leading Democrats in Congress? Prolonged uncertainty within HEW and the administration left room for the bill's congressional sponsors to take the initiative, but left many questions about where the administration stood on the issue. Gilbert Steiner writes: "[HEW secretary Elliot] Richardson and his department simply pulled themselves together too late to face the child development legislative drive effectively," not even staking out a detailed position until the hearings process was almost at an end.[34]

The reason for the administration's uncertainty had to do with the difficulties facing Nixon's welfare reform plan. Facing a welfare system strained to the breaking point, the Nixon administration had made a surprising proposal. Rather than provide more services along the lines of the War on Poverty, Nixon's Family Assistance Plan (FAP) would put more money directly in the hands of the poor. The plan, developed by adviser Daniel Patrick Moynihan, would put a "floor" under the incomes of families with children, guaranteeing every family below the cutoff line $500 per adult and $300 per child, plus food stamps and other benefits. (This cash benefit represented about 40 percent of the income of a family of four living at the federal poverty line.) This plan would expand government welfare spending, including two-parent families and a much larger number of white and working-class families than did existing welfare programs. Indeed, much of Nixon's interest in the plan lay in its potential appeal to lower-income whites, especially in the South. Incentives would reward work, rather than targeting the unemployed for assistance; indeed, "workfare" provisions would require adult recipients to work or forfeit their subsidies.[35]

The FAP was a bold but politically risky idea. While its core idea of a guaranteed income, or a negative income tax, had widespread support among economists and government planners by the late 1960s, it was difficult to explain, much less sell, to Congress and the public. While liberals suspected it was really intended to cut welfare payments, conservatives feared it would bankrupt the treasury, and were aghast at the idea of expanding the welfare rolls in this way. In fact, the FAP's most dramatic effect would have been to bring welfare payments in southern states up to a minimum level; it did relatively little for the welfare poor in the North (where 80 percent of welfare clients resided) or for northern governors, who were clamoring for federal action to reduce their share of burgeoning welfare costs. The National Welfare Rights Organization, which represented mostly welfare recipients in northern cities, fought hard against the FAP, objecting to its work requirement and insisting that its floor was completely inadequate. This opposition dampened support for the plan among many liberal members of Congress, as well as in the older civil rights and poverty organizations, and gave conservative Democrats plenty of cover for voting against it as well.[36] The FAP passed the House in April 1970, but floundered in the Senate, and was ultimately rejected. The measure passed the House again in June 1971, but the White House did little to advance it. Nixon's biographer Stephen Ambrose writes that although the FAP represented Nixon's "bid for greatness" in domestic policy, he was also concerned about the costs of the plan, which most of his advisers had always opposed. After his dramatic introduction of the FAP, Ambrose writes, "He had what he wanted out of FAP, a great PR triumph. He wasn't all that sure he wanted it passed, anyway."[37]

Both of these bold social policy proposals—the FAP and the Comprehensive Child Development Act—were initiated in 1969 with the goal of benefiting working-class as well as poor families, and both expanded the role of the federal government in significant ways. While the child care bill was an expansion of the "service strategy" of the Great Society, the FAP was a Republican alternative, an "income strategy," reflecting the idea that the best solution to poverty was to give people more money. But the two approaches shared a common ground, because the FAP also set aside funding for day care to encourage poor mothers to work. Mothers of preschool children were initially exempted from the FAP's work requirement, but the version of FAP that was still on the table in 1971 would have extended the work requirement to mothers of preschoolers, making child care a necessity.[38] The bill was quite vague about the nature of the child care that would be funded, although Nixon had explained to Congress that he wanted care that was "more than custodial...of a quality that will help in the development of the child."[39] (In an internal memo outlining guidelines for the program, Nixon indicated a different reason for providing day care: "children should not just sit around the house since this leads to their becoming non-workers.")[40]

Given the slim odds of the FAP's passage in 1971, the administration at first opposed the Mondale-Brademas child development bill. Child care under FAP was one thing, but the child development bill "represents the beginning of a general public...program of early childhood," which the administration was not ready to endorse.[41] Nevertheless, debate about the bill continued within the Nixon administration. Elliot Richardson, the secretary of HEW, argued for it, while the Office of Management and Budget's Richard Nathan opposed it, fearing that a separate child care bill would undermine the FAP's chances of passage. The Office of Management and Budget would not clear any bill on the subject, preventing HEW from developing alternative legislative proposals. In fact, Zigler recalls that differences within the administration caused Richardson to cancel his scheduled testimony on the child development bill three different times. Richardson went back and forth between the White House and Capitol Hill, trying to break the deadlock (he had to meet Brademas, who was on Nixon's "enemy list," in hotels away from their offices). By June 1971, Richardson appeared to have won the debate within the administration. In letters to Mondale and Brademas, cleared by the White House, Richardson affirmed the administration's general support for the legislation. The targets, he wrote, should be children in low-income working families and economically disadvantaged children, regardless of their parents' work status. Richardson's letter seemed to give a green light to the legislation, even as the FAP's fortunes remained unclear. Ed Zigler and Stephen Kurzman were sent to deliver friendly testimony before the Senate subcommittee on the bill, with some stipulations about what the administration could accept.[42]

STRUGGLES FOR CONTROL

At this point, the most divisive issue in the child development bill was not *whether* to implement it but *how*. Legislators and advocates disagreed sharply over who should plan and control child care programs. Liberals wanted to encourage community control, while more centrist legislators feared this would lead to chaos, and wanted states (and some large cities) to administer the programs. Marian Wright Edelman's experiences with the struggle for control over Head Start in Mississippi led her to insist on community control. Other members of her Coalition also felt strongly that federally funded child development programs should be administered by nonprofit organizations, ensuring maximum community participation. One recalled: "We were coming out of the 60s, we were all people with civil rights backgrounds, we were people that didn't trust the states...so we were trying to develop a system of getting around them...like the community action programs of the anti-poverty program."[43] Allowing states to administer these programs meant tolerating racial discrimination and depending on bureaucracies where residents of poor communities had little influence. In a statement Edelman made on the House bill in 1971, she presented her position eloquently:

> The heart of this bill is the delivery system....Those of us who have worked with the poor, the uneducated, the hungry, the disenfranchised have had long and bitter experience in how legislative intent is thwarted in the process of implementation; the way money is spent often is more significant than the fact that it is spent. We who are concerned about civil rights and equal opportunity must and will oppose any effort to place principal authority for child development in the hands of the states.[44]

On the other hand, governors opposed the idea of bypassing their authority and limiting their ability to coordinate and consolidate overlapping programs. Testifying in the House in May 1971, current and former governors all pointed to problems with community control of Head Start and other antipoverty programs, and warned against instituting a similar structure for child care programs. Only the states, they argued, had the capacity to manage such a program.[45]

This seemingly technical matter—what entity or unit of government would be eligible to administer programs?—became the bill's major stumbling block. The Mondale bill, which passed the Senate by a vote of forty-nine to twelve in early September 1971, would have allowed any unit of government to sponsor child development programs, reflecting advocates' desire to have these programs controlled by local communities and non-profit agencies. In the House, the Brademas bill originally allowed only states and the nation's largest cities to administer the programs. Due in part to lobbying by members of the Coalition, these provisions were dramatically changed on the floor of the House. Kentucky Democrat and Education and Labor Committee chair Carl Perkins, worried about rural districts like his being deprived of control over federal dollars, pushed through an amendment that allowed much smaller units of local government to administer programs. Minnesota Republican congressman Albert Quie, a cosponsor of the Brademas bill, explained that the original idea was to treat a handful of really large cities on the same level with states. In a compromise with those who wanted to make any unit of government eligible, the bill's sponsors agreed to include other cities as well. To expand it further as Perkins wished, Quie argued, would mean that HEW could be dealing with over 2,000 "prime sponsors" administering child care programs, creating an unmanageable system. Other Republican moderates also warned that a bill that created such a system would lose their support.[46] But the House bill as passed expanded the number of government entities that could sponsor child development programs. When the conference committee reconciled it with the Senate version, that number was expanded even further. Recognizing that this might raise opposition from the White House, liberal New York Republican senator Jacob Javits pleaded: "With so great a reform in prospect, to allow this thing to break up on so narrow a difference would be highly regrettable."[47]

As Javits feared, reducing the requirement for prime sponsorship was a recipe for alienating other congressional Republicans and the White House. Several of the bill's original Republican sponsors defected, fearing that with so many small units of government eligible, legislators would be fighting for towns in their districts all the time. Quie called it "an administrative monstrosity that has no parallel in government" and warned: "All the problems we saw with the inception of the Economic Opportunity Act through OEO are going to be visited upon this program and the way it operates." Other moderate Republicans in the House also turned against the bill. While only sixty-eight House Republicans had opposed the original bill, 135 voted against the conference version, and New York congressman Ogden Reid was the only Republican to sign the final conference report. Although the bill still passed the House, the bipartisanship on which it had been built had collapsed.[48] In the Senate, on the other hand, the balance did not shift much; the conference report passed by sixty-three to seventeen, with support from key Republican leaders.

Another factor influencing legislators was growing opposition to the bill from the conservative right. There had been little indication of this kind of opposition when the bills were first being debated. Indeed, during hearings before Brademas's committee, a representative of the Amalgamated Clothing Workers of America said he was surprised that the committee had spent so much time hearing about the need for day-care facilities, "because this seems to be a little like motherhood. You really can't be against the provision of day-care centers, and it is almost surprising there would be different points of view."[49] New York senator James Buckley of the Conservative Party was one of the few voices raised against the principle of the bill, which he saw as an unwarranted government intrusion into family life. Speaking in the Senate, Buckley said, "It is a program which would revolutionize the concept of child rearing in the United States…a program whose long-term and explicit objective is to extend these federally designed and therefore, federally controlled programs to encompass all American children, regardless of family income." He was particularly appalled by the idea of putting Congress on record as saying that all children have a "right" to such programs, and raised fears of children suing their parents or the government if they were denied access. "Let there be no mistake about it: The enactment of the child development sections of this bill may prove to be one of the most deeply radical steps ever taken by Congress."[50]

The broad and somewhat vague goals of the Child Development Act gave conservatives like Buckley plenty to worry about. Several of the expert psychologists who testified before congressional committees put forth a vision of limitless intervention in the lives of families. When asked to identify the optimal age at which a child might benefit from intervention programs, Urie Bronfenbrenner's answer was two years *before* conception, while others agreed that infancy was the proper time.[51] Wanting to encourage localities to offer a wide range of services for children—from preschool classrooms to home visiting programs, psychological and medical services, parenting education, and nighttime child care—the bill included what Buckley thought was "surely the most exhaustive list of social services ever assembled in a single paragraph of a Senate report."[52] In the House, a few voices similarly warned about "collectivized child rearing" and government interference in family life. Congressman John Rarick, a conservative Democrat from Louisiana, had more dire warnings, saying that the bill heralded "the Orwellian nightmare of 1984" and went beyond even attempts by Hitler or "the most outlandish of the Communist plans" to promote government control of youth.[53]

At first, these were isolated voices of ideological opposition. But in the weeks that followed, conservatives mobilized against the bill on a scale that surprised everyone. Feeling betrayed by Nixon's domestic policy agenda as well as by his planned visit to Communist China, conservatives wanted to put pressure on him. The journal *Human Events* signaled its attack in September 1971 with an article headlined "Big Brother Wants Your Children." After the House passed the bill, the journal urged readers to demand a presidential veto of the "Child Control Law."[54] James Kilpatrick's column, entitled "Child Development Act—To Sovietize Our Youth" was printed in several newspapers, spreading the word that the bill contained "the seeds for destruction of Middle America; and if Richard Nixon signs it, he will have forfeited his last frail claim on Middle America's support."[55]

More significant, however, were efforts to mobilize opposition at the grassroots level. Activist Paul Weyrich (who later established the Heritage Foundation) was surprised to discover a network of parents' groups across the country concerned about the bill's implications. Through talk shows, newsletters, and coverage in different publications, he recalled, "we began to get the word out" to such people to encourage them to campaign against the legislation. The result was an outpouring of letters asking Nixon to veto the bill and asking Congress to uphold the veto. Weyrich wrote that supporters of the bill "were astounded by the level of intensity demonstrated by the people involved and by the sheer numbers who had responded at such short notice—as were we all, for we were not even aware of the existence of these numerous operations." Congressional aide Edwin Feulner wrote later that conservative activists in Washington learned an important lesson from this experience about the power of making alliances with grassroots lobbying groups.[56] By mid-November, congressman John Rarick had received letters from women's clubs, local Republican activists, religious groups, and others raising fears about government-controlled child care.

Outright criticism of mothers working outside the home was quite rare; most of the opposition was framed in terms of imposition of government power on the family. For instance, the Parents of New York United warned:

> The Social Planners are steamrolling ahead to implement what they feel will be the ideal society.... This bill provides federal funds for "experts" to determine the "needs" of all children on a nationwide basis.... S-2007 is the start in the program to federalize America's children.

Iowans for Moral Education asked: "Whose Children? Yours or the State's?" Many raised particular alarm about a small pilot program for "child advocates," whom they feared would challenge parental authority over children. One congressman described receiving mail calling the bill "The Federal Child Control Act" or referring to the "drafting of our children at the age of 1 year."[57]

By the time Congress was ready to vote on the conference version of the bill, such opposition had put its supporters on the defensive, while giving conservatives a common language with which to criticize it. Nebraska senator Carl Curtis noted:

> Senatorial and congressional, Presidential, and Cabinet offices have been deluged with mail from private citizens who are alarmed at what they have heard about plans to minimize their role in raising their children. Their sincerity and their frantic concern are very obvious to anyone who has read some of their letters.

South Carolina Republican senator Strom Thurmond framed the issue as whether parents or the federal government would have the right to shape the young.[58] In the Senate, Hubert Humphrey of Minnesota noted: "many of my colleagues have been bombarded with mail from extremist groups in this country who are trying to stir opposition through scare tactics which have no basis in fact." In December, introducing the conference report in the House, John Brademas carefully listed the national groups who had expressed support for the measure, putting religious groups first. Carl Perkins also took pains to point out that the bill extended no governmental control over children, parents, or the family, as the programs were completely voluntary.[59]

NIXON'S DECISION

The fate of the bill now rested in the White House, and it was not clear how the president would act. While Elliot Richardson and other HEW officials had given friendly testimony on the bill, others within the administration opposed its cost and scope. The FAP was still languishing in the Senate and seemed unlikely to pass. Right-wing opposition to the bill did not stop Congress, but it did create a different context for Nixon's response. Speaking in the Senate in early December, Senator Javits referred to "deep speculation as to the administration's position on the legislation."

Supporters of the bill believed they had a winning issue with a broad constituency, so they did not worry about losing Republican votes in Congress. Zigler recalled that when he worried about the bill's fate, child care advocates said, "Oh, Ed, you don't understand politics. Nixon will never veto this bill in an election year."[60] Similarly, Alice Rivlin wrote in the *Washington Post*, "it would surely be politically costly for the President, who has put such personal stress on the dignity of work, to veto a bill which promises to make work possible for millions of women and better the lives of children into the bargain."[61] Kevin Phillips, Nixon's political strategist in the 1968 campaign, wrote: "politically, President Nixon should be leaping for this issue," as it was a way to build support among young working mothers, "a huge slice of the electorate." Indeed, a broad-based program would mesh with Nixon's strategy of appealing to "working poor" and blue-collar voters, who were often disaffected Democrats in battleground northeastern states. But within the administration, opposition increased as the bill, identified with liberal Democrats, took on the flavor of a community action program and lost the support of moderate and liberal Republicans.[62] Responding to protests from the conservative grassroots, White House aides Charles Colson, Patrick Buchanan, and H. R. Haldeman urged a veto, arguing that Nixon needed to prevent anyone getting to the right of him on this issue.

Nixon agreed and decided to veto the bill. But how would he explain his opposition to the child care legislation? The bill was vulnerable to criticism on many grounds, and if the veto message focused on the administrative problems relating to prime sponsorship, those could be fixed in another bill. Instead, Nixon decided to use the veto to appease the right wing of his party, who felt betrayed by his overtures to China and by domestic policies such as the FAP. Colson advised that a veto message that came down hard against child care as a matter of principle "may be precisely what we need to buy ourselves maneuvering room with the right wing."[63] Similarly, Patrick Buchanan counseled: "Since we are certain to get our lumps from the opposition even with a milquetoast veto, we ought to reap the rewards of an unequivocal one…this is one measure where we *can* get some mileage with the Conservatives."[64] In a veto message that incorporated much of Buchanan's proposed language, Nixon objected to the bill's "fiscal irresponsibility, administrative unworkability, and family weakening implications," as well as its bypassing of state government. In an often-quoted final sentence, he refused to "commit the vast moral authority of the national Government to the side of communal approaches to child rearing over against the family centered approach." (Richardson later said he "went to the mat" to delete this last phrase, but Nixon insisted on retaining it.)[65]

These ideological objections took supporters of the bill by surprise, as no one from the administration had previously voiced them. Wisconsin Democratic senator Gaylord Nelson said a few months later: "Not once during these discussions was there a philosophical attack made on the fundamental proposition of the child development program, so we didn't know we were going to be sandbagged by somebody and neither did the Secretary."[66] There was no sign that the president really believed the federal government should not be involved in child care, although he was critical of the broad scope of this legislation. Indeed, he continued to support day care for children of women receiving welfare, and he made of point of announcing his support for increasing income tax deductions for day care. As a *Washington Post* editorial noted, it was hard to distinguish the day care the president supported from the supposedly radical plan he said he was vetoing. Several other supporters of the legislation noted the irony of the president's sudden distaste for voluntary, community-controlled day care as undermining the family, when his FAP would have forced poor mothers to work and leave their children in day-care centers.[67] Apparently day care was only "family weakening" for families who were not on public assistance.

Nixon's veto energized the growing conservative movement. Not only did he veto the bill in a way that drove "a stake through its heart," so that similar child care legislation would not resurface in the future (in the words of American Conservative Union lobbyist Jeff Bell) but also the campaign against it had shown conservatives how what would soon be known as "family values" issues could mobilize grassroots activists. Paul Weyrich observed later that the lessons learned in this struggle about the power of mobilizing conservative grassroots sentiment informed the New Right's strategy for focusing on issues like abortion in the years that followed.[68]

A POISONED WELL AND A SPLINTERED COALITION

Nixon's sweeping veto message so effectively tainted the concept of universal child care that subsequent efforts to introduce similar legislation gained little support. The Senate voted in December 1971 to override the veto but fell short of the two-thirds majority required. In the years that followed, Walter Mondale and John Brademas continued trying to pass major child care legislation, but they were never able to recapture the momentum the issue had originally enjoyed. A bill with streamlined procedures for sponsoring programs easily passed the Senate in 1972, but its counterpart languished in the House. The following year, Mondale held hearings on "The American Family," trying to establish the idea that day care was a way to support, not undermine, families. In 1974, he and Brademas introduced the Child and Family Services Act, a somewhat more modest version of the earlier legislation. In 1975, they held hearings across the country on an identical set of bills.[69]

At this point, opposition from the far right became especially virulent. Writing in the John Birch Society's journal, Alan Stang warned that the bill would "change Uncle Sam into Big Mama," giving the government total power over child-rearing. "The totalitarians want control of *all* American children as soon as they can talk—before their mothers have a chance to tell them about God, patriotism, privacy, and profit."[70] The article juxtaposed photographs of Mondale and Brademas with images of Hitler Youth rallies and Chinese youth denouncing their parents during the Cultural Revolution, and raised fears of government-sponsored drug experimentation on toddlers as well as a Chinese-style reproductive policy. An anonymous flyer about the bill that was entitled "Raising Children—Government's or Parents Rights?" spread like wildfire in 1975 and 1976 and did even more damage. This flyer did not address the question of day care specifically or point to any actual provisions of the Child and Family Services Act. Instead, it focused on fears that the legislation would give the government power over child-rearing by sponsoring "child advocates" who would help children sue their parents for disciplining them, making them go to Sunday school, or even take out the garbage. Purporting to cite the *Congressional Record*, the flyer used comments made in 1971 about the alleged excesses of some children's rights advocates to smear the bill, which did not actually contain a provision for child advocacy or address the question of children's rights. A *Washington Star* article on the campaign was entitled "Even Nonexistent Parts of Child Bill Draw Fire." Nevertheless, the flyer spurred radio shows, editorials, and TV broadcasts that fanned the flames of opposition, and congressional offices received thousands of angry letters. *Newsweek* reported that Mondale had to hire two additional staff members to handle this mail, which at its height ranged from 2,000 to 6,000 pieces *per day*. Ironically, several news stories noted, the bill that had caused such furor stood almost no chance of becoming law; even if Congress were willing to enact an expensive new program, President Ford had vowed to veto any new social spending, so these opponents were essentially beating a dead horse.[71]

While ideological opposition to child care intensified, the child care Coalition, which had been so effective in 1971, splintered in the years following the veto. The energy of many child care advocates in this period was taken up with a struggle over federal day-care standards. As director of the OCD in HEW, Zigler had worked to develop more specific and enforceable day-care standards for federally funded programs. In 1972, he and Richardson prepared to publicize the regulations, hoping that they would help bolster the Nixon administration's image on children's issues. But they could not overcome opposition from the Office of Management and Budget, which feared the expense of meeting the new standards. Outside the administration, child care advocates attacked Zigler's revisions as an attempt by an administration they did not trust to eviscerate the original standards established in 1968. Loyalty to the 1968 requirements—which set a high standard but were vague and unenforceable—had become a litmus test of commitment to children, and advocates preferred to keep these on the books. The new regulations thus were quietly buried, and Zigler left Washington to return to Yale in the summer of 1972. Although he did not return to government service, he continued to influence debate about early childhood programs and policy in the years that followed.

Another divisive issue was the continuing question of who would control child care programs. In the early 1970s, teachers' unions, facing a decline in K-12 jobs, turned to child care as an expanding sector. Al Shanker, who became president of the American Federation of Teachers in 1974, argued that the public schools should be the main sponsors of child care programs. School-based programs, he contended, would be of higher educational quality than other child care programs, and more accountable to the public. He told an American Federation of Teachers convention in 1975 that support for the early education measure was an example of unions at their best: "a good combination of self-interest and public interest." The delegates at that convention unanimously passed a resolution calling for a national program of universal early childhood education, available to all children starting at the age of three.[72] Shanker advocated revising the 1975 federal child care bill to make schools the default sponsors of child care programs. Speaking to a meeting of the National Association for the Education of Young Children, Shanker's assistant Eugenia Kemble pointed to the political benefits to be gained by allying day care with public education. "Consider what it would mean for the potential combined clout of day care groups," she said, "if all of you had some relationship to the public school system—if all of you were in some way under the public school umbrella."[73]

The idea that schools should be the main sponsors of child care programs raised the ire of Edelman and other civil rights advocates, who had pushed for local community control of programs for children in the 1971 legislation precisely because they did not trust schools to serve minority and poor communities. Edelman wrote: "I'm opposed to giving schools a whole new set of responsibilities when they are so far from meeting the ones they already have."[74] This idea also alienated child care providers and advocates, who saw union interest in child care as a grab for jobs. Organizations representing private and community-based child care providers, including Head Start, saw Shanker's proposal as a threat to their existence, and reacted angrily to the idea that teachers certified to teach older students should replace child care staff.

During hearings on the 1975 Child and Family Services Act, Mondale described the dilemma child care advocates faced. Four years after passing the 1971 bill, containing "what we then thought was the best approach," he explained:

> we have a deficit of $65 billion to $70 billion; we have a coalition facing turf disputes; we have a president who says he will accept no new programs, whose vetoes are rarely overturned…then, we have this new philosophy becoming popular in America that no social services are ever effectively administered.

Recognizing these difficulties, he asked several different witnesses whether it would make more sense to "pass the best comprehensive bill we can fashion" or to "seek to pass something less than that" that might have a better chance of being enacted, and "move this along somehow."[75] As he feared, Congress did not pass any such child care bill in 1975, or for the rest of the decade. The demise of the 1971 child development legislation was a turning point in public policy for young children: universal public child care became anathema, and federal child care programs remained meager and restricted to welfare mothers. The window of opportunity for creating a coherent national system of child care services had essentially slammed shut. Gilbert Steiner wrote in 1976 that unlike other social policy issues (such as national health insurance or federal aid to education), "child development had a quick fling and was gone."[76] Child care, which had started out as a bipartisan issue, ended up as a political hot potato. Political scientist Kimberly Morgan writes:

> At the national and local levels, the right captured the issue of universal public day care and made it so politically toxic that few legislators would come near it. As John Brademas said in a 1997 interview, "Those attacks poisoned the well for early childhood programs for a long time—indeed, ever since."[77]

Even if ideological opposition to child care could have been overcome, the nation's growing economic crisis, rising budget deficits, and a general loss of confidence in government made the 1970s a time of retrenchment rather than expansive innovation in social policy.

A FRAGMENTED SYSTEM

The failure of the Child Development Act in 1971 had a far-reaching impact on the character of early childhood education in the United States. Rather than creating a single publicly funded system of child development centers open to all children, policymakers encouraged the growth of different programs with different purposes, funding, standards, and constituencies. Early care and education grew into a diverse "system" dominated by the private market and supported by parent fees, with fairly minimal government regulation. (In this it came to resemble higher education, although with much less public investment.)

In the wake of Nixon's 1971 veto, federal policymakers focused different child care policies on different social groups. Expanding the federal tax deduction for child care, which especially benefited middle- and upper-income families, was the first of these policies. The day after he vetoed the broad 1971 child care legislation, Nixon signed a bill that broadened eligibility for this tax deduction. Rather than using tax dollars to directly fund public programs, the tax deduction subsidized part of the cost of private care. By subsidizing parents' choices in the private market, this approach avoided the arguments over government provision of services that had been fatal to the 1971 legislation. As one congressional staffer recalled, "We couldn't go through the front door, so we went through the back door."[78]

By expanding the tax deduction for private child care expenses rather than expanding public programs, Nixon helped spur the growth of the private child care market. In the mid-1970s, the federal tax deduction was further expanded, ultimately making it one of the largest sources of federal spending on day care. By choosing to subsidize parents' expenses in the private child care market, policymakers embraced a market that could not yet meet the growing demand for child care, much less assure its quality. The 1972 study conducted by the National Council of Jewish Women, *Windows on Day Care,* reported that an acute shortage of day care across the country was forcing parents to make do with "inferior and often harmful arrangements." Only about 10 percent of children of working mothers were enrolled in licensed centers; many more spent their days in child care homes or with relatives and neighbors, and these children's mothers were far more likely to be dissatisfied with their children's care. Day-care centers were not located in the neighborhoods where they were most needed, and while their fees were higher than many families could afford, they were much lower than would be needed to produce high-quality programs. Proprietary centers were judged to be particularly low in quality (the services of half of these centers visited were judged "poor," compared with 10 percent of the nonprofit ones). Economist Mary Keyserling, who directed the study, concluded: "a large part of the story is a picture of care that is only custodial, some that is bad and too much that is harmful; part of the story is that too many children get no care at all."[79]

A 1972 study of child care in the Los Angeles area highlighted the variety the private child care market produced, with successful centers ranging from home-like to school-like. For instance, a married couple ran a small center out of a house in a Los Angeles suburb, aiming to create a warm, supportive atmosphere in which children could choose activities in a creative environment. Not far away, the owner-director of an elite prep school added a nursery division that emphasized teaching children academic skills and behavior to prepare them to achieve "academic excellence" as they moved through the school's different levels. The director established a small chain of private schools that thrived in the expanding economy of the area, creating economies of scale that helped finance a quality program. Within the city itself, a nursery sponsored by an African-American church offered children a rich physical environment to explore, including a miniature outdoor city created out of crates and boards, a fish pond, and small animals. In another neighborhood, a large for-profit nursery stressed learning through memorization of words and numbers; teachers there spent most of their energy directing children's behavior into approved channels. Whether their centers were run on a for-profit or nonprofit basis, directors struggled to pay their teachers decent salaries, meet their budgets, and find physical space that would satisfy licensing and zoning regulations as well as appealing to parents.[80]

In addition to expanding the tax deduction for child care, members of Congress also agreed to use federal funds to provide some day care for low-income families, hoping to reduce their dependence on welfare. Linking child care to "workfare" and getting more women off the welfare rolls continued to be a strong motivation for policymakers. Title XX of the Social Security Act, which President Ford signed into law in 1975, provided block grants to states for a variety of social services intended to "prevent, reduce, or eliminate dependency." Title XX consolidated different categorical programs and gave states more leeway about how to spend their funds on each type of service, including child care. It provided important funding for child care centers serving poor families, replacing some of the antipoverty funds that had dried up under the Nixon administration. Unlike the Mondale-Brademas bill introduced around the same time, this legislation did not provoke any outcry from conservatives about government interference in family life.[81]

Nonetheless, while federal policymakers agreed to fund some day care for the poorest families, they did not agree about how to regulate it. The 1975 legislation required child care programs to comply with the federal regulations developed in 1968 (which had never really been enforced) and threatened to cut off funds to centers that were not in compliance. Estimating that about half of the child care provided under Title XX would not meet these high standards, caregivers, state administrators, and members of Congress began to protest. For-profit child care centers now comprised two-fifths of the total child care market and were expanding rapidly. Center owners formed a lobby in Washington to convey their strong opposition to any federal enforcement of new staff-to-child ratios. The continued availability of day care, they and their allies argued, depended on keeping costs down. On the other side of the debate stood many nonprofit centers and children's advocates, pressing for more stringent licensing requirements and low ratios. Lawsuits from both sides confronted HEW, and more than twenty bills were introduced to suspend the federal child care regulations. Ultimately, President Ford delayed the deadline for compliance. The regulations were postponed and debated several more times before finally meeting their demise in 1981. Ultimately, attempts to make even federally funded child care meet minimum federal standards failed, leaving the matter of regulation entirely to the states.[82]

CONCLUSION

The federal government's role in child care that emerged during the 1970s was quite different from what advocates and legislators had imagined at the beginning of the decade. Rather than establishing a system of publicly supported child development programs open to children from all families, federal policy helped develop a patchwork approach to child care. Federal funds supported some child care for the poor, which it could not even effectively regulate, and continued to offer Head Start to about 15 percent of the poor children who were eligible. The federal government also subsidized a portion of the child care expenses of middle- and upper-class families through the tax deduction. No federal funds for child care were being spent to help families who fell in between the poverty line and a household income that would enable them to pay for good private care. As in other areas of social policy, funds for the poor were delivered as direct services, while those for the middle and upper classes were funneled through the tax code, making them part of what some scholars have called "the hidden welfare state." In this context, the market came to play a decisive role in child care, producing a great variety of child care arrangements (private nonprofit and for-profit child care centers, family day care, care by relatives and "nannies," nursery schools or preschools) but no way to ensure their quality or accessibility.

What had looked in 1970 like a potentially strong cross-class coalition for child care had become a divided constituency, represented by leaders who disagreed sharply about what strategies to pursue. Rather than a national system for child development, what had been created was a patchwork of programs providing what sociologist Julia Wrigley calls "different care for different kids," varying with their families' economic background.[83] This patchwork had some very good pieces, but many weak ones, and there were significant holes and places where pieces did not meet up. It seemed doubtful that this patchwork quilt could be stretched to cover all the children and families who needed it, but it was the only quilt there was.

CHAPTER 3

Separate Strands

Early Education and Child Care for Poor Children in the 1980s

The failure of the 1971 federal child care legislation, and of subsequent efforts to resurrect it, meant that policy for preschool children would not be addressed as a whole. Instead of bringing together early education and child care needs, policymakers continued to address them as separate issues, if at all. Families with young children encountered a patchwork of public and private programs, with varying types of service, levels of quality, cost, and purposes. This patchwork was stratified along socioeconomic lines; public funding provided some care for the poorest, while other families purchased what they could afford in the private market. Holes appeared in the patchwork where programs were not connected: Head Start remained largely separate from the world of K–12 education, which remained largely separate from the mostly private world of child care.

As separate strands, each of these early childhood sectors struggled for funding and stability during the 1970s and early 1980s. But their position was strengthened during the 1980s by rising concerns about K–12 education reform and the growth of child poverty. Inspired by new research showing the long-term benefits of early education, state legislators launched school-based pre-kindergarten programs for low-income children, while Congress increased support for Head Start and identified "school readiness" as a major educational goal for the nation. At the same time, advocates were pushing child care back onto the national agenda, hoping to improve its quality and make it more accessible through government funding and regulation. Competing visions of child care needs, the proper role of government, public schools, and quality standards ultimately produced a new stream of federal support for child care for low-income families, relying on parental choice in the child care market. By the end of the 1980s, both child care and early education had become stronger and more visible—although still largely separate—strands of policy for young children.

WHOSE BABY IS IT? BATTLING OVER FEDERAL CHILD CARE POLICY

In the mid-1980s, children's advocates succeeded in bringing the issue of child care back onto the national agenda. Debates over child care raised basic questions about who should take responsibility for it: families, the government, the market, or the public schools. With national politics focused on cutting back the federal government's role, this was a contentious question. Ronald Reagan's election in 1980 signaled a triumph for conservatives who sought a stronger role for the private market and a more limited role for the federal government in American society. Conservatives called for lower taxes, less federal regulation, a radical reduction in government programs such as public housing, welfare, and food stamps, and a return to "traditional family values." The nation entered a period in which public spending on social needs was contested, as voters and policymakers were increasingly skeptical of government initiatives.

In the midst of this politically conservative era, economic necessity and opportunity drew record numbers of mothers to the workforce. By the end of the decade, 58.2 percent of mothers with children under age six were working outside the home, as were more than half of married women with a child under age one. (This represented significant change; in 1950 only 13 percent of mothers with preschool-age children were in the paid workforce.) Responding to the growing need for child care, the capacity of day-care centers and private nursery schools doubled (at least) between the late 1970s and the late 1980s.[1] With fewer families able to depend on relatives for care, child care centers and day-care homes were increasingly an important part of families' lives. For-profit providers included "Mom and Pop" owners of small private centers, as well as newer chains and large franchisers like Kinder-Care and Children's World. These chains expanded dramatically in the early 1980s, especially in suburban markets and states with fewer child care regulations, making child care into big business. By the late 1980s, for-profit child care providers made up about half the child care in the United States, with chains constituting about 10 percent of this for-profit market.[2] Nonprofit organizations such as the YWCA, the Salvation Army, and churches and synagogues made up the other half. This expanding private child care sector was only lightly regulated by state laws setting minimal health and safety guidelines for licensed providers. Informal child care arrangements in which women took care of children in their homes also grew, appealing to families who wanted a "home-like" family atmosphere and greater affordability than was offered in many centers. A large proportion of these informal providers avoided state licensing procedures altogether, leaving parents to judge the safety and quality of their arrangements.

Federal policy in the 1980s encouraged the growth of this private market for child care, on the basis of the idea that child care was a family responsibility, not a government one. The Reagan administration cut funding for Title XX of the Social Security Act—the main vehicle for supporting child care for low-income families—and shifted responsibility for child care to the state level. Many states reduced child care slots and staffs, increased fees, or decreased training programs in order to conserve funds; a majority of states lowered their standards and reduced monitoring of child care quality. But the federal government, as it stepped back from both funding and regulating child care for low-income mothers, expanded spending for child care for middle-class families, both by increasing the child care tax credit and by creating tax incentives for employers to provide child care. Employer-sponsored child care programs grew, while the personal income tax credit for child care soared from $956 million in 1980 to $3.4 billion in 1987, making it by far the greatest federal expenditure on child care.[3]

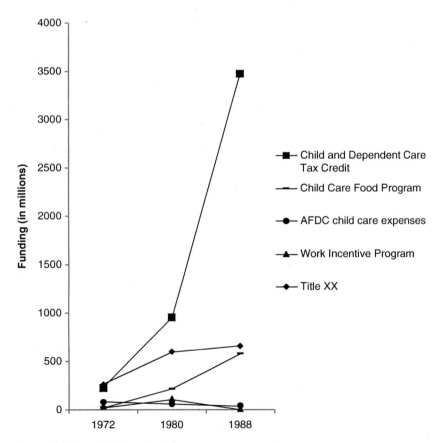

Figure 3.1 Federal Child Care Funding
Source: Testimony of Douglas Besharov, House Education and Labor Committee, *Child Care: Hearings before the Subcommittee of Human Resources,* 134–35.

In the child care market, families' choices were determined in large part by what they could afford to pay. Studying child care arrangements in a small northeastern city, Caroline Zinsser found that they were stratified by social class. Low-income families might be able to enroll their children in one of three publicly subsidized child care centers, which struggled to provide children with care based on child development principles. Professional middle-class parents from nearby suburbs brought their children to one of two private day care centers or paid home-based babysitters or nannies. The private centers charged as much as eight times the fees of the subsidized public centers, though it was not clear whether these higher fees translated into higher quality care. Working- and lower-middle-class families were caught in the middle, not poor enough to be eligible for subsidized care but without the money to pay for a private center. Those who could not arrange care with relatives tended to hire "babysitters" who cared for children in their homes. The quality of these largely unregulated arrangements varied widely; one mother praised her babysitter as being "like a grandmother," but one person watching ten children at a time violated state law and was unlikely to produce the best care.[4]

The fact that working mothers were now a majority (even among those with very young children) drew widespread attention, as Americans sought to come to terms with the change this represented in family life. Families trying to make decisions about work and child care were often caught in the middle of what would soon be dubbed "the Mommy wars," with working mothers carrying a load of guilt about their child care arrangements in addition to their other burdens. Conservative activists like Phyllis Schlafly inveighed against child care and urged mothers to stay home with their children. Researchers argued over whether or not child care had harmful long-term effects, while popular magazines publicized mothers' struggles to find good child care. In 1987, *Time* called child care "the most wrenching personal problem facing millions of American families." A feature article on day care described examples of careless or unreliable babysitters, filthy family day-care homes with children lined up "like zombies" in front of the television, and desperate mothers, like a Los Angeles high school custodian who hid her children in an empty classroom for eight hours while she mopped floors and hauled barrels of trash.[5]

Surrounded by such questions about whether day care in general was good for children, parents' confidence in their own day-care arrangements was often shaky. When child care providers in California, New Jersey, Florida, and elsewhere were charged with sexual abuse in a string of cases starting in 1983, the media spotlight seemed to confirm the public's worst fears about child care, further alarming parents. In the most shocking and far-reaching case, teachers at the McMartin Preschool in California were alleged to have committed multiple sexual assaults against as many as 400 children and forced them to engage in satanic rituals. The fact that this accusation arose in a trusted center with a good reputation in a prosperous Los Angeles suburb underlined the feeling that "no child and no community was safe."[6] The McMartin case was dismissed after seven years for lack of evidence, and several other cases elsewhere were overturned because of their reliance on unreliable testimony. One journalist has written that this wave of abuse cases, arising at a time when Americans were just coming to terms with mothers' employment as the norm, reflected a generalized anxiety about child care: "It was as though there were some dark, self-defeating relief in trading niggling everyday doubts about our children's care for our absolute worst fears—for a story with monsters, not just human beings who didn't always treat our kids exactly as we would like."[7] The intense publicity surrounding these cases also made parents more anxious about using child care. For instance, a woman interviewed in the late 1980s explained that while her son had suffered physical harm in various informal babysitting arrangements (being slapped by a babysitter, not adequately fed, and hit or bitten by other children), she had not considered using a day-care center because television reports of sexual abuse in centers made her afraid of them.[8]

Bemoaning the lack of a national childcare policy, advocates for children and for working women continued to look to the federal government for action. In 1986, Marian Wright Edelman's Children's Defense Fund (CDF) brought together a broad coalition to work on a new federal child care bill. Staffer Helen Blank had become convinced that the timing was right to start pushing for major legislation, building on the successes local advocates had achieved at the state level as they sought to influence responses to Reagan's 1981 child care cuts. Blank worked with representatives of thirty organizations to plan a new bill, with the understanding that it would take several years to get it through Congress. By 1987, this coalition, called the Alliance for Better Child Care, had grown to include more than seventy organizations, encompassing a wide range of children's, religious, women's, labor, and civic groups.[9]

Instead of seeking universal child care, the Alliance focused on providing services for low-income families, who had been hurt the most by Reagan's social policies. Advocates argued that the nation had a special responsibility to aid children in poverty, whose numbers were growing (one out of every five children fell into this category); child care was also an important issue for those concerned with moving poor mothers from welfare to work. In addition to focusing on low-income families, the bill would also seek to improve child care overall by setting aside funds for quality initiatives. Advocates agreed to try for federally mandated standards for child care centers, even though they recognized the political difficulties that might create.

The Alliance's Act for Better Child Care (ABC) started out with strong support in 1987, with testimony from labor unions, women's organizations, public
officials, religious and civic groups, children's policy experts, and early childhood professionals. But fissures among supporters soon became apparent, first
over the issue of vouchers. The ABC allowed states to issue vouchers that parents could use in purchasing child care services, reflecting the Alliance's interest
in using the diverse patchwork of private and public child care provision that
had grown up since the 1970s. Early childhood expert Anne Mitchell wrote in
1989 that good child care policy had to be incremental, building on what
already existed: "It is seductive, but unproductive, to contemplate washing the
slate clean and building an early childhood system from scratch."[10] Some members of the Alliance, however, wanted to create a new, high-quality child care
system within the K–12 public schools. They feared that allowing vouchers for
child care would "open the flood gates for vouchers" for K–12 schooling, and
the National PTA withdrew its support for the bill over this issue. There were
also divisions on the issue of funding religiously based programs. Some groups
were deeply concerned about maintaining separation of church and state in
child care, while others were adamant that religious-based providers be
included. Edelman worked to achieve a compromise. Her willingness to allow
church-run facilities to receive federal funding without detailed restrictions
meant losing support from some Democratic senators and Alliance organizations, and efforts to pass the bill in 1988 eventually failed.

Despite the ABC bill's initial failure, child care was becoming a key issue in
national politics. Both Democratic and Republican party platforms in 1988
addressed child care, and both presidential candidates Michael Dukakis and
George H. Bush held photo ops at child care centers and pledged support for
families with children. One journalist observed that child care centers had
"replaced factory gates for photo opportunities symbolic of political candidates' demonstration of concern for American workers and children."[11] Both
parties were particularly eager to be seen as addressing the needs of low-income
working families, a significant voting bloc whose political allegiances seemed to
be up for grabs.[12] Newly aware of the "gender gap" in national politics, politicians also sought the support of middle-class women voters, and saw child care
as a key issue. A 1988 Gallup poll reported that 39 percent of respondents felt
child care should be a top priority of the next administration, with another
42 percent identifying it as medium priority.[13]

Although both parties highlighted child care, they took significantly different approaches. While Democrats aimed at building a supply of quality child
care through direct government spending and regulation, Republicans preferred to use tax policy to give low-income working families money to spend as

they wished. Liberals who supported the ABC saw high-quality child care centers as the goal, while conservatives sang the praises of grandmothers and neighbors who cared for children in their homes. Opponents of the ABC objected to the idea of setting federal standards for child care, referring to the bill as an "Attempt to Bureaucratize Motherhood" and "Government Nannies for America's Children."[14] George H. Bush's 1988 campaign platform thus included a $1,000 refundable tax credit for low-income families with children under the age of five, whether or not they used child care. This satisfied conservatives who wanted to help "traditional families" where mothers stayed home with their children, while offering an alternative to what they saw as the ABC's overly bureaucratic and regulatory approach. Liberals argued that the Republican proposal to help families purchase child care would not cause child care centers to improve their quality or to locate where they were most needed.

After the ABC's failure to pass in 1988, the child care coalition, in order to consolidate support for the bill in the face of Republican opposition, compromised on both federal standards and church-state protections. These compromises helped produce some bipartisan support, as well as defuse opposition from governors and state legislators. The ABC passed the Senate in 1989, bundled with several other measures aimed to help low-income families. In the House, however, child care supporters were even more divided. Education and Labor Committee chair Augustus Hawkins, a California Democrat, introduced an alternative bill, giving public schools a stronger role. Hawkins's bill placed programs for four-year-olds under the public schools, while incorporating the ABC's approach to child care programs for other children. Hawkins received support from organizations such as the National Education Association, the National Organization for Women, and the American Association of University Women, which looked favorably on public school control of child care and were unhappy with the compromises that had been made regarding vouchers and religious providers.

Hawkins's bill brought to a head the tension surrounding the role of the public schools in child care and early education. Gordon Ambach, who had recently become director of the Council of Chief State School Officers, praised the bill's merging of early education and child care.[15] Montana Democratic congressman John Williams described the task of child care policy as setting up "a new system of education" for young children, comparable to the creation of public schooling in the nineteenth century. Such a system, he believed, needed to be based in the schools. He suggested that Americans would be critical of nineteenth-century school reformers "if they had decided that system was not to be public, but rather a network, a quilt of public/private education all paid for by the taxpayers" and concluded: "the public should continue to do the public's business when it comes to education."[16] Others disagreed. The National Child Care Association, representing 30,000 owners of proprietary child care centers, complained that the Hawkins bill would "legislate a virtual public-school monopoly over care for three- and four-year-olds, impede diversity and thwart parental choice options." Others felt that Hawkins's school-based approach was politically unrealistic. Democratic congressman Thomas Downey of Long Island told the *New York Times* that Hawkins (one of the most senior members of Congress) was living in the past. "He is more wedded to a policy approach that is grounded in the 60's. . . . That would have been great, but Lyndon Johnson is not going to come back and sign a bill for child care."[17] Indeed, President Bush was strongly opposed to placing child care programs under what he called the "traditional education bureaucracy." He also objected to mandates that would limit parental choice, especially of religiously based programs. Despite such criticism, Hawkins got his bill, combined with the ABC, passed by the Committee on Education and Labor in June 1989.

A third alternative, introduced by Democratic congressmen Thomas Downey and George Miller of California, further complicated the legislative picture by building on the traditionally Republican tax policy approach. Instead of creating a new structure for funding child care, the Downey-Miller measure expanded the Earned Income Tax Credit (EITC) and increased Title XX funding for child care. This approach was more palatable to conservatives because it used existing funding streams rather than creating new programs. The child care coalition, however, was completely taken aback by the Downey-Miller bill. Edelman felt that Miller and Downey—her former allies—had betrayed her personally, and the child care cause in general, by introducing this bill rather than supporting the ABC. Neither bill could garner enough votes to form a majority in the House, so action on child care was again postponed until the next session of Congress.[18]

Although the child care coalition was becoming more and more fragmented, supporters undertook what CDF staffer Amy Wilkins described as a "relentless, grinding process" of haranguing the leadership of the House to bring the bill up for a vote. Child care advocates across the country were writing, phoning, and visiting their representatives; a leader in Alabama even cornered members of Congress at an Auburn University football game. In March 1990, the House finally passed a child care bill that combined Downey-Miller's approach with the Hawkins bill, and a conference committee was convened to reconcile it with the version of the ABC passed earlier by the Senate. Although language in the bill allowing religiously based providers caused a number of organizations to oppose it, the CDF worked hard to activate state and local grassroots networks to raise publicity for child care legislation. Supporters in different cities held rallies and created a paper chain that members of the flight attendants' union brought across the country. When it was stretched from the White House to the Capitol in September, it had more than 200,000 links from more than 450 cities, signed by governors and grandparents, mayors and mothers.[19] Larger budget negotiations between the Bush administration and congressional leaders in 1990 ultimately provided the opportunity to move the issue forward. In order to offset the burden Bush's tax increase was placing on low-income families, both Congress and the White House were interested in combining child care with an expansion of the EITC. One budget official explained, "I can't say enough how popular the EITC was [in Congress], it was overwhelming, and there was this sense that you had to take the EITC with child care."[20] The White House was willing to include child care if it incorporated the president's main priorities, such as vouchers, parental choice, and inclusion of religious programs.

In October 1990, the White House and Senate leaders announced they had reached an agreement on child care. The final legislation included the new Child Care and Development Block Grant (CCDBG) as well as the smaller At-Risk Child Care program for families at risk of becoming dependent on welfare. The CCDBG would provide $2.5 billion in funding over three years: three-quarters of the funding would go to provide child care to low-income parents (defined as those earning less than 75 percent of the state median income), while the remaining quarter went to promote quality improvements in child care overall, including a small set-aside for school-based programs. Funding for child care could be provided through vouchers to parents as well as contracts with child care programs.

The CCDBG was the first major piece of federal child care legislation passed since World War II; it was the first ever to address child care as an independent issue, and it provided crucial support to low-income families. Emerging from a protracted struggle in Washington, its passage marked an agreement of sorts about a federal role in child care: providing subsidies to low-income families and helping states upgrade the quality of existing services. The final legislation highlighted the importance of parental choice in the largely private child care market, offering parents vouchers and tax credits (as well as allowing states to contract directly with child care programs). Political scientist Christopher Howard sees this strategy as part of a pattern of a "hidden welfare state" based on tax policies, an alternative mode of significant public spending, especially in areas where direct spending is controversial. Tax expenditures such as the EITC and the child care tax credit, he argues, play a significant role in policy and in the federal budget; they also siphon off political support for more direct forms of aid to families with children, dampening demands for universal programs.[21]

Indeed, earlier decisions to support private child care through the tax code helped to shape the fate of federal child care legislation in the late 1980s. Because so many parents had found child care solutions—however imperfect—in the private marketplace, there was no overwhelming groundswell of public support for a broader approach to publicly funded child care. Some child care supporters were disappointed that the final bill did not provide more help for middle-class families. "We're looking at what fell through the cracks," said a spokeswoman for Colorado Democratic congresswoman Patricia Schroeder. "The biggest gap in this child-care proposal was that the middle class was left out."[22] But polls showed that while 58 percent of respondents supported child care for the poor, only 35 percent favored expanding public funding for all working parents.[23] The idea that child care was a private responsibility, reinforced by the approach the federal government had taken since the early 1970s, had become conventional wisdom, and families who had made private arrangements for their children were unlikely to challenge it. Rather than creating a new approach to child care policy, the CCDBG's funding, along with the expansion of the EITC, helped low-income families to navigate through the lightly regulated private market that policymakers had first embraced in the 1970s.

Advocates and their allies in Congress had made a series of compromises in the long process of getting a federal child care bill passed and signed into law. The CCDBG's quality standards and requirements for states were weaker than those of the original ABC, and the CCDBG provided help to a narrower range of families. Hawkins was disappointed with the final compromise, saying that it left "no meaningful role for the schools." Nevertheless, supporters were delighted finally to have a victory. In a CDF press release, Edelman called it "a historic political win for families," which showed that "the needs of hardworking, struggling American families finally have climbed towards the top of the political agenda." The liberal *Christian Science Monitor* described the bill as both a giant leap in acknowledging a public responsibility for child care and a baby step in its actual impact on the problem.[24]

Child care supporters could not pause long to celebrate the passage of the new legislation; they had to watch carefully how the Bush administration implemented the law. In setting regulations for how states could use the new child care funds, the administration emphasized parental choice above all, evading regulation and standards to a degree that seriously restricted states' ability to set policies that would increase quality. Arguing that parents had the right to use federal funds to purchase whatever care they chose, regardless of its level of quality, administration officials made it difficult for states to provide incentives for better care. These officials also restricted the amount of money states could spend on efforts to raise quality in child care overall, as opposed to direct funding of slots. Child care advocates and legislators, weary from the long fight in Congress, launched into another round of lobbying and publicity in protest. An editorial in the *New York Times* said that the proposed regulations gave child care for families at risk of being on welfare "a green light to be lousy."[25] Downey held hearings in September 1991 lambasting Department of Health and Human Services officials for the liberties they took in drafting the regulations, charging that the clear intent of Congress to set quality standards for child care had been ignored.

Despite these difficulties, the CCDBG played an important role in helping states to subsidize child care expenses for low-income working families. It did not provide nearly enough funding to meet the need—thousands of families were on waiting lists for subsidized child care around the country—but it did provide a framework within which the federal government could help support child care. Responding to the requirement that states have health and safety standards for child care, some states strengthened their child care licensing requirements. Forty states also used some of the new funding to improve quality by increasing the number of staff involved in monitoring local programs or providing funds to help providers meet new requirements. The funds set aside for quality improvement spurred the creation of state programs to improve the training of early childhood care providers and of child care resource and referral services. States also used funds to encourage the provision of good care for those not adequately served by existing programs: infants, school-age children, teen parents, and children with special needs. As the bill's authors had hoped, the block grant thus proved to be a catalyst for improvements in the quality of child care for all children, not just for those directly subsidized under the block grant.[26] But the legislation's ability to raise quality significantly was impaired by its overall focus on parental choice and on working within the existing child care market.

By contrast, Congress did effectively raise quality when it passed a bill to reform the child care system operated by the nation's military. The military's child care had suffered from many of the same problems that beset child care in general: undertrained and poorly compensated staff, inadequate facilities, long waiting lists, lack of quality standards and a way to enforce them, allegations of child abuse, and parents' inability to pay more. But in the hierarchical world of the military, insisting on high standards, systematic training, and frequent inspections of child care centers did not raise nearly as many hackles as it did in the broader society. Following the passage of the 1989 Military Child Care Act, funding for military child care was increased, and new child care centers were built. Staff were paid at the same level as other entry-level jobs on military posts, dramatically reducing turnover rates (from as high as 300 percent on some bases to an average of 30 percent) and received systematic, ongoing training, linked to increased compensation. By 2000, 95 percent of all military child care centers were accredited by the National Association for the Education of Young Children, compared with only 8 percent of centers nationwide. Fees were set on a sliding scale, with military appropriations making up the difference between what parents could afford to pay and what a good quality program actually cost. As a result of these changes, a leading child care advocate noted: "The best chance a family has to be guaranteed affordable and high-quality care in this country is to join the military."[27]

In the civilian society, day care's history as a private enterprise shaped policymakers' approach to the 1990 legislation. The growth of a robust private and community-based sector (including nonprofit and for-profit child care centers, family day care providers, and church-based programs) in the 1970s and 1980s influenced decisions about child care policy at the end of the decade. The growth of this sector both drew on and reinforced the values of parental choice, freedom from government regulation, and the market's ability to meet social needs. Organizations representing the interests of private, faith-based, and community-based providers helped translate these values into policy that embraced market-based solutions such as parent vouchers for child care, rather than government provision and regulation. Federal policymakers had chosen to work within the patchwork system of day care that had been shaped in the 1970s. Although many recognized holes in the quilt, the idea of starting a new one seemed both prohibitively expensive and politically impossible. The most practical course seemed to be one of stretching it to cover poorer families, sewing more patches onto it, and reinforcing some of the threads that held it together.

"THANK GOD FOR THE PERRY PRESCHOOL PROJECT!"

Even as battles over child care legislation in Washington made young children's need for better care more visible than ever, a quieter movement was developing to support their need for education. Research on the long-term benefits of early childhood education for disadvantaged children played a key role, putting preschool education on the national agenda of K–12 education reform and bolstering the fortunes of the Head Start program.

This research had its roots in the debates over Head Start's efficacy in the late 1960s. In the mid-1970s, researchers and Head Start officials were still looking for answers to the pressing question of whether, in fact, early childhood programs like Head Start could be expected to have a long-term impact on children's success in school. In the wake of the Westinghouse study's negative findings, the stakes were high, as the OCD's research director recalled: "A case had to be made for or against the long-term benefits of preschool programs for children in poverty, even though no other program in the history of education, health, or welfare had ever been required before to justify its existence by long-term benefits."[28] In 1976, the OCD funded a group of researchers to create the Consortium for Longitudinal Studies (CLS), pooling data from eleven early intervention projects dating back to the early 1960s. Each of the Consortium projects was a well-planned and carefully researched preschool intervention that aimed to enhance low-income African-American children's cognitive and social development. Each of the studies had used experimental or quasi-experimental designs and tracked children's progress over time, although they differed in the ages of children served, the curriculum used, the duration of the program, and other variables.

This research, which was first published in 1977 (and after additional follow-up again in 1983), found that while differences on cognitive measures like IQ disappeared after a few years, the children who had participated in early intervention programs continued to do better in school and in later "real-life" situations than the children who had not. Those who went through the early intervention programs were less likely to be put into special education classes or have to repeat a grade, and they differed from their peers somewhat in high school completion, occupational aspirations, and employment rates. Discussing the findings, CLS director Irving Lazar wrote: "the independence of the separate studies makes these findings highly reliable. Indeed, few examples of this kind of multiple and independent replication exist anywhere in the social sciences."[29]

Reports about the positive effects the CLS researchers discovered had a powerful impact, establishing the need to look beyond IQ scores in order to discover the long-term impact of early childhood programs. By looking at how these programs affected long-term outcomes like high school completion and employment, the study revisited the most ambitious promises Lyndon Johnson and Sargent Shriver had ever made for Head Start. Head Start advocates had distanced themselves from some of these promises in the early 1970s, seeing them as leading to inevitable disappointment. But the CLS findings suggested that even some of Johnson's extravagant claims for Head Start—that it would lead to success not only in school but also over the whole life span—might be true.[30] The findings also rewrote the story the 1969 Westinghouse study had told of the limited impact of early intervention programs for disadvantaged children. "Research, which almost killed Head Start," wrote Ed Zigler and Susan Muenchow, "would finally help save it."[31]

Convinced that these findings deserved wide attention, the CLS researchers made extraordinary efforts to communicate them to policymakers and to the mass media. In hundreds of personal meetings across the country in the late 1970s and early 1980s, they presented their findings to state legislators, governors, and national associations and urged the expansion of early childhood programs.[32] Particularly prominent in these efforts was David Weikart, who had found some of the strongest effects of any of the CLS studies among the 121 children who attended his Perry Preschool program in Ypsilanti, Michigan. Graduates of this program not only were less likely to be retained or placed in special education classes, but were less likely to have teenage pregnancies or be arrested and incarcerated, and more likely to graduate from high school. Perry Preschool project researchers were the first to conduct a cost-benefit analysis of their early intervention program, finding that the long-term benefits far outweighed the program's cost. As Weikart and his colleagues continued to follow Perry Preschool graduates, they would famously conclude that for each $1 invested in the program, society saved $7 in education, welfare, and criminal justice costs.[33]

The CLS studies documented that specific preschool programs were effective in helping extremely disadvantaged African-American children navigate the world of school during the 1960s and 1970s. Preschool seemed to help these children by enabling them to avoid being placed in special education classes or being "kept back" a grade, setting them on a trajectory of greater success in school. Lazar speculated that preschool intervention produced "a system of mutual reinforcement between the parent and child, the teacher and child, and the combination that 'teaches' that academic success is valuable."[34] While these studies were often invoked to show that preschool is universally beneficial to disadvantaged children (assuming that both "preschool" and "disadvantage" are static categories), it is important to note the specific contexts that shaped children's experiences in these programs.[35] For instance, the Perry Preschool project was inspired by Weikart's frustration with school system practices that he thought pushed low-achieving children into a pattern of school failure. Changing practices in schools, as well as changes in the nature of poverty and family life, could also affect the promise of preschool.

Reporters linked the CLS research directly to Head Start, with headlines such as "Head Start Efforts Prove Their Value," "A Head Start Pays Off in the End," "Head Start Saves Children and Money," and "Head Start Gets a High

Grade."[36] In fact, the CLS research was based mostly on experimental, model programs whose funding, expert supervision, and professionally trained staff far exceeded that of most Head Start programs. The Perry Preschool project was not a typical program. For instance, it spent about $5,000 per child per year and had teachers with postgraduate degrees in early childhood education, while Head Start was spending less than half that amount and often hiring teachers with little formal education. In addition, the carefully controlled nature of the experimental programs could not be replicated in Head Start's 1,300 locally varied sites. Researchers were careful to note that their results showed more about the validity of the early intervention *concept* underlying Head Start than about how this large federal program was implemented: "what Head Start could be rather than what it has been."[37] Nevertheless, the study validated the promise of Head Start for improving outcomes for poor children, and eager listeners often glossed over the details.

In the politically sympathetic climate of the Carter administration, these research findings were translated into increased funding for Head Start. Harley Frankel, a lobbyist for the CDF, began blanketing congressional offices with research summaries of the CLS findings (packaged with a George Washington University study that favorably synthesized some 150 other Head Start research studies), concluding that Head Start had a positive impact on children's cognitive development and health, the family, and the community. The National Head Start Association also fought hard for an increase, visiting legislative aides, sending out copies of newspaper articles about the CLS's findings, and generating thousands of letters from all over the country. Ultimately, Head Start received a $150 million increase in 1978, the program's first significant one in eleven years. Lois-ellin Datta observes that while it is not unusual for a social program to fall "from favor to the abyss" in a relatively short period of time, Head Start may be a rare example of the reverse, with its climb back into political favor inspired in part by this new body of research.[38] In 1980, the White House hosted a fifteenth anniversary celebration for Head Start, at which President Carter spoke of his commitment to Head Start's future. To help guide that future, Carter appointed Zigler to head a committee of sympathetic experts to examine the program. This committee stressed that Head Start was "a social program" rather than a narrowly educational one. "Head Start," they argued, "should never become a sort of junior kindergarten, under the sole jurisdiction of the public schools."[39]

Indeed, as Head Start climbed back into favor, the lines separating it from the public schools became more sharply drawn. Successfully resisting President Carter's attempt to move Head Start into the new Department of Education in 1977, Head Start supporters stressed that the program was about more than just education: it was a community-led, comprehensive effort that included health, nutrition, and social support for poor families. Carter had hoped to include Head Start in the new Department of Education to signal that it would be a center for a comprehensive family policy rather than an agency focused narrowly on K–12 concerns. An administration memo about the proposed move claimed the Head Start program was "one of the clearest examples of Federal success in altering the content of education and the way learning is facilitated...because the Federal government substantially constrained or circumvented the traditional role of schools."[40] But Head Start advocates protested the idea of moving the program. Edelman of the CDF was adamant that Head Start remain a social welfare and community action program and not be joined to the education bureaucracy, which she felt had not served poor and minority children well in the past. A group of prominent civil rights leaders wrote a telegram calling the move a threat to Head Start's integrity, while Edelman wrote to her former ally, vice president Walter Mondale: "If you do this, I and those thousands of poor people in the 1,200 Head Start communities...will view your action as a betrayal. We will fight you in every way we can."[41] The new National Head Start Association joined in the fight; Mississippi civil rights activist Aaron Henry, visiting legislative aides in their congressional offices, would ask: "What is going to happen to black children if Head Start is put into the schools?" [42] Head Start mothers from Hartford and New Haven rode a bus all night to Washington to ask Connecticut Democratic senator Abraham Ribicoff to remove Head Start from the bill creating the new education department. The next morning, Ribicoff—who had previously pledged to support the president on this issue—joined the rest of his committee in voting to delete Head Start from the legislation.

The combination of new research findings and the growing political muscle that Head Start supporters exercised helped protect it during the Reagan administration. The day after Reagan's inauguration, former Carter staffer Harley Frankel placed a call to the Office of Management and Budget, where by luck a high-level official picked up the phone (no secretary had yet been hired). "I know you'll be cutting a lot of programs," Frankel said. "But to avoid bad press, you'll need to save a few, and let me tell you about Head Start: everybody likes it, and it doesn't cost very much." A week later, at the Cabinet meeting, Reagan administration budget director David Stockman proposed that Head Start be placed in a "safety net" of social programs that would not be cut. The new secretary of education, Terrel Bell, and secretary of defense, Caspar Weinberger, both agreed. Not coincidentally, Bell was among the education leaders with whom the CLS researchers had met in the late 1970s to explain their findings, conducting what was "in effect, a small seminar on the study from researchers skilled in presenting results and their implications, confident of the sturdiness of the findings, and assured that they should be put into practice in expansion of quality early childhood programs."[43] At that Cabinet meeting, Bell voiced the view that Head Start was effective in preventing later school failure, and deserving of continuing support.

PRE-KINDERGARTEN AND STATE EDUCATION REFORM

Research about the promise of preschool programs also captured the attention of a growing number of policymakers who were concerned with reforming K–12 schools. A dynamic education reform movement during the 1980s embraced early childhood education as an important tool for improving educational outcomes for poor children. As part of this effort to improve public education, state leaders created pre-kindergarten programs and other initiatives that tied early childhood services more closely to the public schools. In so doing, they opened up a new path to securing public support for preschool.

This broad reform movement was launched when Bell created a national commission to investigate the state of American education, hoping it would be a means of "rallying the American people around their schools" and shaking educators out of their complacency.[44] The commission's influential 1983 report, *A Nation at Risk,* argued powerfully that the weak state of American education was undercutting the nation's economic competitiveness abroad. At a time of severe economic recession, marked by plant closings and widespread unemployment, linking education to economic competitiveness was an effective way to raise alarm. Likewise, in a time of rising Cold War tensions, the report's military language was compelling:

> If an unfriendly foreign power had attempted to impose on America the mediocre educational performance that exists today, we might well have viewed it as an act of war. As it stands, we have allowed this to happen to ourselves...We have, in effect, been committing an act of unthinking, unilateral educational disarmament.

The report hit a responsive chord and had a huge impact. More than a half-million copies were distributed; the *New York Times* said the report "brought the issue [of education] to the forefront of political debate with an urgency not felt since the Soviet satellite shook American confidence in its public schools in

1957."[45] Combined with several other reports on education that appeared around the same time, it galvanized a national school reform movement.

School reform efforts across the country were fueled by concern about the relationship between the deteriorating American economy and the educational system. The education reform agenda was focused on promoting "excellence" in education by raising graduation requirements in academic subjects, lengthening the school day and year, requiring homework, raising teacher salaries, standardizing curricula, reducing class sizes, and expanding early childhood programs. Many southern leaders, anxious to spur economic growth in their states, became champions of improving education as a necessary first step in the revitalization of their economies. Democratic and Republican governors— including Charles Robb of Virginia, Bill Clinton of Arkansas, James Hunt of North Carolina, Richard Riley of South Carolina, William Winter of Mississippi, and Lamar Alexander of Tennessee—embraced school reform both as a means of shifting their states' economies and as a politically winning issue. They took leading roles in school reform movements, establishing reform commissions and sponsoring their own legislative packages. Governor Martha Layne Collins of Kentucky even went so far as to appoint herself as her state's secretary of education in order to help push legislation through in 1985.[46] Some of these governors also became part of a national movement to improve education, working through the National Governors Association and in alliance with business and corporate leaders.

Business leaders became powerful allies for political leaders seeking to change education policies. Employers were concerned about high school graduates' lack of preparation for work; a quarter of youth were not finishing high school, while nearly 13 percent of seventeen-year-olds enrolled in school were functionally illiterate. By contrast, students in Japan, the United States' major economic competitor in the 1980s, had the highest rate of high school completion and literacy in the world and led the world in science and mathematics scores. Japanese students not only spent more time in school but also completed a much more rigorous academic curriculum than their American counterparts. This concern with economic growth captured the attention of business leaders as well as policymakers across the country. For instance, an education reform task force in Oklahoma proclaimed in 1990: "If we do not find a way to create a measurably superior system of elementary and secondary education, we may well be relegated to a kind of domestic Third World status. This will mean decreasing opportunity for us, with only emigration offering a future for our children."[47]

States responded to *A Nation at Risk* with a burst of legislative activity focused on raising the bar for students and teachers. Only fifteen months after the report was released, over 250 state task forces had been created to study virtually every aspect of education; forty-four states raised high school graduation requirements, forty-five strengthened teacher certification requirements, and twenty-seven increased instructional time. Arkansas alone passed 122 separate education bills in a twelve-month period.[48] State legislative activity resulted in new mandates for schools, sweeping legislative packages in more than fifteen states, and large increases in education funding. Although a serious economic recession in the early 1980s had prompted attention to the issue of the nation's economic competitiveness, the country rebounded quickly from this crisis, leaving many states with budget surpluses. The nation's total spending on elementary and secondary education grew 25 percent (after inflation) from 1982 to 1987.[49]

While *A Nation at Risk* had focused almost exclusively on the problems of high school education, the school reform movement that followed it turned to early childhood education as one way to improve the system. Reformers concerned about enabling all students to succeed in school were naturally intrigued by the CLS and other research that found that disadvantaged children who had attended high-quality preschool programs were less likely to drop out of school or be retained in grade. Therefore, promoting "school readiness" became an important element in the education reform agenda. In the National Governors Association 1986 report on education, *Time for Results*, a task force on school readiness endorsed the idea of reducing "at-risk" children's risk of failure by ensuring that they started out school ready to learn. The governors noted that demographic changes in the nation's population meant that schools would be "working with an increasing number of students from groups with whom they have been less successful" in the past, while asking these students to meet a higher academic standard. Studies of programs like the Perry Preschool, showing that quality early childhood programs could have a major impact, promised to offer a solution.[50]

Issues relating to young children were rising on the agenda, tied to long-term concerns about education and the nation's economy. In several states, pre-kindergarten was part of larger education reform packages. For instance, Texas's pre-kindergarten program was introduced in 1984 as part of broad school reform legislation championed by H. Ross Perot along with increased student and teacher testing, a statewide curriculum, and reduced class size.[51] Similarly, Kentucky's 1990 education reform law made a sweeping reform of state education, adding preschool as a means of enhancing school readiness, along with restructuring school funding and creating statewide school-accountability systems, school-based decisionmaking, multiage classrooms, and family resource centers in elementary and secondary schools. In 1987, the Council of Chief

State School Officers included providing pre-kindergarten to all disadvantaged four-year-olds on a list of eleven steps states needed to take in order to give all students the opportunity to graduate from high school.[52] When the Southern Regional Education Board, an influential organization of southern governors, legislators, and education officials, listed twelve goals to improve education in the region, first on the list was that by the year 2000 "all children will be ready for the first grade."[53]

The K–12 reform movement of the 1980s culminated in a national "education summit" held in Charlottesville, Virginia, in 1989, where the nation's governors came together with President Bush and others to work out a common agenda on education reform. The governors created six national education goals, aimed at increasing America's economic competitiveness by improving student outcomes; they were translated into federal legislation in 1994, and they became a focal point of education reform in the 1990s. Although tension among federal and state and local authorities over education would undermine efforts to set a truly national education policy, the goals brought Republicans and Democrats together around a common agenda and energized educators, business leaders, and other organizations around it as well.[54] The first of the six goals was that "all children in America will start school ready to learn." This reflected the extent to which school readiness had been integrated into the education reform movement's agenda during the 1980s. It was not clear how to track progress toward what educator Ernest Boyer called a "bold, hugely optimistic" goal, or even what sector of society was responsible for it. But this national goal recognizing early childhood's importance to education overall was an important step forward. Rima Shore writes: "The fact that young children topped the nation's list of education goals dramatically changed the national debate on early childhood services, shifting the focus from child care geared to parents' work needs to early education geared to children's learning needs."[55]

To improve disadvantaged children's school readiness, state legislators and education leaders launched a range of new initiatives: funding pre-kindergarten programs, launching home-based parent education programs such as Parents as Teachers, improving child care settings, adding state funding to expand Head Start programs, and increasing funding for kindergarten. Some states provided funding for full-day kindergarten, while a few made it mandatory for districts to offer kindergarten or for students to attend. (Despite the fact that kindergarten attendance was only mandatory in a handful of states, over 85 percent of children nationally were attending kindergarten, and the number attending full-day kindergarten grew from 25 percent in 1979 to 40 percent by 1989.)[56] As schools sought to improve overall student achievement, kindergarten curricula became more focused on academic skills; teachers described it as "what first grade used to be," with increasing reliance on paper-and-pencil tasks, individual seatwork, and a curriculum divided into separate subjects.

With kindergarten becoming both more widespread and more academic, concern about "readiness" mounted. Across the country, the age cutoff for entering kindergarten was raised, as older children were more likely to be able to handle the demands of learning. Some school districts conducted readiness screenings of all children entering kindergarten; children deemed "unready" were retained in kindergarten or put in transitional programs before entering first grade.[57] Fearing that schools were overemphasizing academic and cognitive skills and relying on testing and formal, direct instruction, in 1986 the National Association for the Education of Young Children started championing what it called "developmentally appropriate practice."[58] Pre-kindergarten thus seemed an attractive way to help get children ready for school—a role that kindergarten itself had played in earlier generations.

By 1989, thirty-one states were either funding their own pre-kindergarten programs or contributing funds to expand Head Start; almost all of these programs were instituted during the 1980s.[59] These state pre-kindergarten initiatives were typically fairly small-scale, part-day programs that targeted "at-risk" four-year-olds (identified by income, language, and other factors) in order to increase school readiness; some programs also served three-year-olds. For instance, in 1984 the Texas legislature created a pre-kindergarten program to serve high-risk four-year-olds. "The goal was to break the debilitating cycle of costly remediation and school failure in later grades by building a solid foundation of school successes among 4-year-olds."[60] Some states required that children be individually assessed to be eligible for programs, while others determined eligibility based on family or school district characteristics. In a few states, like Oklahoma, programs were not limited to "at-risk" or "disadvantaged" children but were open to any child who was the correct age in districts that were able to offer the program.

Leaders in a few big cities tried to make pre-kindergarten universal, with mixed success. The District of Columbia offered pre-kindergarten in its public schools to all children in the district, starting in 1982; by the late 1980s it was serving more than 60 percent of the city's four-year-olds. In New York City, Mayor Ed Koch announced in 1985 that he would begin to phase in "public education for all four-year-olds" with a program called Project Giant Step, inspired by the Perry Preschool research. Koch's aides were convinced that a high-quality preschool program could help assuage business leaders' concerns about the state of the city's schools, while also helping to ameliorate the effects of escalating poverty among the city's growing minority and immigrant population. They thought that if New York City developed its own version of the

Perry Preschool program and made it widely available, it would bring national recognition to Koch's innovation and leadership. Project Giant Step gained favorable attention and set an important precedent, although it ended up being implemented on a more modest scale than Koch had first envisioned, and was dismantled after he left office.[61]

At the state level, pre-kindergarten programs were strongly linked to public education; they were almost always administered by state departments of education and were typically located in school buildings (although some states allowed other providers to offer the programs as well). Some states incorporated pre-kindergarten into their school-aid formulas and school codes; more states offered a special grant program for which school districts could apply. Including pre-kindergarten in school aid calculations helped provide fiscal stability, but early educators feared that such an approach tended to produce a downward extension of elementary schooling rather than a program appropriate for young children. However, the majority of state pre-kindergarten initiatives looked to early childhood programs rather than elementary school as a model, following standard requirements for good early childhood programs such as teacher-to-child ratios, teacher training, and group size.

Although these state programs were inspired by the CLS and Perry Preschool research on the long-term benefits of early education, they fell far short of providing the level of resources that had helped make these model programs so successful. Research demonstrating short- and long-term benefits of early edu-

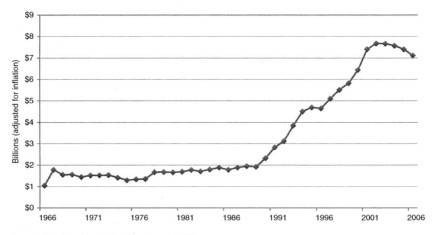

Figure 3.2 Head Start Funding, 1966–2006
Source: Administration for Children and Families, U.S. Department of Health and Human Services, "Head Start Enrollment History—Head Start Program Fact Sheet" (2008), www.acf.hhs.gov/programs/ohs/about/fy2008. html (accessed April 23, 2008). Funding adjusted for inflation (to 2008 dollars) using a GDP inflator.

cation was "the most significant factor influencing legislative support for early childhood education," a report by the National Conference of State Legislatures noted.[62] Researchers' estimate that the Perry Preschool program saved $7 in other spending for every $1 it cost particularly captured the attention of policymakers and the general public, who assumed that any preschool program would produce a similar cost-benefit ratio. Noting the impact of this research, a legislator from Massachusetts said at a symposium on the issue: "Thank God for the Perry Preschool Project!" Strikingly, *every* person that scholar Anne McGill-Franzen interviewed for a 1988 study on early education in New York mentioned the Perry Preschool findings, while some people working in the field acknowledged that its benefits were sometimes overstated.[63] In fact, the state pre-kindergarten programs never approximated the model programs' intensity and quality. Notably, per-child spending on state pre-kindergarten programs was about one-third of what the Perry Preschool program cost. Most were small, part-day programs, and the level of resources they had varied

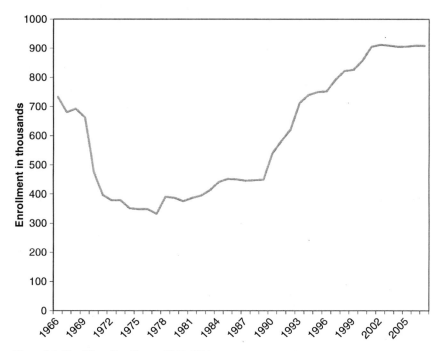

Figure 3.3 Head Start Enrollment, 1966–2006

Source: Administration for Children and Families, U.S. Department of Health and Human Services, "Head Start Enrollment History—Head Start Program Fact Sheet" (2008), www.acf.hhs.gov/programs/ohs/about/fy2008. html (accessed April 23, 2008).

widely, as did their requirements for teacher training, group size, curriculum, and other factors that shaped program quality.

Similarly, although Head Start programs did not have the same kind of staff, funding, or curriculum as model programs like Perry Preschool, they continued to benefit by association. By the end of the decade, it seemed that, as writers for *Newsweek* put it, "everybody likes Head Start."[64] The National Head Start Association—made up of parents, teachers, and supporters of the program—played a crucial role in cultivating support in Congress, even among conservative legislators. By the late 1980s, Republicans and Democrats were almost competing to see who could provide the greatest boost for Head Start, while governors and business leaders lent their strong support as well. For instance, in 1990, the Bush administration sought to add $500 million to Head Start's budget, while Democrats in the Senate were seeking $6 billion in order to "fully fund" the program—to serve three- as well as four-year-olds and to increase the spending per child in order to achieve higher quality.[65] The 1990 reauthorization of Head Start provided the largest budget increase the program had seen; authorized levels were enough to serve all eligible three- and four-year-olds, although appropriation levels were lower, allowing enrollment of about 40 percent of eligible children. The reauthorization also set aside funds for quality improvements, and increased requirements for teachers (mandating that every Head Start classroom have at least one teacher with a CDA credential by 1994).

"NATURAL ALLIES"? EARLY CHILDHOOD AND THE PUBLIC SCHOOLS

At the same time, some children's advocates were also looking to an alliance with the K–12 schools as a promising avenue for improving programs for young children. One national child care advocate remembered realizing in the mid-1980s that "we would never get child care to quality because it was 'child care'" and had to be kept affordable. She saw expanding pre-kindergarten and Head Start—which were both defined as educational and were typically offered without charge to parents—as a way to achieve high quality for more children.[66]

Bettye Caldwell, whose 1960s early intervention program for infants in Syracuse had been an inspiration for Head Start, believed a connection with the public schools could improve the image of child care. A strong connection with public education would help shift day care's image from social service programs for troubled, poor families to educational services that many families would want to use. Caldwell suggested that the very term "day care" should be left behind, offering the phrase "educare" in its place. Day care and education, she noted, were at once "natural allies" and "natural enemies"; each had turned against the other in order to bolster its own standing. But in the end, they needed each other. A stronger alliance between schools and child care would improve day care's image and would help schools serve families better, helping them compete more effectively with private schools. Drawing on her experience developing school-based programs in Little Rock, Arkansas, Caldwell urged schools to adapt to the changing needs of families in the 1980s by offering before- and after-school and child care programs.[67]

Similarly, dismayed at what he considered the abysmal state of child care in the United States, Ed Zigler was drawn to the idea of trying to create support for child care in the public schools. Rather than building a separate, federally funded system for child care as he had tried to do in 1971, Zigler now believed it was more practical to work through the existing system of local public schools. "We can solve the child care crisis by implementing a second system within existing elementary-school buildings and create the school of the twenty-first century," he proclaimed in 1987.[68] This school would offer child care for preschoolers and school-age children (funded by parent fees on a sliding scale), parent education, health and nutrition services, and other services to support families. School districts in Missouri, Colorado, Massachusetts, and elsewhere that were looking for a way to revitalize their schools and serve their changing communities adopted Zigler's model, which was ultimately implemented in more than a thousand schools and became the basis for state-level programs in Kentucky and Connecticut. His colleague Matia Finn-Stevenson later noted that this idea was a direct response to the legacy of previous policy decisions. "We had an opportunity to build a system for child care" back in the early 1970s, when Congress passed the Child Development Act, she observed—

> but we missed the chance. Twenty years after that, in 1990 it was a totally different story because it became such an immense problem...: not only was a larger number of children involved, but also what was built in the interim was this patchwork—family day care, for profit, nonprofit, church-based, and all sorts of things.... So the idea that we could come up with a system, a child care system, and wipe out everything and start from scratch just didn't make sense. And even if it did, there wouldn't be the money that you needed to address it."

Zigler felt he had learned the futility of trying to make social policy along Scandinavian lines in the United States, with its ethos of private family responsibility and of a limited role for national government. Schools, he argued, were where the children already were, and where the stable money was. The school "is the only universal entitlement children in America have, no other, none. And we never have to worry, will the schools open in the fall, they're always going to open." Furthermore, linking child care to education was essential to building public support. He recalled that part of his thinking

> was a growing recognition that the term "child care" is almost pejorative in America.... Make it education, then you've got something to sell.... There's absolutely no difference between good child care and an educational setting except the length of the day.... So if you want it to be educational and help the kid, make it education. Climb into the education tent, that's where the action is. That's what people want to pay for, what they see the value of.[69]

Other school districts in the 1980s were also starting their own early childhood programs, independent from any state or federal policy. They were motivated by multiple goals: to help meet needs for child care, to attract families to their communities, and to prepare children for kindergarten. For instance, a district near Reading, Pennsylvania, started a child care program in 1983 because district officials were concerned about both declining enrollments and children's difficulties when they started school. A school-based child care classroom promised to provide a higher quality experience for children than the local private centers offered, keep more families in the school district, and even prevent the closing of an elementary school.[70] At the same time, changes in federal special education law required school districts to provide a "free and appropriate public education" to handicapped preschoolers, extending the services required under the Education for All Handicapped Children Act. This move provided a boost to school district preschool programs by providing a framework within which to provide preschool to economically disadvantaged as well as physically handicapped children.[71] Researchers at the Bank Street College of Education reported in 1989 that schools were mixing public and private funding for early childhood programs in various ways, including Head Start, Chapter I (of the Elementary and Secondary Education Act), special education, subsidized child care, state-funded pre-kindergarten, magnet school pre-kindergarten, and tuition-supported child care and nursery schools. Although school-based programs represented a small fraction of all early childhood programs, they were clearly an expanding part of "the early childhood 'ecosystem.'"[72]

State education leaders and their allies increasingly paid attention to early childhood education, urging an expanded role for the schools. In 1988, the Council of Chief State School Officers declared that "the single most important investment to be made in education is the provision of high-quality programs for the nation's youngest children," and called for every at-risk four-year-old to be guaranteed an opportunity to attend a publicly funded pre-kindergarten program.[73] The National Association of State Boards of Education called for stronger ties between public schools and the early childhood world in order to improve the nation's "diverse, underfunded, and uncoordinated system for delivering programs to young children." The Association recommended that elementary schools create early childhood units to focus on children aged four to eight and develop partnerships with existing early childhood programs in their communities to better organize the patchwork of services. Just as college presidents and business executives were becoming involved in strengthening the public schools, the Association argued, school leaders needed to become advocates for strengthening early childhood programs, whether or not they were located in public schools.[74] The Committee on Economic Development, a business think tank that had played an important role in cultivating business support for K–12 education reform, wrote in 1987 that school reform could not succeed if it ignored the plight of educationally disadvantaged children. Only "an early and sustained intervention in the lives of disadvantaged children, both in school and out," would help build the educated workforce that business needed. This meant funding quality preschool programs for all disadvantaged three- and four-year-olds, a "superior educational investment for society."[75]

Growing support for pre-kindergarten seemed to offer the chance to weave together the separate strands of child care and early childhood education. Economist W. Norton Grubb wrote in 1987 that since most states were just beginning to formulate public policy for young children, they had the unique opportunity to create policy "from scratch," erasing outdated distinctions between child care and education and reconciling K–12 and early childhood educators' different teaching philosophies. Parents sought *both* care and education for their children, and good early childhood programs could combine multiple goals with sound pedagogical approaches.[76] But state policymakers generally did not approach the issue with this goal of integrating care and education. Rather, they started part-day pre-kindergarten programs as an education reform, and they addressed child care as a separate issue, without creating any ties between these two types of early childhood services. Furthermore, the growth of private child care and preschool programs since the early 1970s meant that the blank slate on which Grubb hoped policymakers could write new policies for young children was in fact already crowded with existing providers ready to defend their turf.

For their part, early childhood educators and providers were often suspicious of public school leaders' newfound interest in offering early childhood programs. Fearing that schools were trying to take over the finite resources that existed for young children's programs, they argued that the public schools had an unfair advantage in competition with private providers. Remembering the American Federation of Teachers' campaign for school-based child care in the mid-1970s, many believed that the public schools were trying to take over child care in order to claim new jobs for teachers. Some child care providers warned that independent child care programs would go out of business if public pre-kindergarten forced them to concentrate exclusively on serving infants and toddlers (typically the most expensive age group to serve because of child-to-staff ratios). Organizations of private providers were not afraid to fight against proposals they saw as threatening, and they lobbied at both state and federal levels to protect their interests.

Early childhood providers also objected to school-based programs on peda-gogical or philosophical grounds. Head Start and child care providers questioned whether schools could muster the flexibility needed to work effectively with parents, collaborate with other agencies, and offer a range of services. Many doubted the schools' ability to offer developmentally appropriate programs for young children and feared that school programs would simply provide a "pushed-down" first-grade curriculum taught by teachers who did not understand young children's development. For instance, Zigler cautioned against extending academics downward, proclaiming: "Our four-year-olds do have a place in school, but it is not at a school desk."[77] Early childhood educators feared that school-based programs would overemphasize academics and direct instruction rather than nurturing children's overall development and sense of competence. Grubb noted that while this criticism of rigid and didactic school classrooms was overdrawn, it was based on a real distinction in peda-gogical approaches. While most early childhood programs were organized around child-initiated activity and exploration in a range of domains (social, cognitive, and physical), most elementary classrooms were oriented toward teacher-directed instruction in academic subjects. The 1989 Bank Street study of public school-based programs for young children addressed these fears, finding that most school-based programs aimed to provide "developmentally appropriate" classrooms and were appropriately furnished with materials for children to explore. But such schools did struggle to reconcile a holistic, developmental approach with district goals of raising scores on school readiness assessments. Others—often in urban districts with large minority populations—had a teacher-centered, direct instruction focus rather than a developmental one.[78]

During the 1980s, the separate strands of K–12 education and early childhood moved closer together, spurred by the spread of research findings about the promise of preschool on the one hand and a growing sense that programs for young children needed a stronger foundation of support on the other.

Interest in strong early education programs now developed among K–12 educators who had previously not thought much about children below the age of kindergarten, while some children's advocates turned to the schools as the best avenue for gaining public support and legitimacy for young children's programs. It was still not clear, however, whether schools and early childhood providers could overcome their tradition of competition in order to build a strong alliance.

CONCLUSION

By the end of the decade, the question of public responsibility for young children was being intently debated within the separate policy worlds of K–12 education reform and child care. The education reform movement of the 1980s drew preschool closer to the world of public education, making school readiness a central part of school reform. States launched pre-kindergarten programs; leading reformers and education groups called for a coherent system of early education for disadvantaged children; and federal policymakers seemed united behind expanding Head Start. At the same time, child care, which had been largely invisible as a political issue since the mid-1970s, briefly became a focus of national politics as Congress wrestled with competing approaches. In neither education nor child care were the policy responses adequate to address the need: state pre-kindergarten programs, Head Start, and subsidized day care served only fractions of the poor families who were eligible, while the needs of middle-class families were not directly addressed at all. But these new commitments to young children's care and education strengthened the different strands of policy for young children, creating the possibility that they might later be woven together.

CHAPTER 4

Opening Doors to Universal Preschool in the 1990s

Most of the state pre-kindergarten programs created in the 1980s remained relatively small ones focused on "at-risk" children. But during the 1990s, a few states moved to make pre-kindergarten programs available to a much wider population. An explosion of public interest in young children's brain development, as well as accumulating research showing the positive long-term impact of early childhood education, drew attention to the promise of preschool. Another type of promise—that offering preschool to all children would increase political support for public programs—also inspired governors, legislators, and education officials. Georgia, New York, and Oklahoma made publicly funded pre-kindergarten "universal," open to all children whose parents chose to enroll them. Each of these states pioneered the idea that preschool should be available to all children, laying the groundwork that would lead to a national movement for "preschool for all." At the same time, courts in New Jersey required the state's poorest school districts to offer preschool to all children as part of an unprecedented effort to address inequality in the state's schools, reinforcing the idea that public preschool should be targeted to those who needed it most.

In each of these states, the intersection of economic opportunity and education reform spurred creative leaders to turn to pre-kindergarten, although different individuals and priorities shaped each state's approach. In Georgia, Governor Zell Miller latched onto the idea of pre-kindergarten as a means of improving education and boosting his state's economy. When the success of the state lottery for education created the opportunity to expand the program, he did it in a way that would "touch all Georgians," creating a broad constituency. In Oklahoma, pre-kindergarten was part of a reform the state legislature demanded when the K–12 system faced a fiscal crisis. Here education officials and legislators took the lead, quietly expanding their school-based program to make it universal without much public fanfare. In New York, early childhood advocates mobilized to implement a universal program at a time of economic growth but were stalled for a number of years by fiscal crises and the opposition of their governor. Legislators protected the program from the budget axe, arguing that pre-kindergarten should be available to all as part of the state's education system. New Jersey's preschool expansion, on the other hand, was driven by a court's ruling that the state must provide more funding to children in its most disadvantaged school districts. Concluding that other state leaders had failed to equalize educational opportunity in this wealthy state, the court played an active role in shaping the preschool program that resulted.

INSPIRING RESEARCH

In explaining how legislators in New York state came to the idea of expanding pre-kindergarten in 1996, one advocate commented that they would have had to be "hiding under a rock" not to have heard about early childhood education. Another recalled: "In 1996, as you may or may not recall, you couldn't pick up a newspaper without reading about brain development."[1] Indeed, the mid-1990s saw an unprecedented surge in media and public attention to neuroscience research about brain development that supported the idea that the first few years of life were a crucial period for brain growth. New imaging techniques that allowed researchers to map brain activity, such as functional magnetic resonance imaging and positron-emission tomography, attracted great attention. The prospect of being able to see "inside the brain" was tantalizing, enlivening the idea that babies' brains undergo massive change.[2]

Descriptions of this research—combining high-tech science and phrases like "hard wiring" with a message about the importance of nurturing—had wide appeal. Parents eager to increase their children's intellectual potential were an important audience for this message, which also reinforced folk wisdom about the importance of early childhood in the shaping of individual destiny and character. When *Newsweek* ran a cover story in 1996 entitled "Your Child's Brain," it was greeted with an overwhelming public reaction; the magazine received over a million reprint requests, more than for any article it had ever published. First lady Hillary Clinton hosted a White House conference on young children's cognitive development in 1997, declaring that new discoveries about the brain were as important as earlier discoveries about protecting children's physical health.[3] In tandem with the conference, actor-producer Rob Reiner organized a national media campaign entitled "I Am Your Child" to increase public interest in the needs of children during the first three years of life. This campaign used slogans such as "The first years last forever" and "The early years are learning years" to stress the importance of nurturing and stimulating babies and toddlers. Celebrities ranging from basketball star Shaquille O'Neal to actor Tom Hanks appeared in a prime-time television special focusing on the importance of the first three years of life. Building on this momentum, national and local media, parenting magazines, and teacher publications put forth a steady stream of articles on the implications of the new brain science.[4]

Significantly, publicity about brain research emphasized the needs of *all* children for stimulating and healthy development. It provided a basis for talking about the common needs of all children, not just the poorest, and its potential audience included every family in America. Entrepreneurs capitalized on the new interest in babies' intellectual development, promising parents that educational toys, Mozart recordings for the crib, and black-and-white graphics for decorating the nursery would help stimulate their babies' mental development. State policymakers also paid attention; the National Governors Association focused its 1998 conference on early development, and early childhood initiatives were under way in twenty-five states. Twelve governors mentioned brain research in calling for early childhood development programs during the 1998 legislative session. Legislative presentations and agency reports on the need to increase funding for early childhood programs often included copies of *Time* and *Newsweek* articles on brain development.[5]

Advocates sought to build on this remarkable public interest in early childhood development to create support for policies aimed at infants and toddlers such as Early Head Start, home visiting programs, expanding parental leave, health insurance coverage, and standards for child care programs. But garnering support for public funding for these programs often met with resistance from those who felt that care of these very young children was a private family responsibility. Moreover, the way child care policy had so far evolved made it difficult to raise quality standards. When the 1996 welfare reform pushed thousands of poor mothers into the workforce, additional funds were used to serve larger numbers of children rather than investing in the kind of nurturing and stimulating care for which the brain research seemed to call. In fact, the funds the CCDBG originally set aside for quality improvements were drastically reduced in order to channel more federal money into expanding the number of available slots for children to be served. Although more federal funding was available than ever before, the demand for child care continued to outstrip the supply.[6]

Interest in early childhood development was instead channeled into expanding opportunities for preschool education. Although the brain research emphasized the first three years of life, preschool advocates called attention to children's learning in their first *five* years of life. For instance, in 1998, California voters approved a measure backed by the Reiner Foundation instituting a 50-cent cigarette tax to fund a variety of programs for children from birth to age five, including universal pre-kindergarten programs for four-year-olds. Nationally, funding for state pre-kindergarten programs grew, resulting in an enrollment jump from about 290,000 to nearly 725,000 by the end of the decade, while Head Start also continued to expand.[7]

Support for expanding preschool was also bolstered by accumulating research on its long-term benefits for disadvantaged children. By the late 1990s, important findings from longitudinal studies of several different early child-hood projects, as well as several rigorous reviews of this literature, had been published. Researchers had found long-term benefits not only from small, experimental programs like the Perry Preschool program but also from the large-scale, publicly funded Chicago Child-Parent Centers. This program had been started in eleven public schools in the late 1960s with Title I money to provide economically disadvantaged children with preschool education, health, and social services. With additional state funding in the late 1970s, it expanded to include services through third grade, including reduced class size, full-day kindergarten, parental involvement, health screenings, and free meals. Participating children had higher achievement scores, lower rates of retention in grade, and higher rates of parental involvement even years after the end of the program. Another significant piece of research was a study of the Abecedarian Project, which operated from 1972 to 1985 in Chapel Hill, North Carolina. The program worked with at-risk African-American children from infancy through the early elementary grades, providing full-day, year-round educational child care and health services, as well as enabling parents to support their children's learning at home. Studies of the project published in 1995 revealed that the preschool component of the program had the strongest effects on IQ, while the school-age components helped maintain higher achievement test scores and reduce special education placement and retention in grade by more than 20 percentage points. Both the Chicago and Abecedarian studies found that while IQ effects disappeared with time, there were longer lasting effects on achievement scores and other educational outcomes such as grade retention and the need for special education.[8]

Longitudinal studies like these allowed researchers to devise cost-benefit figures for early childhood interventions, following the lead of the Perry Preschool researchers. Economists calculated that by helping children to succeed in school, these programs saved society much more in special education, crime, and welfare costs than they cost to operate. For each $1 invested in a high-quality early intervention program, society saved between $2 (Abecedarian) and $7 (Chicago Child-Parent Centers, Perry Preschool) over the long term.

Such cost-benefit analyses captured the attention of policymakers and the public, and were frequently cited in discussions of early childhood initiatives, as if every early education program, no matter how it was designed and whom it served, would have similar results. However, as economist Janet Currie wrote, "cost/benefit analysis should not be regarded as an exact science."[9] Taken collectively, these studies provided strong support for the idea that investing in such programs was not only morally right but also fiscally responsible. This economic argument would come to play a crucial role in the growth of public pre-kindergarten programs, appealing to business leaders and policymakers looking for evidence that their investment of public dollars would bring a worthwhile return.

"A PROGRAM THAT WOULD TOUCH ALL GEORGIANS"

Georgia was the first state to make preschool universally available, shifting in 1995 from a program aimed at disadvantaged children to one that was open to all. Democratic Governor Zell Miller made a bold move to open up preschool programs to every four-year-old in the state, believing that this was the best way to broaden support for his pre-kindergarten program for poor children. While research findings originally led Miller to the idea of pre-kindergarten, it was political instinct that inspired him to make the program universal, creating a broad constituency for state-funded pre-kindergarten.

During his campaign for governor in 1990, Miller had championed a new "lottery for education" as a means of bringing badly needed resources into the state's education system, which consistently ranked toward the bottom in the nation. Miller made his gubernatorial campaign a referendum on the lottery idea, promising that ticket proceeds would be used to supplement public education funds, and won. The *Atlanta Journal and Constitution* wrote: "In the public mind it will be Mr. Miller's lottery. Few politicians have ever been so totally identified with a single issue. That puts the results—good or bad—squarely on his shoulders."[10] Determined that the new lottery funds would not get "lost in the education bureaucracy," Miller specified that the money be earmarked for distinctive programs that could have broad impact and appeal: a pre-kindergarten program for disadvantaged four-year-olds, college scholarships, and funds for technology and equipment in K–12 schools. These funds would not go through the normal budget process in the legislature but would be administered by an independent commission that the governor controlled.[11]

A former educator with a missionary zeal for improving education in the state, Miller was familiar with national education trends, and saw a preschool program for disadvantaged children as an effective way to improve educational outcomes. Drawing on research such as the Perry Preschool and Abecedarian studies, he touted the pre-kindergarten program for poor children as a solution to the state's high dropout rate, as well as to problems of like teen pregnancy and crime. Georgia's pre-kindergarten started as a pilot program in September 1992 and grew to serving 15,500 low-income children by 1994. The new program had much in common with Head Start: a developmentally appropriate curriculum, emphasis on community collaboration, health and social services, and relatively low requirements for teacher training.

When the lottery ended up producing almost twice as much money as had been expected, some early childhood experts advised the governor to use the money to extend the program to disadvantaged three-year-olds. But Miller, a Democrat, had been reelected in 1994 by a narrow margin in an increasingly Republican state, and he decided that building broader support for his education programs was more pressing. In 1995, he announced that all four-year-olds in Georgia would be eligible to attend the voluntary program. At a press conference later that year, he declared:

> Today we become the first state in the country, indeed the first state in the nation's history, to offer Pre-K for every four-year-old who wants it. No longer will the program just serve at-risk students. The benefits of Pre-K now belong to every Georgia 4-year-old; the benefits of Pre-K now belong to every Georgia parent who has a 4-year-old.[12]

Miller clearly hoped to strengthen both the pre-kindergarten program and his own political base by opening it up to more families. Adviser Mike Volmer reflected:

> With the political conservative environment that we are living in, if we come out and try to push a program for poor kids, we're not going to get a whole lot of support. And so, what we made the decision to do is push a program that would touch all Georgians. So I don't know whether middle-class or upper-class people really need the program. But we needed their support.[13]

Middle-class families had, in fact, been pushing for access to Georgia's Pre-K program, asking their state representatives why they should have to pay for preschool when the governor had promised a lottery-funded program for Georgia's four-year-olds. By 1996, the program was even larger than Miller had envisioned, serving about 60,000 four-year-olds at cost of $200 million. A program administrator noted that the governor was right when he predicted that opening up the program to middle-class children would end up benefiting poor children as well; 25,000 low-income children were being served in 1996, 5,000 more than were being served when it was limited to the disadvantaged.[14]

Opening the program to all created huge logistical problems, of which the most immediate was finding space to house thousands of preschool programs. Since the state's school facilities were already crowded, administrators launching the smaller pre-kindergarten program for disadvantaged children in 1993 had decided to contract with private child care providers and Head Start programs to offer pre-kindergarten. Head Start providers were initially fearful that the state was coming to take away "their" four-year-olds (as they felt it had done with their five-year-olds when kindergarten was funded during the 1980s). But Head Start and the state pre-kindergarten program ultimately worked together well. Private, for-profit providers, however, showed little interest in participating in the state pre-kindergarten program as long as it was limited to disadvantaged children. According to one Department of Education staffer, not a single for-profit child care provider applied to be part of the first year's pilot program in 1992. Associations representing for-profit child care centers, anxious about the state taking over their business, had lobbied to keep the public program focused on low-income children. But when Miller opened up the program in 1995, Georgia Child Care Council president Susan Maxwell explained, private providers "knew they had to get in the game."[15]

Private providers need not have worried about being excluded, for the state needed them to make the experiment of universal pre-kindergarten work. Miller wanted to roll the program out quickly, so there was no time to spend constructing new buildings even if he had wanted to spend the money that way. Working with private child care providers who had available space made it possible to implement the program quickly, inexpensively, and on the large scale Miller had in mind. Furthermore, Miller and his advisers were surely aware of the political pressure that the for-profit child care industry, a powerful lobby in the state, could bring to bear. Maxwell said that private providers "would have tried to kill the program if they had not been allowed to participate," and others warned Miller that excluding private providers would hurt small businesses. Hundreds of private providers were part of the pre-K program the first year it was opened up; by 1997, 57 percent of the children in the program were being served in sites located outside the public schools, making Georgia's pre-K program "one of the nation's most extensive public-private education ventures."[16]

While Miller's decision to open up the Pre-K program to all four-year-olds seemed popular with parents, it was controversial elsewhere. Some educators and advocates feared that expanding the program would mean denying slots to low-income children, while conservatives sought to limit costs by keeping it focused on the poorest children. A Republican legislator from Atlanta said later that year: "There are just not going to be enough lottery dollars to float this program forever. It needs to be for at-risk children." Miller feared that an advisory committee studying the program in late 1995 wanted to take it back to four-year-olds at risk. "Over my dead body," he told reporters.[17]

Believing that he had to act quickly to save the program, Miller moved it out of the jurisdiction of the hostile state school superintendent and put it under the direction of his adviser Mike Volmer, who had a reputation as a "politically astute fix-it man." Volmer saw his main task as one of marketing and public relations: convincing the public that Pre-K was an educational program rather than a babysitting service. He and his staff developed a glossy brochure explaining the program's learning goals and presented Pre-K as an ambitious experiment in school choice—a cherished part of the conservative agenda. Volmer also worked to change the tone of the state's relationship with private providers running Pre-K programs, making the monitoring process more consultative and supportive. Marketing the program as an educational one also meant scaling back its social service components, which had seemed appropriate in a program for disadvantaged children but now seemed overly intrusive (as well as expensive). Full health screenings and transportation services were also cut, as was funding for extended day and summer programs, reducing the per-child cost of the program significantly (from about $5,000 to about $3,500).

Several of those close to the pre-kindergarten program believe that the decision to make it universal helped protect it. One administrator observed that while low-income children may be the most important beneficiaries of early education programs, "you can't mount a sustainable program without support from the middle class that votes." Volmer recalled:

> Legislators were shooting holes in this program [in 1996]. Now if you talk to them, I don't think they'd say anything negative—in a public manner anyway. Because they've got too many [middle-class] families…that are utilizing the program. And that's what we were aiming to do—make sure this was perceived as a middle-class program. It just so happened [to be] helping 30,000 at-risk children.

Because of the program's expansion, administrators heard from the "very verbal, very educated" middle-class parents who are committed to Pre-K and understand the kinds of strategies (such as calls and letters to representatives or organized rallies) that will help ensure the program's survival. Evaluator Gary Henry has concluded that "the big lesson" of Georgia's experience is that making programs available to a broad array of children "probably will increase geometrically the support for the program over time."[18]

Parents of different economic circumstances appreciated the ways the program helped them by lifting the financial burden of providing a good preschool experience for their children. A 2000 *Washington Post* article focused on Lori Pierce, a divorced mother of two who worked in the billing office of an Atlanta hotel. Pierce moved from Texas to Georgia in part because of Georgia's funding for preschool, which she believed would give her children a better start in life. In Texas, preschool cost her $115 a week per child, but with Georgia's state funding, her costs were half as much. "It means food and electricity to our family," she said. "It helps a lot, especially for single parents. In lots of states, they only help people in the lower income brackets. The middle-income people get no assistance. If you don't get any help, you end up struggling."[19]

Certainly Georgia's program garnered enormous popularity and acclaim, both within the state and nationally. A 1997 poll found that 85 percent of the Georgians who responded were supportive of using lottery revenues in support of Pre-K. Parents—including both "working" and "stay-at home" mothers—were lining up in the wee hours of the morning to register their children for pre-kindergarten at public school buildings, child care centers, YMCAs, recreation centers, converted grocery stores, military bases, and churches throughout the state. Some parents, competing for slots at the "best" programs (often those offering extras such as foreign language or ballet instruction) camped out at schools or traveled long distances to register their children.[20] (In 2008, parents in Atlanta who had been camping out for three days in the hope of getting their children into a particularly sought-after pre-K program were outraged when they learned that the campout line would be disbanded by police and not used for the registration process. The line had become such a tradition that the PTA had been auctioning off the use of trailers and RVs as a fundraiser.)[21] Harvard University's John F. Kennedy School of Government awarded Georgia's pre-K program the prestigious Innovations in American Government Award in 1997. *Atlanta Journal and Constitution* columnist Jeff Dickerson wrote: "For generations, the South has followed the lead of Massachusetts and other states in innovative, forward-looking programs. With Pre-K, we're on top."[22] *Education Week* concluded that Miller's push to open up both the pre-K and the HOPE college scholarships to all Georgians "is considered one of his wisest political moves." Both programs, funded by the lottery, were widely popular, were endorsed by Miller's successor, and were imitated by other states. Zell Miller left office in 1999 as one of the nation's most popular governors, and was named "Politician of the Year" by *Governing* magazine. In a 1998 article in the *New York Times*, he said of his popular education programs: "They are broad-based and you can see them. It touches your family, or it touches someone's family that you know."[23]

OKLAHOMA: QUIETLY ADDING A GRADE TO THE PUBLIC SCHOOLS

Oklahoma's pre-kindergarten program—which now serves a higher proportion of the state's four-year-olds than are served in any other state—was not the result of a visible campaign for universal pre-kindergarten or of active gubernatorial leadership. Rather, it was built by education officials and legislators who, during a crisis in the K–12 system, made preschool part of education reform and enabled it to grow through the school aid formula. More than any other state, Oklahoma has made pre-kindergarten part of its system of public education, essentially adding a grade to the public schools. While Georgia launched its program quickly by relying on the existing infrastructure of community early childhood programs, Oklahoma built up its program more gradually, making it part of the public schools from the beginning and ensuring high quality standards.

Oklahoma's pre-kindergarten program started on a small scale in 1980, but with a broad vision. When the state superintendent asked early childhood specialist Ramona Paul to create a model early childhood program, she hoped to extend the benefits of the public education system to programs for young children. She worked with Cleta Deatherage, a young legislator who had risen quickly to chair the key Appropriations and Budget Committee and had strong commitments to children's and women's issues. The fact that the programs were designed to be open to all children was a selling point in the legislature, Paul recalled, as it seemed unusual at a time when much federal aid to schools was restricted to serving children from specified groups. Indeed, Deatherage later said she would not support a program "if it were just another imitation of Head Start," wanting rather to provide something that would benefit all children. She worked to get Paul's model—with programs based in the schools, staffed by early childhood–certified teachers, and open to all children—funded as a small pilot program in 1980. Deatherage later explained: "We stuck it in through the back door," in a thick bill passed on the last day of the session. The legislation, which passed without much public discussion, provided for ten pilot pre-kindergarten programs in districts across the state.[24] As state funding increased over the next several years for the program for four-year-olds, it expanded to support thirty-four programs serving 1,400 children.

Oklahoma's preschool program grew as a part of a reform in the K–12 education system that the state's legislators demanded during a period of fiscal crisis. Schools were facing a funding crisis in the late 1980s, as the state's economy was rocked by a steep fall in oil prices and an agricultural depression. As other states responded to the *Nation at Risk* report with a wave of education reforms, Oklahoma was one of only two states in the nation where per-pupil spending decreased; by 1989, it had dropped to forty-sixth in the nation.[25] In 1989, the Republican governor, Henry Bellmon (fearing a court challenge and a teachers' strike), called a special session of the legislature to focus on education. Legislators made it clear they would not support a tax increase for schools without school reforms, and they appointed a task force to propose a revenue and reform package. Among other proposals, the task force called for an expansion of early childhood education, claiming that it "directly correlated to improvement in ultimate educational achievement." A preschool program for four-year-olds should be available to all children "regardless of socio-economic circumstances" and should be taught "by early childhood learning specialists in developmentally appropriate ways."[26]

The task force's proposed education reform bill became the focus of intense public debate and controversy in Oklahoma for the next two years. A local journalist wrote later: "In Oklahoma's history, possibly no single piece of legislation has inspired as much hope and as much controversy."[27] In April 1990, teachers' protests of the legislature's failure to pass the bill closed school systems throughout the state and brought thousands of teachers and supporters to demonstrate at the capitol. Oklahoma City schools flew the state flag upside down as a sign of distress—until veterans' groups objected. "It's kind of like the state has gone berserk," said the Tulsa school superintendent. "Everybody just [went] to lobby the legislature." Governor Bellmon supported the bill, which raised taxes on income, sales, and corporations in order to add about $200 million of revenue to the budget for schools, paying for early childhood programs as well as teacher salary increases, reduced class size, curriculum revisions, and school district consolidation. Many of Bellmon's fellow Republicans, however, opposed the bill. The service industry mounted an intense lobbying effort against the proposed tax, and the *Oklahoman* ran two front-page editorials against the education bill. Finally, in 1990, after struggle and delay in both houses of the legislature, HB 1017 was passed, as teachers watched from a packed Senate gallery.[28] But opponents of the law, including Stop Taxing Our People and the Oklahoma Taxpayers Union, waged a vigorous campaign to repeal the bill, collecting enough signatures on a petition to force a statewide referendum on repealing the law. This referendum became the top issue in the state, marked by intense debate and grassroots campaigning on both sides of the issue. The campaign even took a violent turn when a bomb exploded at the office of the Taxpayers Union and the organization blamed pro-1017 forces for the attack.[29]

Finally, in a record turnout in 1991, the referendum failed, and voters upheld the bill. The law had a significant impact on early childhood education in the state. Kindergarten attendance became mandatory, and preschool programs for four-year-olds, now funded through the state aid formula, spread to more schools than had been possible under the earlier pilot program. The standards Ramona Paul and her colleagues had written in 1980 continued to apply, including the requirement that preschool teachers be certified in early childhood education. The legislation gave priority to children who were eligible for Head Start, allowing them to attend free of charge; in practice, most of the children enrolled in these programs were from low-income families. By the 1992–93 school year, approximately 10 percent of all four-year-olds in Oklahoma were enrolled in a publicly funded pre-kindergarten program.[30]

In contrast to the public controversy and debate over the education reform bill, relatively little public attention was paid to the expansion of preschool programs in the mid-1990s. This growth in public preschool was part of a gradual building up of efforts by "passionate bureaucrats, savvy state politicians, and public-spirited business leaders" who followed a strategy of "doing good by stealth."[31] In 1996, Democratic legislators sought to expand the program for four-year-olds to a wider range of children by giving priority to children who were eligible for free and reduced-price lunch (rather than using the more restrictive Head Start eligibility measure). Since more than one-third of the children in the state would qualify under this guideline, this would have been a significant expansion.[32] Republican governor Frank Keating vetoed the bill, however, explaining that since "the challenge of educating kindergarten through twelfth grade has yet to be fully met," it was not the time to expand early childhood programs, possibly creating "a new unfunded liability in our education system in excess of Fifty Million Dollars." While Keating's main objection was fiscal, he also flagged it as an issue of cultural values: "The business of educating four-year-olds should be the responsibility of the parents, not the state." Legislators supporting the bill called Keating's $50 million figure "ridiculous," saying that that would be the cost if every single four-year-old in the state enrolled; the actual funding in the bill for early childhood programs was only $1 million. Keating's spokesman warned that public programs

> can start off small and become a cash-eating monster. . . . The liberals think, gee, what a nice idea, and then they rush off and create a new program with public

money that is like the Energizer bunny. It just keeps on going and going, costing more every year.[33]

But even legislators who opposed increasing state spending became persuaded to support the program for four-year-olds on the grounds that it was less expensive than kindergarten, where many of these students were being placed. A loophole in the school funding formula allowed school administrators to enroll four-year-olds in their kindergarten classes when there was space available. Since the maximum kindergarten class size was quite high, and there were morning and afternoon sessions of kindergarten, the opportunity to put four-year-olds into kindergarten classes was tempting, especially in rural districts whose overall enrollment was declining. Kay Floyd, who in 1996 was a lobbyist for the Oklahoma State School Boards Association, remembers talking to legislators about the issue: "We went over there and said, 'This is what's happening. Is this what you want?' People are serving four-year-olds anyway, why not have their own program for it?"[34] Legislators chose to fund the program for four-year-olds while closing the loophole that had allowed districts to enroll preschoolers in kindergarten.

Some also saw this as an opportunity to open up the program to serve all children. For Democratic legislator Joe Eddins, a staffer explains, this was a natural step. "It did not seem logical to him to have restrictions on something that is in the public schools, [and] is supposed to be for all children."[35] Statewide education groups also lobbied to make the program open to all children. Kay Floyd, the lobbyist for the Oklahoma State School Boards Association, remembers that the Oklahoma Department of Education "was behind us on this; they felt that anything that was part of the public schools, funded through the state aid formula, should be for all children." Similarly, the director of the state school administrators' association pushed for removing the income restrictions on the pre-kindergarten program. Talking with his members, he frequently heard that there was not much difference between children who qualified and those who didn't, and separating out the "poor" from the "near-poor" for enrollment in the program caused problems in communities.[36]

The desire to close the funding loophole that districts were using to enroll four-year-olds in kindergarten, along with increasing public attention to early education, was enough to gain support for a bill that would put the program for four-year-olds on firmer footing. In 1998, the legislature opened the program up to all four-year-olds, increased the funding weight for the program in the school aid formula, and prohibited enrolling underage children in kindergarten.[37] Despite his opposition to expanding the program two years earlier, Keating signed this bill without objection. His secretary of education later explained that since school administrators were already spending almost the amount of money it would take to have a program for four-year-olds, he felt the state "might as well go ahead and do it."[38]

In Oklahoma, making pre-kindergarten universal was a quiet revolution. Legislator Joe Eddins explained: "Some states have made a big deal and the governor and the legislature say, 'let's do something big.' That's not the way we did it here in Oklahoma."[39] Randall Raburn of the state school administrators' organization recalls that there "really was not much discussion of the budgetary impact of expanding four-year-old program," speculating that it may have "under the radar" for many people. Floyd concurs, noting that it was done quietly on purpose. "It was never the education coalition's approach to publicize issues beyond the legislature.... The stealth approach is the best way to get things done in this state." Rather than launching a public campaign to build support for the program for four-year-olds, it was more effective to "go to the people that support it and can make it happen."[40]

Unlike Georgia's highly publicized education lottery, Oklahoma's funding of universal pre-kindergarten was nearly invisible. Because it was funded through the state aid formula rather than as a line item in the budget, its costs were not as apparent and were not discussed annually in the legislature. As one legislator put it, the program was "funded by dilution," depending on money that might have gone elsewhere in the state's education budget. Since overall education spending was rising, however, it did not seem to have a negative impact.[41] Raburn observed that if every district had expanded its programs at once, it could have had quite a damaging effect on school budgets, but it grew gradually, so its impact was not as noticed. "This wasn't a way to get it funded," he explained. "It was a way to get it done."

In fact, by adding four-year-olds to the K–12 student population, the program helped some districts offset declines in overall enrollment. Statewide, K–12 enrollment dipped by about 1 percent between 1998 and 2007, but with the addition of pre-kindergarten, overall enrollment grew by about 2 percent. For some rural districts whose enrollments were declining, the opportunity to secure funding for four-year-olds was an incentive, even though the amount of state funding ($2,409 per child in 2003) was relatively low compared to that in other states.[42] The district of Yukon, for instance, decided to start a pre-kindergarten program in 2002 in part because of the funding, although school officials had originally hoped to start full-day kindergarten first. "'There's a big pile of money there,' the superintendent said. 'The money follows the students.'"[43]

Within five years, Oklahoma was serving 59 percent of its four-year-olds in state-funded pre-kindergarten—more than any state in the nation. (Georgia was the only other state to serve more than half its four-year-olds in 2003.)[44] The 1998 legislation spurred a dramatic expansion in the number of programs for four-year-olds across the state. Statewide preschool enrollment, which had already grown substantially during the mid-1990s, doubled in 1998, and by 2005 it had more than doubled again. By 2007, almost all of the state's 540 school districts were offering classes for four-year-olds, reaching 68 percent of the state's four-year-olds at a cost of about $118 million.[45] (See the map in fig. 6.2 showing pre-kindergarten enrollment by state.)

Thousands of parents were clearly eager to enroll their children. A teacher in one of the new pre-kindergarten programs in Tulsa said that parents "feel good it's being offered in a public school. I've heard a lot of people say, 'I wish they had this when mine was this old.'"[46] When the district of Moore launched a preschool program in 1999, responding to "continuous calls from the community for the last two or three years," demand far outstripped supply, with 300 children signed up for 160 slots. In 2003, officials decided they could no longer allow parents to camp out the night before pre-kindergarten enrollment to get their child a spot, citing security concerns raised by the local police.[47] Ramona Paul of the state education department explained that superintendents are glad to have a program that is popular with local parents. The strong base of support among parents for the program for four-year-olds seemed to promise its continuation even during periods of budget crisis.

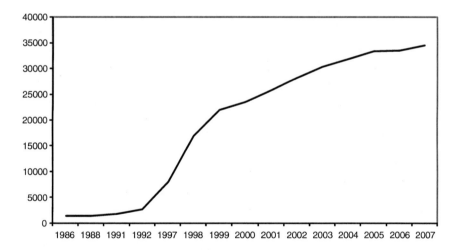

Figure 4.1 Oklahoma Pre-K Enrollment, 1986–2007
Source: For 1998–2005, data are from *Investing in Oklahoma* (Okla. State Dept. of Education, 2005), www.sde.state .ok.us/home/defaultns.html (accessed January 25, 2006), and "Oklahoma Pre-Kindergarten Enrollment," www.sde .state.ok.us/announcements/Enrollment/Pre-K%20Enrollment.jpg (accessed January 26, 2006). The 1986 figure is from Terry Gnezda and Susan Robison, "State Approaches to Early Childhood Education," *State Legislative Reports* (National Conference of State Legislatures, 1986) 11, no. 14, App. A; the 1988 figure is from Anne Mitchell, Michelle Seligson, and Fern Marx, *Early Childhood Programs and the Public Schools* (Dover, MA: Auburn House Publishing: 1989); the 1991 figure is from Adams and Sandfort, *First Steps, Promising Futures*; the 1992 figure is from Jim Killackey, "Early Childhood Classes Grow in Popularity," *The Oklahoman* (March 1, 1992); and the figure for 1997 is from Kay Floyd, Michael Jones, and Jeff Alexander, "Systems Integration for Successful School Readiness in Oklahoma," presentation to the Head Start State Collaboration Directors Meeting, Potomac, MD, May 6, 2004, p. 12.

With funding secure through the state aid formula and enrollment opened to all, the program for four-year-olds became an integral part of the public schools in most Oklahoma districts. More than any other state, Oklahoma has provided universally accessible pre-kindergarten by working through the structure of the public schools. State education officials maintained high quality standards in part by treating pre-kindergarten like other grades in the public education system: districts had to hire teachers certified in early childhood education, and to compensate them at the same rate as their other teachers. There was no mandated curriculum (though the state did develop voluntary curriculum guidelines for pre-kindergarten programs and required use of a standard report card) and no extensive system for monitoring classrooms. Rather, the strategy was to hire well-trained teachers and give them some flexibility about meeting their goals. The attention that Oklahoma has garnered from national organizations for its success in creating universal pre-kindergarten has also affected attitudes in the state. The *Oklahoman*, commenting on the failure of California's universal preschool ballot measure in 2006, said proudly: "Oklahoma has done pre-K the right way in making it part of the every day education system for as many children as possible. Just as elementary, middle and high schools must work together, so must pre-K be part of the continuum."[48]

Evidence for the effectiveness of Oklahoma's approach came from a series of studies conducted in Tulsa (the state's largest school district) by Georgetown University researchers in 2002–3. Using a research design that reduced the problem of selection bias, the researchers found that the test scores of children who had completed pre-kindergarten increased significantly, especially their prereading and prewriting skills, compared to those who did not attend the program. The size of the effects—the equivalent of as much as seven months' difference—was larger than had been found in other studies of state pre-kindergarten programs, and approached that of some of the well-known model intervention programs such as the Perry Preschool one.[49] Moreover, children from different backgrounds all benefited from the program, although benefits were greater for children from poorer and minority families. The Georgetown researchers observed that Oklahoma's unusual combination of universal access and high quality standards had created these results. They warned that states that did not have such high requirements for teacher training and the willingness to retain skilled teachers by compensating them at the same level as K–12 teachers might find weaker results.[50]

Essentially, over time and without public fanfare, Oklahoma has added pre-kindergarten as a grade to its public education system—albeit one that remains optional for both families and districts. Both the scale and the quality standards of Oklahoma's program for four-year-olds make it stand out among other state efforts. The program's integration into the system of public education in

Oklahoma is evident from its requirements for teachers to its funding through the state aid formula. Because the program was built up over time, starting as a small pilot in the 1980s, and because declining enrollment in some areas meant there was space available in school buildings as well as an incentive for school districts to launch programs, the program developed within the existing school system in ways that did not seem possible in other states. Making pre-kindergarten part of Oklahoma's system of public education has made it universally available, while mandating high quality standards. In a conservative state that struggles with poverty—51 percent of its K–12 students now qualify for free or reduced-price lunch—expanding preschool quietly through the schools has helped extend quality preschool opportunities on a scale that few imagined fifteen years ago.

NEW YORK: STRUGGLING TO MAKE "UNIVERSAL PRE-KINDERGARTEN" UNIVERSAL

Georgia's lesson about building political support by expanding its pre-kindergarten program to everyone was not lost on other states. In New York, a group of children's advocates and organizations concerned with early education held a legislative breakfast in Albany in 1997, hoping to build momentum for action on the issue within the next several years. They wanted to highlight both the universal pre-kindergarten program in Georgia and a newly released Carnegie Corporation report that called for a broad public investment in prekindergarten. At the breakfast, a speaker from the Georgia Business Education Roundtable spoke so compellingly about the success of universal preschool in Georgia that, one of the organizers recalled, "I think our legislators were a little embarrassed that Georgia had this and we didn't."[51]

If New York did not have a universal program, it was not for lack of trying. As already mentioned, the New York Board of Regents had called for universal preschool thirty years earlier and had proposed several times during the 1980s to incorporate pre-kindergarten into the state's school aid formula. The New York State School Boards Association had recommended expanding pre-kindergarten to all areas of the state in 1986. Mayor Ed Koch had launched Project Giant Step to make pre-kindergarten universally available in New York City in 1986, and Democratic governor Mario Cuomo had called for making pre-kindergarten available to all four-year-old children. Although these previous efforts had fallen short, they had helped build significant support for expanding pre-kindergarten. A universal program could appeal across class lines, increasing access to preschool for poorer families while also relieving middle-class families of the expense of paying to send their children to private programs. As one scholar wrote, providing preschool for all was seen as both "popular in the suburbs and good for the poor."[52]

New York already had a public pre-kindergarten program that was "good for the poor," although it did not reach enough of them. Established in 1966 as part of Governor Nelson Rockefeller's efforts to improve urban education in the state, the Experimental Pre-kindergarten program was targeted to children from poor families. It operated alongside Head Start, with which it shared similar goals. Indeed, Rockefeller's speech announcing this program could have been modeled on Johnson's speech describing Head Start the year before: "The real victims of poverty are poverty's children.... [This program is] designed to break the tragic circle of poverty that dooms so many of the children of the poor to cultural deprivation, lack of achievement in school, dropping-out of school, unemployment and more poverty."[53] As the name suggests, the program started as an experiment in providing preschool and other services to poor children within the public schools, and as such was generally deemed to have succeeded. A longitudinal evaluation published in 1982 found that the children in the program gained significantly in reading and math skills and were less likely to be referred for special education or retained in grade.[54] Long after it ceased to be an experiment, however, New York's Experimental Pre-kindergarten remained a small program, serving roughly 9 percent of low-income three- and four-year-olds in the mid-1990s.[55]

By the time New York legislators sat over breakfast and listened to the speaker from Georgia, the issue of universal pre-kindergarten had become prominent again in the state. Democratic leaders in the state assembly had been calling for an expansion of early education programs (including both pre-kindergarten and full-day kindergarten) to serve all children. Assemblyman Steven Sanders, chair of the Committee on Education, said in 1996: "It's absolutely mind-boggling that these programs aren't available in this state, especially given what we've learned from research on the development of children in the last 10 years, research that's shown what children are missing if we don't take advantage of these years."[56] Democratic assembly leader Sheldon Silver and his staff incorporated the idea of universal pre-kindergarten into the larger education bill they were working on, packaging it with funding for full-day kindergarten, reduced class size in grades K–3, technology, and capital improvements for schools. The bill's passage in 1997 was part of a budget deal between Assembly Democrats and Governor George Pataki, which traded increased funding for education for local property tax cuts. This trade was attractive to both Republicans and

Democrats; with the luxury of a budget surplus, both could take credit for simultaneously increasing school funding and restraining property taxes.

New York's universal pre-kindergarten program (known as UPK) pre-kindergarten was to be phased in over five years, eventually expanding to serve all four-year-olds across the state. The part-day programs, run by school districts, were intended to promote all aspects of children's growth and development, especially literacy in English, through developmentally appropriate activities. Unlike earlier proposals, the 1997 legislation had the support of child care providers and Head Start advocates, whose fears of competition from the state were eased by a provision in the law that required school districts to contract out 10 percent of the funding to community organizations. Children's advocates had pushed for this provision, recognizing that schools alone could not provide the space for a universal program. They also knew that delivering pre-kindergarten in child care settings would enable programs to meet families' needs for child care while giving child care centers resources with which to improve their educational quality. They had also pushed to make the program universal—an idea that seemed to arouse very little opposition, despite its hefty price tag (which was to reach $500 million a year when the program was fully phased in).

Like Georgia's, New York's UPK program was launched quickly, and it depended on extensive collaborations between public school districts and other providers (both nonprofit and for-profit) to provide both space and infrastructure for pre-kindergarten programs. Indeed, the initial implementation of UPK relied on the efforts of several nonprofit organizations whose members were eager to make this collaboration between school districts and other providers work. The state's education department had limited capacity to launch the new program, and there was no money or time for extensive planning, but many of the same individuals and organizations that had planned the legislative breakfast in Albany now "rallied to promote the program." A Pre-K Directors Association (consisting mostly of Experimental Pre-kindergarten directors) helped to present the idea to school districts, while others worked to provide information that would smooth collaboration between districts and community-based providers. The Early Childhood Strategic Group published technical assistance materials with information about the legislation, part- and full-day program models, blending funding, advisory boards, and other implementation issues. Foundations helped underwrite efforts to distribute these materials widely and to reach out through professional organizations to all the relevant constituencies. This concerted effort helped the UPK initiative start off strong; in the first year, programs across the state succeeded in enrolling as many eligible children as they could fund.[57]

Despite its goal of universality, UPK initially emphasized serving low-income children. The first set of districts eligible to participate were chosen on the basis of economic need, and the legislature added a requirement in1999 (later phased out) that districts give preference to economically disadvantaged children in allocating pre-kindergarten slots.[58] Early education consultant Anne Mitchell explained that since the program was not fully funded, any school board "in their right mind" would focus on disadvantaged kids, "because they're the ones who really need it."[59] In communities where the poorest children were already well served, however, the UPK program could address the needs of other families. Denise Gomber, the director of early childhood services for the Ithaca school district in upstate New York, said in 2000 that UPK was reaching more lower-middle-class families—those who might not qualify for programs that serve children in poverty but could not afford to send their children to private preschools or child care centers. "There is a whole community of children and families that I felt we weren't getting to because of fiscal reasons," Gomber said. "This has allowed us to get to families who didn't have options."[60]

Though it started off strong, UPK in New York stalled on the road to actually becoming universal, largely due to struggles between the governor and the legislature. Unlike Zell Miller, who saw Georgia's pre-kindergarten program as his pet project and primary legacy, Republican governor George Pataki never championed UPK. He tolerated it when the state budget was flush, even praising it in his 1998 "State of the State" address. The following year, however, he proposed freezing its expansion, along with other substantial cuts to education. Democrats succeeded in defeating this proposal, but the program's future remained unsure, with the governor unwilling to lock it into law permanently. With an eye on national office, Pataki was more interested in keeping taxes and spending down than in expanding pre-kindergarten.[61]

Despite the governor's lack of support, the legislature was able to increase appropriations for UPK for several years, according to the original phase-in plan. But in 2001, following a very acrimonious legislative session, lawmakers passed a "bare bones" budget. This was meant as a temporary measure that would allow legislators to continue negotiations with Governor Pataki.[62] When the attacks of September 11, 2001, sent New York's budget into a tailspin, however, restoring funding for education was not possible. The planned expansion of UPK was frozen halfway through the process, leaving the program in place in about one-quarter of the state's school districts. Then in 2003, faced with a state budget gap of $9.3 billion, Pataki proposed eliminating the program altogether as well as making other deep cuts in education and social services.

Although the UPK program was a small part of the budget, it became an important cause, especially for Assembly Democrats. Committee on Education chairman Steven Sanders vowed: "there will not be a budget agreement without the restoration of pre-K.... Politically and substantively, it's not a good thing to be going after 4-year-olds."[63] Speaker Sheldon Silver accused Pataki of "slamming the door of the school house for 60,000 four-year-olds" and spoke to audiences across the state on the topic—in just one week in early March, he called three separate news conferences in Albany to rail against the governor's proposals to eliminate early education. As a *New York Times* headline put it, Silver "Wields Preschool Education as a Sword."[64]

Pre-kindergarten advocates "whipped into action" to save the program. Karen Schimke, who helped to coordinate this campaign from Albany, recalled: "We had thousands of inches of media attention, thousands of parents, grandparents, and others wrote letters, made phone calls, sent in postcards, we had 225,000 petition signatures, all people saying, 'we really have to have pre-K, it's essential.'" The organization Fight Crime/Invest in Kids held a press conference to highlight their prediction that crime would rise in New York if the state cut pre-kindergarten programs. Groups of four-year-olds used little red wagons to deliver petitions bearing 150,000 signatures asking the legislature not to eliminate funding.[65] In lobbying for the preservation of UPK funding, the fact that the program was intended to be universal, rather than limited to the poorest families, was an advantage. This increased the political support that backers could call on in the legislature and spurred activism by parents of different income levels. For instance, Julie Gates, a production supervisor and part-time college student from central New York, got involved in fighting for the program in 2003. Gates gathered hundreds of signatures on a petition to save UPK and called the governor's office on a "weekly, sometimes daily, basis."[66]

Pataki's Republican allies in the Senate joined Democrats in the Assembly in objecting to the proposed budget cuts, which they argued would simply drive up local property taxes while cutting important services. In an unusual show of unity, the legislature passed a spending plan that restored funding to education and health care. Determined to protect his record as a tax-cutting leader, Pataki vetoed the plan, but the legislature overrode the veto, handing Pataki one of the biggest governing defeats of his career.[67]

For pre-kindergarten supporters, fighting these budget cuts alongside other education advocates had an unexpected silver lining. Advocate Karen Schimke commented: "Because everybody was under attack, and it really was a phenomenal attack, the education community gathered and banded together...[and] pre-K became a part of the banding together." Parents, teachers' unions, school boards, students, and policemen marched to the state capital to voice their opposition to education cuts. At a massive rally in Albany protesting the cuts, pre-kindergarten was clearly part of the agenda, with Schimke included as one of the speakers. She reflected:

And so I think what happened is that pre-K really got on the education map.... Pre-K has an identity as a part of education in New York state. And regardless of these miserable battles, and all the things that we have to do, that is something that once it is well established, once it's there in people's minds, it doesn't go away. It is something that for kindergarten, probably took a hundred years.[68]

A colleague of Schimke reflected that Pataki's move to eliminate UPK "was the best gift that we could have had because it mobilized everyone. We realized how strong the support was."[69] Their "Winning Beginning" campaign, which had started out aiming to achieve full funding for UPK and to "see early education take its rightful place as a public responsibility in New York, alongside K–12," found that fighting for the program's life had actually helped bring them closer to that broader goal.[70]

Shortly after declaring victory in this budget battle, advocates saw another path opening up to securing stable funding for UPK. In June 2003, the New York Court of Appeals handed down a decision in a decade-old school finance equity lawsuit to the effect that New York had to restructure its system for school finance to ensure that every child in the state receives "a sound basic education." While the decision was limited to the New York City school system, many saw it as an opportunity to revise the state's school funding formula to include pre-kindergarten. Advocates argued that pre-kindergarten was an essential part of the "sound basic education" the state constitution guaranteed. At community forums around the state, parents and teachers highlighted the issue of pre-kindergarten, stressing its importance in the educational process. In testimony before a joint legislative committee, Karen Schimke said: "Early education programs for 3- and 4-year-olds are not optional enrichment programs. They are the foundation tier of learning, through which children gain the essential cognitive, sensory-motor coordination and social-emotional skills without which learning cannot take place." Using cost-benefit studies to appeal to legislators' fiscal concerns, she argued: "School funding equity is not just a matter of how much money we put in, but how much learning comes out. Dollar for dollar, pre-kindergarten 'buys' more student achievement than any other form of public education spending."[71]

The state's initial responses to the court's ruling in the school funding lawsuit seemed promising. Both the commission charged with recommending ways of meeting the court's mandate and an independent board set up by the plaintiffs in the case recommended incorporating pre-kindergarten funding in the state aid formula. But Pataki and many legislators, faced with the need to find billions of dollars to add to New York City's school aid and to address the complicated issue of revising the school aid formula, preferred to stall for time.

Pataki completed his term as governor without directly addressing the school funding lawsuit, though he did approve a $50 million increase for UPK in his 2006 budget.

Universal pre-kindergarten had been saved from the budget axe, but it remained far from universal. In the 2005–6 school year, it served about 30 percent of the state's four-year-olds, mostly in disadvantaged school districts. While all of the major city districts participated, many districts in this largely rural state did not, lacking space and qualified teachers and fearing that state aid would not cover the costs of the program. Often children in these rural communities had few other opportunities to attend preschool.[72] Even within participating districts, there were not enough slots for all the children whose parents might want them to enroll. In the Syracuse area, a reporter wrote in 2005, six districts used a lottery, with principals literally picking names from a hat, basket, or cardboard box. The reporter, highlighting the difference between pre-kindergarten and the public school's normal practice of serving all children, wrote that in this lottery, "the winners get to go to school." She subtitled her article "If You Want Your 4-year-old in State Pre-K, You'd Better Be Lucky."[73]

There was growing consensus among policymakers that pre-kindergarten should be incorporated into the K–12 education system, even though progress toward this statewide goal seemed slow. Rather than waiting for state aid, the New York City Board of Education decided to use its own funds to expand pre-kindergarten slots. At the same time, the state's Board of Regents asked legislators to use the state aid formula to fund pre-kindergarten for three- and four-year-olds in all the state's school districts. "Early childhood programs can no longer be an issue for debate at State and local budget times," the Regents wrote.[74]

With the election of Democrat Eliot Spitzer as governor in 2006, the fortunes of pre-kindergarten started to change. He campaigned on a platform that included "pre-K for all" along with other educational measures. In his first budget, he proposed increasing pre-kindergarten funding dramatically, and he promised to fully fund the program over four years. The nearly 50 percent increase in funding for pre-kindergarten in 2007 spread the program to more school districts, as well as allowing others to expand enrollment. It also integrated UPK funding into a restructured state education formula, and folded Experimental Pre-kindergarten into UPK. Spitzer's scandal-induced resignation in 2008 meant yet another hurdle for pre-kindergarten advocates as they worked to maintain momentum on the program's planned expansion. Now UPK serves about half of the state's four-year-olds, and supporters continue to defend its growth in the face of statewide budget cuts.

Over the ten years since the legislature first passed the UPK legislation, the program's fortunes have risen and fallen with those of K–12 education in general. Originating in a bill expanding education funding, UPK was threatened when state education faced severe cuts. In 2003, as pre-kindergarten supporters and other education advocates fought Pataki's budget cuts, pre-kindergarten became even more tightly bound to K–12 education. Although pre-kindergarten classrooms are often located outside schools, the pre-kindergarten program has become closely intertwined with public education. Though not yet universal, UPK seems to be on the road to being recognized, as advocates have long hoped, as children's entryway into public education in the state.

NEW JERSEY: A CONSTITUTIONAL RIGHT TO PRE-KINDERGARTEN, FOR SOME

Unlike other states, where governors and legislators created universal pre-kindergarten, in New Jersey it was created in a series of rulings by the highest judicial branch. In 1998, preschool became part of the court-ordered remedy in the landmark *Abbott v. Burke* decision, which declared that unequal spending by poor urban and affluent suburban districts violated the state's constitution. As the state Supreme Court became convinced that preschool was a necessary part of the "thorough and efficient education" to which children in the state were constitutionally entitled, judges ordered the state to build a system of high-quality preschool education for children in its poorest school districts.

New Jersey's extremes of wealth and poverty had produced legal struggles over unequal school spending extending back more than twenty-five years. In the 1970s, the state Supreme Court shut down schools across the state, declaring the financing system unconstitutional, and legislators adopted an income tax in order to deliver more revenue to the neediest school districts. The problem persisted, however, and from 1988 to 2001 the high court issued ten different rulings in the *Abbott* case, attempting to fulfill the state constitution's promise of providing a "thorough and efficient education" to all its students. The attorneys from the nonprofit Education Law Center who argued the case saw it as a continuation of civil rights struggles to ensure that minority children had an equal education. Representing a group of twenty schoolchildren from Camden, East Orange, Irvington, and Jersey City, they argued that funding disparities between affluent and poor school districts in the state meant that the entire system of state funding for schools was unconstitutional.

In its key 1990 decision, however, the court did not accept this conclusion; rather, judges focused their attention on twenty-eight of the state's poorest urban districts, which were "failing abysmally, dramatically, and tragically." Rather than establishing a statewide standard of what constituted a "thorough and efficient" education, the high court took the unique step of ordering the state to ensure that the poorest urban districts were able to spend at the same level as those in the wealthiest suburbs, enabling them to "wipe out disadvantages as much as a school district can." The state's poorest children, the court ruled, were entitled to be as well prepared for citizenship and labor market competition as their most affluent peers. Furthermore, these children also needed special services, beyond what children in wealthy districts had, to help "redress their extreme disadvantages." Advocates called the *Abbott* decision a "Magna Carta for urban schoolchildren" and proclaimed: "New Jersey's urban school children now have the most comprehensive set of educational rights anywhere in the nation."[75] While the decision's call for equal spending was bold, its impact was restricted: it did not apply across the board, or even to all poor children in New Jersey, but only to those who lived in the specified urban districts, which became known as the *Abbott* districts.

In the years that followed the 1990 decision, legislators struggled with what one state official called its "difficult political calculus," which required shifting resources to 28 of the state's 527 school districts without angering the majority of the electorate. Democratic governor Jim Florio's efforts to implement the decision led to a taxpayer revolt, which resulted in a Republican sweep of the legislature in 1991, a compromised school funding law, and the election of Republican Christine Todd Whitman as governor in 1993.[76] The court struck down the legislature's first efforts in 1994, providing an opening for Whitman to reframe the issue. Her administration proposed that the state define a "thorough and efficient education" not by spending levels but by creating statewide standards for students and establishing a core curriculum, for which state aid would pay. School funding legislation based on this approach passed in 1996, but in 1997, the court found that it did not provide equal resources for children in the special districts, include programs poor children especially needed, or address these districts' serious physical facilities needs.

In its 1998 *Abbott V* decision, the court went further. Citing the legislature's repeated failures to fully comply with their rulings, the justices took on the role of making detailed policy prescriptions for how to reform urban schools. In addition to approving "whole school reform" in all the *Abbott* elementary schools, the court focused on early childhood education as a well-documented method for improving children's success in school. Indeed, the evidence supporting early childhood education seemed to be stronger than for many other education reforms. "Empirical evidence strongly supports the essentiality of preschool education for children in impoverished school districts," Justice Handler wrote. He went on to refer to the Perry Preschool and Abecedarian studies, as well as to the Carnegie Task Force's 1996 report calling for increasing access to preschool, and to studies showing the role that preschool could play in enhancing poorer children's language development. "This Court is convinced that pre-school for three- and four-year-olds will have a significant and substantial positive impact on academic achievement in both early and later school years." The court stopped short of concluding that there was a constitutional right to preschool (the state constitution specified a responsibility for educating only children between the ages of five and fifteen). Since the legislature and the commissioner of education had clearly "understood and endorsed the strong empirical link between early education and later educational achievement" in other legislation, the court wrote, "we need not reach the constitutional issue."[77] But the court had concluded that preschool education was needed in order to provide the "thorough and efficient" education that was guaranteed by the state constitution. The 1998 decision thus required that the targeted school districts offer half-day preschool programs for three- and four-year-olds (as well as full-day kindergarten) by the beginning of the next school year. These districts could cooperate with existing early childhood and day-care programs in order to offer preschool to all children in the district, and the state was to make construction of preschool facilities a priority.

This mandate for "well-planned, high-quality preschool" in the 1998 *Abbott V* decision created a new battleground in the ongoing struggle between education advocates and the state. The Whitman administration saw the *Abbott* preschools primarily in terms of child care, while the plaintiffs and districts focused on educational quality. Whitman went beyond the court's mandate by requiring that the preschool programs operate for as many as ten hours a day in order to meet families' needs for child care, and encouraged districts to collaborate with existing center-based programs run by the Department of Human Services. She did not, however, include quality improvement measures such as renovating child care facilities, reducing class size, or upgrading teachers' credentials. Districts planning to ensure quality by hiring certified teachers and getting national accreditation had their plans rejected by the state.[78] Advocate Cecilia Zalkind, of the Association for Children in New Jersey, became concerned that collaboration with child care providers was being used "to save money instead of being used to raise standards."[79]

According to economist Steven Barnett and colleagues at the Rutgers Center for Early Education Research, neither the quantity nor the quality of preschool programs was meeting the court's expectations of making a difference in children's education. *Abbott* districts were enrolling, on average, less than 40 percent of eligible children, and observations of preschool classrooms found them wanting. Teachers were de facto exempted from meeting the certification requirements, and they were inadequately paid. The state's insistence that programs provide up to ten hours of care without increasing funding, the researchers warned, meant sacrificing quality. Overall, they wrote, "state preschool policy has been to try to create the appearance of compliance with the court while minimizing state spending and continuing to treat early education as little more than babysitting."[80] Advocacy groups worked together, under the leadership of the Association for Children of New Jersey, to establish standards for "high-quality" preschool, brokering agreements among private providers and others on requirements for teacher training and other matters and testifying in the court proceedings. The *Abbott* plaintiffs returned to court, and in 2000 the court issued another decision, redirecting the state to implement preschool and prescribing more detail about what it meant by "high quality." This decision reaffirmed the importance of curriculum, made it mandatory for pre-kindergarten teachers to have bachelor's degrees, and specified a teacher-to-child ratio of one to fifteen. In 2001, the court ruled again on a timetable for decisions on district preschool plans, budgets, and administrative appeals. In 2002, the weary court issued yet another ruling clarifying issues of enrollment, educational standards, and facilities.

By 2004, the *Abbott* preschool program looked like a success. Abbott districts were enrolling 74 percent of the eligible children in full-school-day pre-kindergarten programs in public schools, Head Start programs, and private child care centers. The *Abbott* pre-kindergarten program had some of the highest quality standards in the country, including comprehensive curriculum standards, certified teachers in every classroom, comparable teacher salaries for public schools and private providers, and a maximum class size of fifteen.[81] It was also the most expensive program in the country, spending more per pupil on its preschool program than any other state. A concerted effort to raise teacher education levels pushed the percentage of teachers with a bachelor's degree up from an estimated 38 percent in 1999 to 99 percent in 2005; over 200 master teachers were designated as mentors.[82] Teacher salaries had risen substantially along with training requirements. Overall classroom quality rose between 2002 and 2004, and literacy assessment scores increased by 20 percent, reflecting strong emphasis on teacher training in oral language and early literacy. A follow-up study published in 2007 found that classroom quality scores continued to rise, and quality teaching practices were found equally in school- and community-based classrooms. Significantly, children's substantial gains in language, literacy, and mathematics learning in Abbott preschools were largely sustained during the kindergarten year.[83]

Despite the preschool program's success, policymakers were questioning the future of the whole *Abbott* enterprise, seeking a way to restructure state education aid to eliminate the need for special funding for the *Abbott* districts. In 2006, the state Board of Education called for an overhaul of the state's school funding, noting that poor rural as well as middle-wealth districts had been shortchanged. The *Abbott* districts enrolled 21 percent of New Jersey children but received half of all state education aid. Non-*Abbott* districts were forced to rely more heavily on property taxes in order to fund their schools, and the state's property tax rate was twice the national average. Rather than add a few more districts to the *Abbott* category, the board said, the state must fashion a funding system to ensure a quality education as guaranteed by the state constitution in *all* of the state's 600-plus districts.[84] That same year, Democratic governor Jon Corzine surprised some of his liberal allies by filing a suit in the state Supreme Court to freeze aid to the *Abbott* districts, and restart litigation. Meanwhile, Democratic lawmakers were working on a new school funding formula that would address the imbalance in state education aid. One explained: "I'm a Democrat. I'm an African-American. I am not going to do something which will be a detriment to black and brown children across this state, but we need to recognize that children who have hurdles before them in terms of their education live all over this state."[85] In January 2008, the legislature narrowly approved Corzine's new school funding formula, which apportioned funds to districts on the basis of student demographics (including family income, language ability, and special educational needs).[86] Since many needy children lived outside the *Abbott* districts, this meant spreading state money around the state rather than concentrating it in these poor urban districts.

The new law also expanded preschool, requiring school districts to offer full-day preschool for all three- and four-year-olds in eighty-two additional high-poverty districts, and to all disadvantaged children residing elsewhere in the state. This expansion widened the circle of children eligible for state-funded preschool (from 55,000 to approximately 85,000), partially realizing the hopes of children's advocates who wanted to use the *Abbott* preschools as the basis for a statewide system open to all children.[87] Corzine called the phased-in expansion "an exciting and promising opportunity to replicate the gains that have been made in the *Abbott* districts in other communities across the state." Corzine also sought to convince the state Supreme Court that the new child-based funding formula eliminated the need for continued special funding for the *Abbott* districts.[88] In May 2009, the court ruled that the new funding formula was constitutional, marking not only the end of a long struggle over funding for the *Abbott* districts but also the beginning of a commitment to provide preschool for all disadvantaged children in the state.

The first court-ordered preschool program in the nation, *Abbott* has achieved successes that have inspired action elsewhere. Prekindergarten has become part of school finance litigation in twelve other states, where plaintiffs have argued that preschool needs to be considered as part of an adequate education, especially for disadvantaged children.[89] Court decisions may be a blunt instrument for policy, but in New Jersey they produced important results. With specific mandates and designated funding to achieve high quality, the *Abbott* preschool programs have gone beyond those of most other states in upgrading the skills and compensation of the teaching force, using community-based as well as school-based programs to deliver pre-kindergarten, and requiring other quality standards. Having built a high-quality system of preschool for some of its poorest children, New Jersey is now poised to make it available it to children across the state.

CONCLUSION

In New Jersey, Oklahoma, New York, and Georgia, policymakers in the 1990s, inspired in different ways by research findings, educational priorities, and opportunities in their states, expanded publicly funded preschool. The avenues they used to do so shaped their thinking about whom they would serve, and how. While legislators in Georgia, Oklahoma, and New York approved "preschool for all" with an eye toward building a broad political constituency, court action in New Jersey focused on the poorest children. Oklahoma built its program as part and parcel of the public schools, while Georgia, New York, and New Jersey relied on extensive partnerships with private and community-based providers to create preschool classrooms for growing numbers of four-year-olds.

While leaders in Georgia, Oklahoma, and New York shared the belief that a universal approach would build broad-based political support and enable them to serve more children with higher quality programs, their experiences differed in important ways. Governor Zell Miller made pre-kindergarten a visible and well-known part of his agenda in Georgia, while advocates in New York struggled to keep the pre-kindergarten program alive in the face of opposition from their governor. Meanwhile, legislators and state officials in Oklahoma quietly expanded an existing pre-kindergarten program without launching public debate. Funding structures also made a difference: Georgia's new lottery provided a dedicated stream of funding, while New York depended on legislative appropriations, and Oklahoma's program was folded into the state education aid formula. New Jersey spent more than any other state, in part because of specific court mandates that governed the *Abbott* preschool program.

Combining attention to research about the promise of preschool with attention to its political and constitutional ramifications, these states were the first to move toward "universal" preschool. As leaders responded to moments of opportunity and crisis in their states, they turned to pre-kindergarten as a type of education reform that held the promise of boosting economic growth and equalizing opportunity by improving children's early learning. Prekindergarten thus became more closely tied to public K–12 education as it expanded, even though pre-kindergarten classes were not always located in school buildings. Each of these four states helped lay the foundation for a broader movement for expanding public pre-kindergarten. The questions leaders in these states faced as they worked to open doors to preschool—who needed preschool, how to pay for it, what made for quality, and how to garner political support for it—would find different answers in other states as the pressure to expand pre-kindergarten grew.

CHAPTER 5

Preschool for All

Building a Movement in the 2000s

In the late 1990s, the idea of universal preschool pioneered by states like Georgia, New York, and Oklahoma started to draw national-level attention. Foundations, educators and business leaders working on K–12 school reform and children's issues embraced the idea of a universal approach to preschool. Providing "preschool for all," they believed, would produce broad political support, leading to better funding and higher quality programs in the long run, and with a greater impact on children's educational success. In 2001, the Pew Charitable Trusts, a nonprofit with over $5 billion in assets, committed its significant resources to the cause of universal pre-kindergarten. Pew's involvement served as a catalyst, as it poured funding into selected state campaigns, brought together different constituencies across the country, and focused unprecedented attention on pre-kindergarten as a solution to educational and social problems.

This move toward universal programs represented an important departure for both policymakers and advocates. Since the 1960s, policymakers had worked from the assumption that most children did not need publicly funded preschool programs; their only purpose was to give disadvantaged children extra help, a "head start" or at least a means to catch up with their more advantaged peers. Thus, the federal Head Start program was limited to children whose families lived below the poverty line, and almost all the state pre-kindergarten programs created in the 1980s were targeted to low-income and at-risk children. Although millions of nonpoor children attended private child care and preschool programs, the emphasis in *public* programs was on the disadvantaged. Since funding for young children was so limited, it made sense to target it to those most in need, who were likely to benefit the most from preschool. Advocates for children focused mostly on the disadvantaged, calling for the expansion of Head Start and child care subsidies for low-income families.

Over the course of the 1990s, however, some advocates and foundation leaders began to question the limitations of this approach. Even with significant growth during the Bush and Clinton administrations, Head Start was only able to serve about 60 percent of eligible children. Ruby Takanishi of the Foundation for Child Development commented in 2003:

> it seems to be that after all these years and even now, Head Start is never going to serve all of the eligible population, it's just not going to. So we have to figure out something else.... And I think we really need to think about, you know, what can be done today to reach the same goals that people had for Head Start in 1965."[1]

Similarly, John Merrow wrote in 2002 of the "failure" of Head Start to close the achievement gap between poor and middle-class children and urged a different approach: creating a preschool system "that's good enough for those with money" but available to all.[2]

The idea of creating preschool for all also appealed to those who were frustrated with the limitations of publicly-supported child care. Federal child care funding was more directed at quantity than quality, especially after the 1996 welfare reform legislation pushed thousands of mothers into the workforce, and the funding could not keep pace with demand. Even as she fought for child care funding in the late 1980s, one key advocate recalled: "I realized we would never get child care to quality because it was child care" and had to be kept affordable. Pre-kindergarten, however, was seen as educational, and expanding it could be a path to securing higher quality programs for three- and four-year-olds.[3] Unprecedented public interest in young children's brain development, combined with research studies documenting the promise of preschool, and concern with K–12 school reform, had generated support for educational programs for young children. Public opinion research showed that while the public generally saw "child care" as a private responsibility of families, they looked favorably on preschool programs that were seen as "educational."

Advocates and reformers across the country paid attention to Georgia's experiment with offering preschool to all four-year-olds. Zell Miller's commitment to having a program that would "touch all Georgians" seemed to be a textbook example of the political benefits of a universal approach. By appealing across class lines, universal preschool could increase access to preschool for poorer families while also relieving middle-class families of the expense of sending their children to private programs. Furthermore, advocates believed that universal preschool programs would ultimately develop more political support, more stable funding, and higher quality services than programs limited to poor children. As one scholar wrote, providing preschool for all could be both "popular in the suburbs and good for the poor."[4] This approach was intriguing to politicians, policy experts, and advocates looking for new ways of garnering support for young children.

They also looked to historical examples of universal programs that had become part of America's social contract. Particularly influential was sociologist Theda Skocpol's argument that only universal social policies have, over time, succeeded at garnering enough political support to be sustainable and successful. Programs like Social Security, Civil War soldiers' pensions, and public education proved popular because they benefited broad categories of people. Once created, these universal programs both built broad coalitions of support and provided a framework within which extra benefits could be offered that helped the poor more. Similarly, sociologist William Julius Wilson wrote that the best way to benefit "the truly disadvantaged" was to develop universal policies, such as family allowances and employment programs, that a large segment of the population would benefit from and support. Targeted programs, which tended to be perceived as benefiting poor minorities rather than white taxpayers, were both less effective and more vulnerable. Noting that Social Security proved over time to be a much more effective antipoverty tool than War on Poverty programs, Skocpol and Wilson both urged policymakers to look for universal programs rather than narrowly focused, targeted ones.[5]

Supporters of a universal approach also pointed to the example of France, where the system of *écoles maternelles*, open to all children, enjoyed strong public support. In the 1970s, when American policymakers were settling on a private approach to child care, French officials were hastening to expand preschool in response to increased parent demand. By the mid-1970s, 80 percent of three-year-olds, 97 percent of four-year-olds, and 100 percent of five-year-olds were attending these noncompulsory schools, which operated with highly trained teachers as part of the national system of public education. The *écoles maternelles* were well developed by the time the economic crises of the 1970s and 1980s set in, and they were little affected, as the Ministry of Education, parents, and teachers agreed that preschool education was a right of all children. In fact, access to these schools improved during the 1980s, with three-year-olds being guaranteed spaces by the end of the decade.[6] Delaine Eastin, California's superintendent of education, while visiting French preschools with a group of U.S. experts in 1999, asked a local mayor which of France's political parties would suggest cutting funding for preschool during a recession. He laughed and said, "No one would dare!" Eastin commented: "It's as if someone here were running for office and wanted to discontinue public education. You'd run him out of town."[7]

American experts were particularly interested in how the French system combined the benefits of universal and targeted approaches by offering children in poor neighborhoods more intensive services and earlier access to the *écoles maternelles*. Rather than creating a separate program for disadvantaged children—like Head Start or targeted pre-kindergarten programs in the United States—the French used the infrastructure of universal education but provided schools in disadvantaged areas with greater resources in order to help poor and immigrant children meet educational goals. (The concept was similar to the American Title I program of supplementary funding for schools serving disadvantaged children, but the centralized French system actually provided greater funding to schools serving poorer students, while the decentralized U.S. system, reliant primarily on state and local funding, struggled to meet this goal.) Within designated "priority education zones," schools received extra resources that allowed them to reduce class size, provide teacher bonuses, strengthen ties to providers of health and social services, and enroll more two-year-olds in preschool. Starting disadvantaged children (often immigrants) in preschool at the age of two, French officials believed, gives them the boost they need for an "equal start," as well as immersing them in French language and culture and promoting social cohesion by educating all children together. To the visiting American experts, the French approach seemed to bring together the advantages of both universal and targeted programs.[8]

American K–12 education reformers were also drawn to the idea of universal preschool, seeing improved early education as a key to overall reform. In 1996, the Carnegie Task Force on Learning in the Primary Grades recommended a dramatic expansion of preschool programs for 3- and four-year-olds. Failure to provide a high-quality, coherent system of early learning, the task force argued, was one key reason why American children were not achieving as much as they could or needed to in school. "Make no mistake," the report warned, "underachievement is not just a crisis of certain groups. It is not limited to the poor; it is not a problem afflicting *other* people's children." Americans had created "a non-system of early care and education" that left millions of children "caught in a maze of unstable, substandard settings that compromise their chances of succeeding in school."[9]

Carnegie's proposal of making quality preschool available to all children was fairly novel in 1996, but it would soon gain momentum from both education and business leaders. The Council of Chief State School Officers, under Gordon Ambach's leadership, lent its support to the idea of universal preschool in 1999, having concluded that improving early education for all children was crucial to efforts to reform and strengthen K–12 education. What was needed were not just new programs but an early childhood *system* in each state, providing continuity as children moved from early childhood through the first years of elementary school.[10] The National Association of State Boards of Education formed a network in 2001 to help selected states build such systems, while the Education Commission of the States also focused on early childhood education at its 2001 conference, culminating a year of work on increasing access to quality prekindergarten.[11] *Education Week*'s annual *Quality Counts* report for 2002 focused on early childhood education, further raising the issue's visibility among those concerned with K–12 education. Teachers' unions also endorsed the idea. In 2001, American Federation of Teachers president Sandra Feldman called for universally available preschool, with first priority given to needy children; the larger National Education Association followed suit in 2003, calling for publicly funded universal pre-kindergarten for three- and four-year-olds.[12]

Business leaders concerned with education reform were also drawn to the idea of universal pre-kindergarten. The Committee on Economic Development (CED), a prominent national group of business and education leaders, took up the issue of preschool in the late 1990s. The CED had been among the strong business voices calling for reform in K–12 education during the 1980s and 1990s and had come to see preschool as an important component of school reform. Janet Hansen of the CED noted the trustees'

> growing awareness of the fact that so many kids enter school at uneven places, that some of the kinds of things that [CED trustees had] been working for in terms of K–12 reform and narrowing achievement gaps and improving achievement for all kids and so on, just aren't going to happen if one doesn't pay attention to those gaps that exist as kids enter school.

The CED had a long-standing commitment to "human capital investments" in young children, and trustees recognized that early education was a promising issue that could garner support from many different constituencies.[13] In *Preschool for All: Investing in a Productive and Just Society*, CED trustees called for a nationwide system of publicly supported universal preschool. This 2002 blueprint provided the most detailed and systematic vision of preschool policy to be found anywhere. Calling the nation's current patchwork approach to early education "haphazard, piecemeal, and under-funded," *Preschool for All* urged each state, with support from the federal government, to develop a system for offering a full school day of preschool to all children whose parents wanted it. In the past, the CED had recommended targeting early education programs at disadvantaged children. Now the group urged making early education open to all children, writing: "Just as we have long seen elementary and secondary education for all as a societal responsibility, we must now undertake to extend educational opportunity to all children age 3 and up."[14] Janet Hansen, who worked on this report, explained that while a few of the CED trustees would have preferred a recommendation for a more targeted program...the majority really felt that this ought to be a universal program, that it would be a higher quality program if it were a universal program, that programs that are targeted on the poor tend to always be, you know, kind of on the sidelines. And that a lot of children need this, and that it's hard to just break out who needs it neatly by something like income, which you'd do in a targeted program.[15]

Another important push for universal preschool came from groups concerned with the children of the "working poor." In response to the 1996 welfare reform legislation, the New York–based Foundation for Child Development decided to focus its work on advancing policies that would help the increasing number of families who were working but poor because of low wages and an eroding social safety net. High-quality preschool was an important part of this agenda, and a universal approach seemed to be the best strategy for ensuring that all families could access it. Foundation president Ruby Takanishi later explained:

> A lot of our grant-making was focused on having every child have access to good quality early education, because rich kids already have it, we pay for it for our children, some low-income children have it because they are in Head Start or certain kinds of special programs, but that huge number of kids maybe above the poverty line or below the poverty line...they're the people who essentially are not getting good quality programs, because their parents can't pay it, and they get no help, basically. And universal pre-K is really kind of a strategy to get those kids into better quality programs.[16]

Advocates for poor children had long been concerned that targeted programs excluded children in families just above the poverty line. Takanishi's colleague Fasaha Traylor observed:

> There is probably no significant difference between kids who are eligible for Head Start and the next couple of quintiles.... So it was really sort of like a Swiss cheese thing that was mostly holes. It seems like only universality will be able to really fill those holes.[17]

Through sponsoring research, policy analysis, symposia, and work with the media, the foundation hoped to push the idea of universal pre-K "higher on the agenda" so that bigger foundations and interests could pick it up.

That goal seemed to be achieved when in September 2001, the Pew Charitable Trusts announced plans to spend about $10 million a year for ten years to promote universal, voluntary, early education for three- and four-year-olds.[18] This turn to pre-kindergarten came partly out of Pew's frustration with its efforts to reform both K–12 schools and social services for children. Pew had been involved in efforts to restructure and reform the Philadelphia schools, giving nearly $40 million to the school district from 1985 to 1995 in one of the largest philanthropic donations ever to a single district.[19] However, board members were frustrated with an apparent lack of results and were considering ceasing grantmaking in education altogether. (They were in good company; several other major foundations also cut back on efforts to reform K–12 education around this time, in part due to frustration that more had not been accomplished.)[20] Susan Urahn, who had recently come to Pew as education director, suggested that the board consider early childhood education as an arena in which to make change. Pushing for universal pre-kindergarten was attractive, Urahn wrote later, because it was "substantial enough to make a difference in children's lives, but also well-enough defined so that the public, media and policymakers could readily understand it and follow progress towards the goal."[21] This made it different from another large Pew project, the Children's Initiative, which started in 1992 with the ambitious aim of helping states revamp and coordinate fragmented human services programs to improve education, health, and social outcomes for children. Only a year into the projected ten-year Children's Initiative, Pew decided to terminate it, having concluded that it was not likely to meet its goals. "The balance is in trying to select a system that is large enough to achieve significant goals, but manageable enough to be feasible," a foundation official explained.[22]

Promoting pre-kindergarten seemed to be an area where philanthropic efforts could bear fruit. Early education was important enough to make a difference but small and focused enough that philanthropic efforts would be well spent. Since substantial research evidence documenting the benefit of quality pre-kindergarten programs for disadvantaged children existed, the issue fit the Pew Trusts' mission of bringing sound research to bear on important policy questions. No other major foundation had staked a claim to the issue, and an infusion of foundation money could make a difference. Policymakers were interested, and public opinion research showed that there was support for preschool if it was framed as an issue of education rather than day care. Urahn also believed that the relatively undeveloped infrastructure of early childhood education was more amenable to change. In K–12 public education, she explained,

> You've got the unions, you've got the principals, you've got the superintendents, you've got the school boards, you've got a substantial public investment and a real vitriolic policy scene...change is very difficult from a philanthropic perspective.

Because what you want to drive change in philanthropy is the ability to find a lever, or a small number of levers, that with limited dollars you can kind of make happen, that will then generate broad change. It's very hard to find that in K–12 education, and I think responsible people simply acknowledge that. It's not that you can't change K–12; it's just that it's a very long and complicated process. It struck us that in the early education field, that structure was much more nascent and less recalcitrant, if you will.

The way early education had developed—with limited public investment and infrastructure and relatively weak professional or stakeholder organizations—made it a good candidate for philanthropic involvement. Pew thus decided to shift all its education grantmaking into the early childhood arena, making "a pretty fundamental shift away from K–12 and higher ed." Although Pew understood the value and importance of K–12 education, Urahn said in 2003, board members and staff had "concluded that pushing for expanded access to early education would be more productive."[23]

For Pew's board and staff, taking a universal approach was an important strategy for building broad-based political support for early education programs. Urahn explained:

From our perspective, if you don't have an investment in universal, you will never get the quality across the board that every kid deserves, nor will you get the environment that the disadvantaged kids need to really improve. And I think the long experience we've had with Head Start sends a pretty clear message that when the programs are designed for poor kids, they never develop the constituency, and they never reach the level of quality that we, in the middle class, would want for our kids. And I think that if you want a good program then you make it something that the middle class develops an investment in.

Moreover, the problem of finding high-quality pre-kindergarten programs was not limited to the very disadvantaged; working- and middle-class parents also had trouble getting truly educational programs for their preschoolers, so a broad-based solution seemed necessary.[24]

SHAPING THE PRE-KINDERGARTEN CAMPAIGN

The Pew Charitable Trusts' involvement transformed universal pre-kindergarten from a promising idea being pursued on a relatively small scale to a national movement. Following a pattern of its work in other areas, Pew invested in research, advocacy, and public awareness campaigns, establishing the National Institute for Early Education Research (NIEER) at Rutgers University and the Trust for Early Education in Washington. Separating research efforts from advocacy work was important, Urahn explained, in order to ensure that the research—which advocates would rely on in their efforts—would be independent and credible.[25] The NIEER, directed by Rutgers economist Steve Barnett, funded and published relevant research, created policy briefs and testimony about the components of high-quality programs, and published state-by-state rankings of pre-kindergarten programs, quality standards, and funding levels. In Washington, advocacy efforts at the Trust for Early Education were initially connected to the Education Trust, a nonprofit focused on closing the achievement gap. In 2005, the Trust for Early Education was reorganized with the name Pre-K Now, under the leadership of Libby Doggett, who had worked for the National Head Start Association and the federal Department of Education when she had come from Texas to Washington with her husband, congressman Lloyd Doggett. Since 2001, Pew has spent more than $83 million to advance the cause of high-quality, voluntary pre-kindergarten for all three- and four-year-olds.[26]

Pew's initial approach was to start with "the low-hanging fruit" of the states that were already moving toward the goal of universal pre-kindergarten. Urahn explained in 2003 that she hoped to get a handful of states "over a period of time to really move aggressively towards this, and then make clear to people what the benefits are," in order to encourage other states to follow suit.[27] Pew president Rebecca Rimel explained her overall strategy: "If ten states adopt universal pre-K [by the end of Pew's ten-year commitment], then the advocates will pick this up and we'll move on. Even if three of the programs are cruddy, it's a win." Picking the states in which to invest, Doggett commented, "was almost a science. We had reams of data on the political climate, the budget situation, the child advocacy organizations. I was looking for two things: experienced advocates and someone high up in government who could make something happen."[28] Initial states included Illinois and Massachusetts, where advocates and political leaders were working to expand early education, as well as New York and New Jersey, where existing programs could be expanded or more fully funded. In addition, organizations in Arkansas, North Carolina, Oklahoma, and Wisconsin were given planning grants based on the assessment that these states had the potential to make progress despite tight state budgets.[29] Over time, Pew has funded campaigns in nineteen different states.

Pew's involvement also attracted other foundations to the idea of universal pre-kindergarten. In 2003, the David and Lucile Packard Foundation, one of the nation's largest private foundations, decided to fund efforts for universal preschool in California over a period of ten years. The foundation had lost a significant part of its endowment in the high-tech market collapse and needed to focus its efforts in order to have a greater impact. Children's program director Lois Salisbury commented: "It is important to lead where there is strength. Right now that is with universal preschool." Mirroring the thinking that had taken place at Pew, the Packard board embraced the goal of providing pre-kindergarten for every three- and four-year-old in the state of California.[30] The foundation supported the advocacy group Preschool California to push for universal pre-kindergarten at the state level and funded a variety of education and children's groups to work on advancing this cause. Preschool California's founder explained that getting all these groups to focus on this one issue was not easy: "Ideally, initiatives come from the bottom up, but this one came from the top down."[31] Other foundations also targeted preschool efforts in specific states or regions. Some of these predated Pew's initiative, such as the Schumann Fund's support for work on New Jersey's *Abbott* preschools and the Schott Foundation's support for preschool advocacy in Massachusetts. Others followed Pew and built on its efforts; for example, the Joyce Foundation worked in Illinois, Michigan, and Wisconsin, and the Bill and Melinda Gates Foundation in 2005 pledged $90 million to provide model early childhood centers reaching most of the young children in two Washington state communities.[32] In 2003, the W. K. Kellogg Foundation announced it would spend $43 million over five years to improve school readiness by bringing early childhood and K–12 systems closer together.[33]

In both its carefully targeted state campaigns and its efforts to build a national network of pre-kindergarten advocates, Pew-funded work paid particular attention to "messaging" and communication strategies. Polling research (a strong feature of Pew's work overall) had convinced Pew board members that pre-kindergarten could be a popular cause, and it continued to shape the campaign and its messages as it unfolded. For instance, on the basis of polling data, advocates changed the way they described their goal: from "universal preschool" (with its connotations of government compulsion) to "preschool for all." Supporters shared information via national teleconferences, satellite conferences, and frequent electronic communication and learned about shaping messages to appeal to policymakers and voters. They also worked to "frame" pre-kindergarten as an essential element of public school reform that would boost student achievement rather than as child care. Bruce Fuller, a critic of Pew-funded efforts, charges that the preschool movement's effort was "dominated by strategy, polling, and arguments aimed at piecing together public credibility" rather than by open-ended dialogue about children's needs.[34]

Having identified the expansion of preschool as their goal, advocates zeroed in on securing support for it, using all the techniques of modern political campaigns.

Pew worked to broaden the circle of support for pre-kindergarten beyond the educators and children's advocates who had typically backed such causes. Indeed, Urahn explained that she deliberately sought to reach beyond the "usual suspects" to groups "that could reach more centrist and conservative policy makers and audiences with different messages."[35] Pew staffer Sara Watson noted the importance of finding "champions from many sectors—police chiefs, business leaders, seniors, physicians, school board members."[36] Pew funding enabled the Committee for Economic Development to mobilize support for pre-kindergarten from business leaders in selected states, and the National Governors Association to spotlight the importance of gubernatorial leadership on preschool. Pew support also spurred the Council of Chief State School Officers to work on identifying early education "champions" among state school superintendents, helped Fight Crime/Invest in Kids mobilize law enforcement officials who saw early childhood programs as an effective means of reducing crime, and sponsored efforts by the New Jersey–based Education Law Center to include preschool as a remedy in state school finance and equity awsuits.[37]

Business leaders were a particularly influential group to bring into the pre-kindergarten movement, for these "unlikely messengers" commanded the attention of legislators in a way children's advocates did not. While legislators tended to perceive (mostly female) children's advocates as well-intentioned but partisan, they saw (mostly male) business leaders as levelheaded, conservative, and fiscally responsible. A business leader reflected: "I think the legislators were actually scratching their heads a little bit and saying to themselves, 'What's going on here? We have these business people advocating [for children's programs] and there is nothing in it for them. It must be good. It must be good.'"[38] Pre-kindergarten advocates traded ideas on how to engage business leaders as allies, noting that they were often attracted to the issue by the strong research base and promise of securing a better educated workforce through long-range investment.[39] In Oklahoma, oil billionaire George Kaiser (listed by Forbes as the twenty-sixth richest person in the country) was inspired by reading about brain research and the Abecedarian study to get involved in early childhood education. He was joined by the CEO of the state's largest oil company, Pete Churchwell, and the head of the Tulsa Chamber of Commerce; all of them became important activists for early childhood causes in Oklahoma. After visiting Ed Zigler at Yale University to learn about his Schools of the Twenty-First Century, these Tulsa business leaders launched early childhood programs funded by a combination of public and private dollars.[40] In Mississippi, business leaders raised funds in 2008 to start a pilot pre-kindergarten program, hoping to spur the state to create a statewide program.

Other business leaders also saw pre-kindergarten as a promising education reform that could help prepare the future workforce for an increasingly competitive and knowledge-based global economy. In 2003, the Business Roundtable and Corporate Voices for Working Families issued a joint "call to action from the business community" on early childhood education. Business leaders, the two organizations wrote, had invested time, expertise, and resources over a period of twenty years to improve K–12 education. (The Business Roundtable, an association of 150 CEOs of leading corporations, had been particularly involved in standards-based reform of public schools, and strongly supported the passage of the No Child Left Behind Act in 2001.) But school reform efforts "to develop a world-class workforce will be hampered without a federal and state commitment to early childhood education for 3- and 4-year-old children." Like the CED, these business leaders called for states to develop systems of early education for three- and four-year-olds and for the federal government to support and provide leadership for these efforts. The Business Roundtable also called for programs to be open to families regardless of socioeconomic status, noting that middle-class children as well as poorer children stood to benefit from quality early education.[41] In 2008, the National Association of Manufacturers added its endorsement, calling pre-kindergarten a crucial part of preparing children to succeed in the competitive global economy.[42] In 2003, PNC Financial Services announced it would spend $100 million over ten years to promote school readiness in the five-state region where it operated. On a smaller scale, a group of businesses in Fairfax County, Virginia (including PNC Bank), decided in 2006 to spend $300,000 on preschool education in the county, hoping to improve the caliber of the local workforce to better meet the needs of the region's "knowledge-based economy." The regional president of PNC Bank noted that it had traditionally contributed to high school and college programs but had been convinced by research showing that early learning can have dramatic effects, making it "clear that the investment here was more appropriate than anywhere else."[43]

Business leaders' attention was especially captured by economists who concluded that early childhood programs were an effective long-term investment. Most influential was Art Rolnick of the Federal Reserve Bank of Minneapolis, who urged policymakers to consider early childhood education as an economic development measure. He had been drawn into the issue of preschool when listening to a presentation about the need to support Minnesota's pre-kindergarten program. He observed that while moral arguments on behalf of programs for children were compelling, "I just think you're not going to make much headway without making the economic case for it." Researching the subject, he became convinced that there was in fact a strong economic case to be made. He calculated an internal rate of return to compare the value gained by different kinds of investments, and concluded that investing in early childhood development under the right conditions "yields an extraordinary return, far exceeding the return on most investments, private or public." The Perry Preschool program could claim a 12 percent public return on investment— about twice the historic rate of return on the stock market, and much higher than could be gained through conventional economic development measures such as public subsidies for building sports stadiums or for relocating retail stores and corporate headquarters.[44] Rolnick became a sought-after speaker (one colleague described him as "almost a rock star of early childhood"), addressing the National Governors Association, the National Conference of State Legislatures, the World Bank, and audiences of business leaders and policymakers in different states.

Rolnick's talks drew a different audience from the "usual suspects"—educators and advocates for children. For example, a business columnist for the *Hartford Courant* wrote in 2004: "The forum was on early childhood development. And a funny thing happened. Men in gray suits showed up. Lots of them."[45] Connecticut Republican Governor Jodi Rell noted that although she had been involved with the issue before, participating in a forum with Rolnick was "an eye-opener for me," convincing her of the importance of getting "the economic people and the early childhood people together to talk with a common language." Business leaders were willing to champion early childhood programs when they perceived them as a social investment with a high rate of return rather than as "wasteful government spending."[46] Similarly, a reporter for the *New York Times* wrote that an event organized by Pew, the Committee for Economic Development, and PNC Financial Services in 2006 aimed to "reframe the warm, fuzzy image of early childhood programs, transforming them into a hardheaded, quantifiable matter of economics and work force efficiency." The event included the release of a poll of Fortune 1000 and other top executives, showing that they overwhelmingly favored pre-kindergarten as a means of improving the workforce.[47] National Public Radio's *Marketplace* correspondent Chris Farrell explained in a 2006 interview that CEOs had become frustrated by giving money to education without seeing a significant effect. "So they're putting pressure on their people, saying 'what's the biggest bang for my buck?' What their people are coming to them and saying is the biggest bang for the buck is to invest in early childhood education for at-risk kids between birth and age five." Business leaders were coalescing around the issue, their commitments fueled by research findings, especially Rolnick's calculations of a rate of return on investment "that leaves the stock market way behind."[48]

Emphasizing the economic benefits of preschool to communities and states sparked interest from many policymakers and business leaders, broadening the circle of those who saw preschool as a promising solution. The Pew Trusts supported research estimating the economic benefits of universal preschool in several states, reporting that in each case benefits exceeded the costs of the program, even when it offered preschool to all or most children. For instance, Clive Belfield estimated the cost savings to New York's education system of implementing universal early childhood education. Even assuming that the impact of a universal program would be only a quarter of that documented for programs targeted at disadvantaged children, Belfield calculated that savings from reducing grade retention and special education costs, as well as increased classroom productivity, would be significant (partly because New York had high rates of special education placement and overall higher per-pupil spending), and would recoup between 40 and 60 percent of the initial expenditures within about ten years.[49]

Urahn wrote in 2006 that this kind of economic research "has had such a remarkable impact on the preschool policy debate" that the Pew Trusts were exploring whether the approach could be applied to other social programs benefiting children, such as health care and after-school programs. Evidence that spending money on effective programs for children could translate into large-scale economic impacts, she wrote, could help "make investments in children the top economic priority in the United States."[50] The importance of this investment argument for preschool efforts is captured in the title of David Kirp's recent book on the pre-kindergarten movement, *The Sandbox Investment*. While earlier efforts, such as Head Start, focused on improving the lives of poor young children as a moral imperative, recent efforts have appealed to societal self-interest by focusing on the economic benefits of improving the future workforce.

DEBATING WHO NEEDS PRESCHOOL: TARGETED VERSUS UNIVERSAL APPROACHES

While these economic arguments have been crucial in building support for expanding preschool, they do not necessarily lead to pushing for preschool for all. Indeed, advocates today differ about whether public programs should be universal (that is, offered to all children) or restricted to the neediest in a targeted approach. Experts who are focused on achieving the greatest return on investment tend to push for programs targeted to the poorest children, citing the research on the benefits of pre-kindergarten for disadvantaged children. Those more attuned to the political aspects of policy formation argue for a universal approach, arguing that pursuing "preschool for all" is a more effective strategy for gaining broad political support and ultimately securing higher quality, more sustainable programs.

Proponents of targeting, such as economist Art Rolnick, argue for investing public resources where they will make the most difference: in programs for the most disadvantaged children. A significant research base documents that these children stand to benefit most dramatically from a good preschool experience. Some also argue that smaller, targeted programs may be better able to provide the quality, intensity, and duration of service that can make a difference for children with the greatest needs. Because targeted programs are smaller and serve children whose families cannot afford to purchase good preschool on their own, they are also an easier "sell" for policymakers. Economist Greg Duncan, writing in *The Future of Children* in 2007, recommended a targeted, two-year program for economically disadvantaged three- and four-year-olds, staffed by college-trained teachers, using a proven curriculum combined with family outreach, and with a generous adult-to-child ratio. Such a program, he estimated, would have a better cost-benefit ratio than a blanket universal program, reducing future poverty by 5 to 15 percent.[51] University of California professor Bruce Fuller is another proponent of targeting, seeing universal programs as a misguided effort to create a new entitlement for the middle class. He wrote in his 2007 critique of the pre-kindergarten movement: "Policymakers need to act in surgical fashion, focusing public resources on the children who will benefit the most from quality preschool."[52]

Proponents of universal programs, such as economist Steven Barnett, argue that a universal approach is likely to receive greater public support and ultimately create better programs. Successful social programs need a constituency that can exert some political muscle, and if preschool were universal, "a broader and more influential cross-section of the nation would have a direct stake in [program] quality." Central to this argument is the conviction that targeted programs do not usually live up to the promise of high quality; as Barnett put it in 2004 (combining two policy aphorisms), "Programs for the poor tend to be poor programs," since "beggars can't be choosers."[53] In a recent book on pre-kindergarten, Edward Zigler and his coauthors emphasize the strategic benefit of a universal approach. Providing preschool for all, they write, "may be the best way to attract the political will needed to mount and sustain these programs.... For quality in state pre-kindergartens to be high and stay high, a broad constituency is needed—one that includes the political clout of the middle class."[54] Education journalist John Merrow wrote that instead of creating programs to help the poor,

> we ought to be creating a system that would be good enough for the well-off. . . . Design a preschool system the way we built our Interstate highway system. We didn't create separate highways for rich and poor. Instead, we built an Interstate system that was good enough for people behind the wheel of a Cadillac or a Lexus, a Corvette or a Mercedes, and there were no complaints from those driving a Chevy or a Ford.[55]

Supporters of a universal approach argued that preschool, like public K–12 education, should be made available to all children. "Back in the late nineteenth century, this same fight was being waged over free public high schools. Let the state pay only for so-called 'pauper schools,' opponents argued, while the well-to-do can educate their own. That idea now seems quaint," observed David Kirp and Deborah Stipek.[56] In New York, preschool advocate Karen Schimke often gets asked: "Do you really want to pay for pre-K for a kid in Scarsdale?" She replies, "Well, why do I want to pay for the second grade for a kid in Scarsdale? Why is it different?"[57] Similarly, Marc Tucker of the New Commission on the American Workforce said in 2007:

> To my knowledge, no one is proposing that the state should fund K–12 public schools only for low-income children. We have now established that, from a strictly educational standpoint, pre-kindergarten education is no less vital to a young person's growth and development than kindergarten or grades 1–5. So it is hard for me to understand the logic of saying that the state should fully fund K–12 education but not fully fund the education of younger students.[58]

Furthermore, scholar Richard Kahlenberg notes, a universal preschool system, linked to the schools, would have real staying power:

> Under a universal system, these teachers would ally with middle class parents . . . to ensure the program's survival, even in times of budget cuts. Teacher unions would bargain for better wages for preschool teachers, and higher teacher standards—like the requirement of a college degree—and reduce teacher turnover. Universal pre-K would look like universal Social Security and universal public schooling. These are not the "tragedy of American liberalism" [as one critic contended], but rather liberalism's glory: programs committed to the common good and frustratingly difficult for conservatives to dismantle.[59]

Since so many young children were already enrolled in preschool or child care, universal preschool seemed attractive as a way of bringing children together into a single system. Steven Barnett wrote: "the nation is quickly moving toward universal preschool whether we plan for it or not." In a context where 75 percent of four-year-olds were receiving some sort of child care (56 percent in center-based care) and children were increasingly enrolled in preschool whether or not their mothers were employed outside the home, he wrote, "to continue to treat preschool as an enrichment program for the disadvantaged would appear to be a form of denial."[60] Furthermore, the problem of school readiness was not restricted to poor children, as the Carnegie task force had noted in calling for a universal approach in 1996. Kindergarten teachers surveyed in 1991 reported that at least one-third of their students were not "ready" for kindergarten, lacking not only specific academic skills but behavioral skills like knowing how to follow directions or take turns.[61] In 2004, the Trust for Early Education assembled national data showing that problems with school readiness were widespread. For instance, half the children who entered kindergarten without knowing the alphabet came from middle- or upper-class families. Steve Barnett of the NIEER found that many children whose families were *above* the poverty line had problems with school readiness, low achievement, and dropout rates and could benefit from high-quality preschool education. Although he found a nearly linear relationship between family income and school readiness skills, meaning that poorest children's needs were greatest, Barnett documented significant needs for middle-income children, concluding: "There is no clear cut-off where the gap dramatically declines and ceases to be important." Finally, a universal approach eliminated the problems associated with screening families for eligibility, as well as the stigma associated with programs limited to poor and troubled families.[62]

But one problem for advocates of a universal approach to preschool was the initial lack of research showing specifically how middle- and upper-class children benefited from preschool. An evaluation of the Georgia universal pre-kindergarten program found no significant differences between middle-class children who attended pre-kindergarten and those who did not. Looking at the effects of child care in general, a large government study found significant cognitive benefits for middle-class children attending child care centers, though it also reported a small but significant increase in aggressive social behavior among children who spent many hours in child care. Looking more specifically at preschool, one small study found that in an "educationally advantaged" setting, preschool attendance had a significant impact on boys' (but not girls') achievement in elementary school, especially on language indicators. An analysis of the much larger Early Childhood Longitudinal Study found benefits in early language and prereading skills for white children attending preschool, and larger benefits for Latino children. While the benefits for poorer children were sustained in elementary school, those for middle-class children tended to fade by third grade.[63] The Georgetown University study of pre-kindergarten students in Tulsa, described in the last chapter, produced a similar result. Researchers found that children from all backgrounds benefited, though not equally. Hispanic and Native American children seemed to benefit the most from the program, while African-American and white children saw smaller, but still significant, improvements. Similarly, while children in all income brackets (as measured by free lunch eligibility) benefited, the poorer children in the sample showed more improvement in scores than did those who came from more affluent families.[64] Indeed, in their first study, using a test designed to screen entering kindergarten children for problems, the Georgetown research-ers did not find any benefit to white children or to children who did not qualify for free lunch. It was only in their second study, when they used a more sophis-ticated standardized test that could measure a full range of abilities, that they detected benefits to all subgroups of children. Commenting on their initial findings in 2003, the Georgetown researchers noted that the more disadvan-taged children may have benefited precisely because the program included more advantaged children. "Oklahoma's relatively unique emphasis on univer-sality…may contribute to classroom mixes of children that foster the gains we have demonstrated, particularly for children of color and those from disadvan-taged families."[65]

Indeed, bringing together children from different backgrounds in the same classroom could have important value. A growing literature on socioeconomic integration in K–12 settings shows that disadvantaged students benefit from being in classrooms with more affluent students, and another body of research shows that children with disabilities benefit from being in classrooms with their abled peers. The question of peer effects in preschool has been little studied, in part because early childhood programs tend to be segregated along socioeco-nomic lines. One small-scale study in Connecticut found that low-income chil-dren in economically integrated preschool settings had much larger language gains than their counterparts in economically segregated settings. Because pre-school children spend the same amount of time talking to each other as talking to the teacher, the language skills of other children are an important aspect of the learning environment.

Staking out a third position in this debate are conservatives and libertarians who ideologically oppose government involvement in family life and therefore see "preschool for all" as government intrusion into child-rearing. While they do not oppose expanding preschool for disadvantaged children, the idea of publicly funded preschool for all four-year-olds raises alarms. For instance, the president of the Palmetto Family Council wrote in 2006 that South Carolina should provide pre-kindergarten intervention only to "seriously at-risk kids," just as "we don't prescribe radiation or other aggressive therapies for healthy people."[66] Universal preschool raises fears of increased governmental involvement in children's lives—what Darcy Olsen of the Cato Institute called "the advancing nanny state"—and decreased parental responsibility.[67] Conservative talk show host Laura Schlessinger wrote in 1999 that the idea of universal preschool reminded her of a scene in George Orwell's *Animal Farm* where a mother dog's puppies were taken away from her by the government. "Any time a government entity tells parents that it knows more about the welfare of all children than the caring, involved, nurturing and attentive mother and father," Schlessinger wrote, "be afraid. Be VERY afraid."[68] Some also raised fears that voluntary programs would quickly become mandatory, following the historical path of public education more generally. Thus the Virginia Family Foundation warned in 2006 that Democratic governor Tim Kaine's plans for universal preschool were a cover for the ultimate goal of "the state forced education of 2, 3, and 4 year old children."[69] To those who mistrust government, expanding public education to include preschool seems a poor idea. They fear that universal preschool will give rise to greater bureaucracy and will give more power to teacher unions, rather than improving education. For instance, during the 2002 campaign for the universal preschool ballot initiative in Florida, a Jacksonville newspaper declared that it was wrong to expand "the public education empire" when not all children need preschool; children should be with their parents rather than "turned over to a government program."[70] Skepticism about the efficacy of public schools also plays a strong role in generating opposition to universal pre-kindergarten. In Pennsylvania, the president of the free market-oriented Commonwealth Foundation wrote a newspaper opinion piece titled "Waiting at the Cradle: The Well-meaning Folks Who Care about 'The Kids' Want State Government to Raise Your Children."[71]

Some ideological critics of the universal approach also argue that preschool's promise has been inflated. There is little hard evidence, they say, of how preschool benefits middle-class children, and the academic benefits that have been documented for other children are no longer significant by the fourth grade. Darcy Olsen of the Goldwater Institute wrote in 2005: "For mainstream children, there is little evidence to support the contention that formal preschool and kindergarten are necessary for school achievement." Despite its extensive Pre-K program, Olsen and others claim, overall test scores for Georgia students and fourth-grade scores on the National Assessment of Educational Progress have not gone up in the past ten years. Looking abroad, they argue that despite universal preschool, elementary school students in European countries do worse than their American peers on international tests; it is in the older grades that European students outperform Americans. In fact, they say, American children are well prepared for kindergarten; it is the schools that fail them, and that is where attention should be directed, rather than on expanding preschool.[72] These claims can all be disputed; both national fourth-grade reading scores on the National Assessment of Educational Progress and test scores in Georgia have in fact increased somewhat in recent years, and factors other than preschool go further in explaining why U.S. high school students fare worse in comparisons on international tests.[73] But since so much of the support for expanding preschool rests on research evidence, opponents who use research on student achievement to question whether too much has been promised for preschool will certainly draw more attention than those who object to it on ideological grounds.

CONCLUSION

During the first decade of the twenty-first century, Pew and other funders helped build a national movement for universal pre-kindergarten and launch a carefully designed campaign to expand state preschool programs. This coalition for expanding public pre-kindergarten brought together social liberals and fiscal conservatives, reaching out to education reformers and business leaders who were drawn to the idea of investing in the skills of the future workforce. Support for expanding preschool relied on a strong research base that documented the promise of preschool for improving the life chances of disadvantaged children. The movement's vision of providing "preschool for all" was also inspired by another promise—that a universal approach would be more politically effective in the long run, resulting in stable funding and higher quality programs. But this commitment to a universal approach to preschool was challenged both by those who preferred to target scarce resources to the neediest children and by critics who feared increasing government's role in raising children in general. This general debate over government's role in educating preschoolers—should it provide preschool for all, for some, or not at all?—set the stage for specific political struggles in the states, where the preschool movement was taking shape.

PART II

Where We Are Going

CHAPTER 6

"Preschool for All" or Preschool for the Needy?

Universal and Targeted Approaches in the States

In the previous chapter, we saw that a national movement for "preschool for all" has built a broad education-business coalition favoring expanding publicly funded preschool. The next three chapters explore the key questions that preschool advocates and policymakers today face as they try to expand access to high-quality preschool: determining which children publicly funded preschool should serve, how it should be delivered, and how to ensure that it is of high quality.

As advocates and policymakers at the state level sought to translate the promise of preschool into practice, they had to wrestle with the practical question of whether their preschool programs should serve all children or be targeted to the neediest, like Head Start. Backers of a universal approach believed that offering preschool to all children would create a broad constituency and gain greater public support, ultimately producing stronger, higher quality programs. They sought to secure for preschool the kind of legitimacy and longevity enjoyed by Social Security and public K–12 education, universal programs that had prospered in part because they benefited broad categories of people. The legislative success of universal pre-kindergarten programs in several states in recent years (including Florida, West Virginia, Illinois, and Iowa) seemed to confirm the wisdom of this strategy.

But although the idea that universal programs would be more politically popular and result in higher quality programs was widely shared, it was not always a useful guide in practice. Attempts to enact universal pre-kindergarten in several states ran into opposition precisely because the idea of providing "preschool for all" seemed a questionable use of public dollars when many families were already paying to send their children to private preschools. Earlier decisions to rely on the private sector to provide preschool and child care thus influenced the options that policymakers now faced, diminishing the demand for universal, public solutions. Not only was the promise of broad political support often misleading, so was the promise that universal programs would necessarily produce higher quality than targeted ones. Indeed, one of the largest universal pre-kindergarten programs, Florida's Voluntary Pre-kindergarten, operates with some of the nation's lowest quality standards.

In practice, the universal preschool programs that states have designed have had mixed success at generating broad political support and high quality standards, while some more incremental efforts to expand targeted programs have been quite successful. Advocates and policymakers today are torn between pushing for "preschool for all," which they believe will provide greater political support and lead to higher quality in the long run, and "preschool for the needy," which is less expensive, more easily justified by research evidence, and more politically feasible in the short run.

BUILDING POLITICAL SUPPORT

In making the case for a universal approach to preschool, advocates often pointed to history, citing the example of Head Start's ongoing struggle for funding as proof that programs targeted to the poor cannot gain sufficient political support to prosper. They frequently cited the slogan "No more poor programs for poor people" as a way of explaining their commitment to a universal approach.[1] Graciela Italiano-Thomas, who spent ten years working in Head Start and directed Los Angeles' universal preschool effort, commented in 2006:

> We are at a point where we need to go beyond Head Start.... If we are going to aim at high quality we have to aim at all children.... When you only aim at those in greatest need, history tells us that the programs lose the political support they need to survive, and therefore those in greatest need don't benefit."[2]

Head Start champion Edward Zigler has written recently that the program's history shows the dangers of developing a program just for the poor. "Programs for poor children are susceptible to the whimsical support of policy makers, changing national priorities, and political strategizing—events that middle-class parents would not stand for if they affected their children's care and education." Universal programs, he argued, would benefit from the clout and knowledge of middle-class parents accustomed to exerting pressure on policymakers.[3] But recent developments in several states call into question the idea that universal programs necessarily garner broader political support. Most notable is California, where in 2006 voters rejected the "Preschool for All" ballot initiative.

Prior to this ballot defeat, California had been gradually moving toward universal preschool; it was written into the state's master plan for education in 1998, and some counties chose to use funds from the "First 5" cigarette tax passed that year to develop universal programs. But finding the money to finance public preschool for all was a daunting challenge, and advocates hoped that taking the question directly to the voters would spur action. Actor-director Rob Reiner, who had made early childhood development his political cause since the early 1990s, developed and championed the "Preschool for All" ballot measure in 2006. The initiative promised to provide preschool to all four-year-olds in the state, raising $2.4 billion annually by increasing the income tax on the wealthiest taxpayers (individuals making more than $400,000 and couples making more than $800,000). Advocates like Reiner sought a universal measure because they believed it would garner broad political support, ensure access to

Figure 6.1 Actor Rob Reiner, chair of the First 5 California Commission, plays with preschoolers at the Turnbull Learning Academy in San Mateo, California in 2003. The commission's decision to use funds raised by the First 5 cigarette tax to support universal preschool programs helped pave the way for the 2006 "Preschool for All" ballot initiative. *AP/Wide World Photos, photographer Ben Margot*

the wide range of families who needed preschool, and gain a constituency over time that would ensure its quality, funding, and survival. Universality was also attractive to those who wanted to see preschool become part of the public education system, including school leaders and teachers' unions. School districts would administer funds, which could go to public, private, and parochial preschools. Preschool teachers would be required to have a bachelor's degree, would be paid at the same level as K–12 teachers, and would have a right to collective bargaining.

Initial polls in 2006 seemed to favor the measure, which garnered a long list of business and education supporters, including both the Los Angeles and San Francisco chambers of commerce. (This was the first time the Los Angeles Chamber had endorsed any income tax increase in its 188-year history, and the first time the powerful California State Teachers Association supported any measure based on parental choice.)[4] Law enforcement groups such as the California Police Chiefs and state sheriffs' associations, as well as Fight Crime/ Invest in Kids, also endorsed the measure.[5] Supporters pointed to the RAND Corporation's estimate that the state would save $2.62 for every dollar spent providing preschool to 70 percent of its four-year-olds. Several commentators speculated that Reiner might move from a victory on this issue to launching a political career in the state. Rather than leading the campaign to victory, however, Reiner ended up derailing it when charges surfaced that he had improperly used First 5 Commission funds to air ads promoting preschool during the signature-gathering phase of the campaign for the ballot initiative. Although Reiner stepped down from the Commission in March, the political damage had been done.[6] Senate leader Don Perata (whom reporters called "the state's most powerful Democrat") announced around this time that he was withdrawing his support from the measure, saying it was too costly and not focused on those who needed it most.[7]

Opponents of the "Preschool for All" ballot initiative argued that a universal program would benefit families who did not really need help. "Rather than focus resources on the state's most pressing needs or helping parents of low-income families who need the most help sending their kids to preschool, this flawed measure creates a subsidy for rich and middle-income families that already send their kids to preschool," said Larry McCarthy, president of the California Taxpayers' Association.[8] Bruce Fuller, a policy expert at the University of California, Berkeley, lent his scholarly weight to this charge. Noting that 65 percent of California's four-year-olds were already attending preschool, Fuller argued that the measure would not make a substantial difference in preschool enrollments. Fuller was a visible critic, publishing not only policy briefs but also newspaper opinion pieces with provocative titles like "Preschool Reform Measure

Won't Close Learning Gap for Poor," "The Preschool 'Spin,'" and "Universal Preschool: Democrats' New Embrace of Big Government."[9] Supporters of the measure said that Fuller's charge was misleading, since most children were not enrolled in the high-quality programs the initiative sought to create but in ordinary day-care centers. Federal Reserve economist Art Rolnick, whose analysis of preschool as a social investment had sparked so much interest from business leaders around the country, also raised questions about the "Preschool for All" measure. Cautioning that it would be wiser to expand preschool for at-risk families rather than offering it to every child, he told a reporter: "The business community is willing to write checks for poor families, but there is concern that Preschool for All is another subsidy for the middle class."[10]

Opponents also feared that the universal preschool measure, backed by teachers' unions and administered by school districts, would extend the reach of the "education bureaucracy" in the state and leave out private providers. They framed their public message around this fear of big government, which resonated with voters and opinion leaders, and argued that preschool, while a worthy idea, should not be legislated through ballot initiatives. All the major papers in the state editorialized against the measure. The *Los Angeles Times* declared that it would "set up a cumbersome bureaucracy and place it under the State Department of Education, which has done a disappointing job with K–12 schools."[11] *New York Times* columnist David Brooks chimed in that the initiative "seems to have been devised under the supposition that it takes a bureaucratic megalopolis to raise a child."[12] Television commercials opposing the initiative capitalized on those fears, consistently warning the measure would do little to raise preschool enrollment but would create a new "preschool bureaucracy."[13]

At the polls in June 2006, California voters soundly rejected the measure, by a margin of 61 to 39 percent. One San Jose resident who voted against it explained: "Prop. 82 sounded really good, but the more I looked at it, the more I realized it was subject to shenanigans. Kids should go to preschool, but it didn't sound like Prop. 82 would help the families who most needed the help."[14] Many of the initiative's opponents claimed they did not object to the idea of publicly funded preschool, but rather to the way the initiative would have organized and funded it. The president of the California Business Roundtable and cochair of the No on Prop. 82 Campaign said after the election: "If you want to have a discussion about whether universal preschool should be approved in California, that's a good discussion to have. It should probably be funded through the normal K–12 public financing system.... People are tired of ballot box budgeting."[15]

The failure of the "Preschool for All" initiative suggests that a universal approach carries political risks as well as benefits. Promising universal pre-kindergarten may help build a broad base of support, especially over the long term, but it also carries a big price tag, and it raises questions about why public dollars should go to those who are already paying to provide preschool for their children. In postmortem analyses, several observers suggested that the initiative's universal approach, rather than building broad political support, had in fact doomed it. Former federal education official Nina Rees wrote in *Education Week* that advocates should learn from the initiative's failure about the importance of targeting funds to the neediest children.[16] *Washington Post* columnist E. J. Dionne also questioned whether universality was the best strategy.

> In principle, programs that cover everyone—Social Security and Medicare are prime examples—are usually better programs and command broad political support. Programs for the poor alone are often less generous and have a shakier foundation in public opinion. But universal programs carry large price tags. In retrospect, Reiner might have gotten closer to his honorable goal with a smaller program directed at the poorest kids and requiring a smaller tax increase.[17]

Indeed, three months after the rejection of the "Preschool for All" measure, the legislature passed a much smaller bill targeting $50 million for low-income children to attend preschool programs in underperforming school districts. The funding was a small fraction of what would have been provided under "Preschool for All" and did not address concerns about quality. As he signed the legislation, Republican governor Arnold Schwarzenegger referred to the work of his Democratic father-in-law, Sargent Shriver, in creating Head Start. Schwarzenegger's promisethat preschool would help those children who were "behind the starting line" get a "head start on their education and their lives" showed that Head Start's approach of targeting public dollars toward the most needy children in the 1960s continued to resonate in twenty-first-century California.[18]

In other states across the nation, attempts to promote universal pre-kindergarten ran into some of the same difficulties that advocates in California had experienced. Advocates in these states have found it easier to promote preschool for the needy than to achieve "preschool for all." In Illinois, Democratic governor Rod Blagojevich succeeded in building legislative support over several years to expand early education for at-risk children. He made early childhood education a key issue in his gubernatorial campaign in 2002 and shepherded three major funding increases (totaling $90 million) through the legislature. "Not since the Chicago School Reform Act was passed in 1988," a local education journalist wrote at the time of the first of these increases, have so many diverse groups rallied around a single issue in Springfield. Early childhood advocacy groups have joined forces with child care providers, school districts, state board of education officials, business leaders, even police organizations to map out an early childhood education system and build the public will to make it happen.[19]

But in 2006, Blagojevich's proposal to make Illinois the first state in the nation to promise universal access to preschool for three-year-olds as well as four-year-olds met with more resistance. The *Chicago Tribune* applauded the idea of "Preschool for All" but also asked for "a reality check." Noting the many educational needs in the state—a fifth of the state's school districts were on the state's financial warning or watch lists, and another funding crisis in the Chicago schools was looming—the editorial board proposed limiting public preschool to families with incomes under $75,000. Children who rode to preschool in their families' Mercedes, the editorial board wrote, should not be funded by public dollars. Although "Preschool for Some" did not make as good a slogan as "Preschool for All," it was a more responsible approach.[20]

In response to concerns that the universal program would be a "giveaway" to wealthy families, the governor's office agreed to give priority to disadvantaged children and to working-class families who could not afford private preschool. Blagojevich was particularly concerned with working families whose incomes were above the eligibility line for the state's existing pre-kindergarten program but too low to afford high-quality private programs for their children. His director of education reform explained: "We intend to serve all kids, but we agreed that at-risk kids needed to be funded first." One of the legislators who helped draft the bill explained that his own priority was "making sure at-risk children were reached before we go on to higher income levels."[21] The measure enacted by the legislature thus implemented "universal" preschool in a "targeted" way, giving priority first to at-risk children and then to children of working families meeting certain income guidelines. More affluent families could not expect to benefit from the program until the governor's plan was fully implemented (at least five years away).[22] The Illinois program, then, uses "universal" programs to link the needs of working-class and lower-middle-class families, but does not reach further up the socioeconomic ladder. One might describe this as a program aspiring to universal access, taking one step at a time to achieve that goal.

Preschool for the needy has also been a more effective approach in Tennessee than has the idea of preschool for all. Democratic governor Phil Bredesen, long an advocate of children's issues, wanted to push for universal prekindergarten. According to his education commissioner, Bredesen hoped to be remembered for having an impact on education, and "there does not seem to be a better place to go than pre-K, which has a fundamental effect on our education system."[23] Finding insufficient support in the legislature for a universal program, he proposed in 2005 using $25 million from the new state lottery to expand the state's pilot pre-kindergarten program for at-risk children, which had high quality standards and had been showing good evaluation results. To support Bredesen's initiative, advocates formed a broad coalition of more than 100 organizations, including business leaders, health industry organizations, community organizations, and unions, and received funding from Pre-K Now to hire a public relations firm to assist in its advocacy work.[24] When the state department of education testified before the state Senate on the bill, it pointed out that the bill had the support of groups that included the Tennessee Association of Chiefs of Police, the sheriffs' and district attorneys' associations, and business leaders.

The combination of this broad-based coalition and Bredesen's leadership produced strong support in the legislature for a pre-kindergarten program aimed at low-income children. Every school district that requested pre-kindergarten funding when the program started received it, ensuring that the program would be spread around the state. By 2006–7, about a third of the state's eligible children (those whose family incomes were within 185 percent of the federal poverty line) were enrolled in the program. Ninety percent of school districts were participating, and almost all the counties that had not yet participated were planning to apply for funding.[25] Commissioner of education Lana Seivers noted: "Not too long ago, pre-K was not on the public radar in this state. Today, we are celebrating the breakneck expansion of pre-K classrooms."[26] At a national conference on advocacy in the pre-kindergarten movement in 2006, Libby Doggett of Pre-K Now praised Tennessee's strategy of establishing a high-quality program and increasing it incrementally, rather than rushing into a universal program.[27]

Although Bredesen was willing to focus the program's expansion on low-income students, he was not shy about his goal of pushing for universal access in the long run. He told a reporter in 2005 that he hoped to have a program open to all four-year-olds by the time he left office.[28] He explained that he planned to request $25 million in lottery funds for the program every year, plus an increase from state revenue growth.

> I look at this a little like paying down a mortgage. Every year you do a little bit and you wake up one day and suddenly you have a lot of equity in your house. I want to do that with education. I think we will look up in four, five, six years from now and there will be an absolute national model pre-K program in our state.[29]

Although some key legislators felt the program should continue to focus on at-risk children, Bredesen made his pledge of "pre-K for all" part of his reelection campaign in 2006. "It is really important to open this," he said. "I mean, kindergarten and first grade are not available only to at-risk students."[30] By June 2007, the legislature had increased funding for pre-kindergarten, which was operating in ninety-four out of the state's ninety-five counties and serving 17,000 children.[31] But it remained a targeted, rather than universal, effort.

In Virginia, the same debate also greeted Timothy Kaine's efforts to provide preschool to all of the state's four-year-olds. He made pre-kindergarten the centerpiece of his education platform during the 2005 gubernatorial election, and in late 2006 he proposed piloting a universal pre-kindergarten program in six communities in the state. "The needs of at-risk kids will be paramount, but early childhood education benefits all kids," Kaine said, explaining that he hoped to have universal pre-kindergarten in place before leaving office in 2010. Universal programs, he contended, are less susceptible to "the political winds," and children benefited from being in diverse classrooms. Some legislators, however, objected to the idea of a universal program. Republican House majority leader H. Morgan Griffith said it made sense to provide preschool to children from poor families, but he didn't want to invest millions on early childhood education for middle- or upper-class children. "We have lots of other needs," he said. "The vast majority of students who aren't at-risk are going to be fine without it." Another Republican legislator, a teacher who described himself as "solidly middle-class," asked, "Why would you want to subsidize me? Where does the money come from? Does it come from tutoring? Does it come from algebra-readiness?"[32] Republican legislator Scott Lingamfelter argued that the state's current policy toward preschool—providing public programs "for those who can't afford it and a free enterprise solution for those who can"—was effective and should not be changed.[33] At a public forum in Charlottesville, state secretary of education Tom Morris argued that a universal program would end up serving children more effectively than the existing targeted program did, since a universal approach would garner more support from community groups and business leaders. "Public programs for just at-risk students don't have the broader constituency of support as one that includes all children," he said. But a member of the local school board suggested that it would be more effective to increase funding for low-income three-year-olds in order to narrow the achievement gap: "It seems to me that in a world of limited funding, it would be better to put it toward at-risk 3-year-olds, so those kids have two years of preschool."[34] When the legislature did not produce the funding Kaine had requested for pre-kindergarten expansion in 2007, he decided to focus on doubling the number of disadvantaged children served by the state's existing pre-kindergarten program, rather than pushing for universal access. The new plan would extend free pre-kindergarten to four-year-olds who qualified for reduced-price lunches, making an additional 17,000 children eligible. "We're coming at it a little differently," Kaine explained, "because the experience of other states has convinced us to work within the existing system we already have."[35] Even this more modest approach met opposition in the legislature, although legislators did agree to increase the pre-kindergarten program's budget in 2008.

A different kind of compromise was under way in Massachusetts. In 2006, building on several years of careful advocacy work by the Early Education for All campaign, the legislature passed a bill establishing a universal pre-kindergarten program for three- and four-year-olds, to be fully phased in by 2012. Despite bipartisan support (two-thirds of the legislature cosponsored the bill), Republican governor Mitt Romney vetoed it in August 2006, saying the program was unproven and could cost taxpayers up to $1 billion a year.[36] Advocates went back to work, commissioning a team of economists from Northeastern University to establish a solid cost estimate. By cutting back on hours and abandoning the idea that the program would be available free of charge to all families, they came up with a figure that was half the original estimate for the program. Instituting sliding scale fees enabled them to provide "universal" access, but with differential costs. Under the more politically friendly administration of Democratic governor Duval Patrick, in 2008 the state committed itself to building a universal preschool program, funded with parent fees as well as state funds.

In California, Illinois, Tennessee, Virginia, and Massachusetts, then, a universal approach generated both political opposition and support. While politicians are certainly interested in a policy that benefits as many of their constituents as possible, they are also keenly aware of the need to balance competing budget priorities. Given that so many families already pay to send their children to preschool, there is often stronger political support for using public dollars for low-income children who clearly "need" it than for building a bigger and more expensive universal system. Indeed, the development of a strong private sector providing early childhood education and care influences today's debates about where public funds should be spent. Journalist John Merrow argued for building a single, universal preschool system, noting: "We didn't create separate highways for rich and poor." But this is in fact what we have done for preschool and child care over the past forty years. The question that policymakers now face is whether we should now go back and try to integrate these systems into one.

STRIVING TO IMPROVE PROGRAM QUALITY

Just as these examples demonstrate that universal programs do not necessarily attract broader political support, we must also question the conviction that universal programs lead naturally to higher quality. The most striking example is Florida, which has one of the nation's largest state pre-kindergarten programs and some of the nation's lowest quality standards.

Frustrated by the legislature's opposition to enacting universal pre-kindergarten, advocates in Florida launched a petition campaign to put a constitutional amendment for universal pre-kindergarten on the ballot in 2002. David Lawrence, former publisher of the *Miami Herald*, and Alex Penelas, the Democratic mayor of Miami-Dade County, spearheaded the effort. An aide to Penelas explained: "It was clear...that if there was ever going to be any serious hope of getting universal pre-k passed in the state of Florida, it was via a citizens' initiative....No one [in the legislature] wanted to be responsible for bringing an item forth that could possibly have a substantial price tag."[37] Backers raised $1.8 million and flooded South Florida's media market, knowing that strong support there would carry the state. In the fall 2002 election, voters approved an amendment to the constitution stating that every four-year-old in the state "shall be offered a high-quality pre-kindergarten learning opportunity by the state" at no cost to parents; the program was to be "established according to high quality standards."

However, the legislature passed a program that did not set standards at all for class size, teacher training, staff-to-child ratios, or length of the program day.[38] The task force charged with making recommendations for the pre-kindergarten program had envisioned a six-hour day with certified teachers, costing about $4,320 per student, but the legislature approved funding for a three-hour day at about $2,500 per student and did not require teachers to have college degrees. Private providers who did not want many strings attached to participating in the state program applauded this approach, as did advocates of school choice and limited government. But children's advocates and others who had worked for the passage of the universal pre-kindergarten referendum urged Republican governor Jeb Bush to veto the bill. One national advocate described it as "pre-K on the cheap," commenting, "It looks like child care, but they call it pre-K. If they're going to do that, then I will take down the flag. The whole point of pre-K was to raise quality."[39] In response to Governor Bush's veto, legislators agreed on a compromise bill—one with only slightly higher standards—that served as a foundation for the state's new program.[40] The Voluntary Pre-kindergarten program, which began in the fall of 2005, met only three of the NIEER's ten quality benchmarks, giving it the second worst quality rating of any state pre-kindergarten program in the country. In fact, several states required as much or more from their licensed child care centers as Florida did from its pre-kindergarten program. These problems with the program's quality standards did not set off any great outcry from Florida parents, but it may have kept some away. In the program's first year, there was less enrollment than expected; it served just over 40 percent of the state's four-year-olds in 2005–6 rather than the 66 percent predicted, and returned $158 million to the state's general fund.[41]

Advocates of universal pre-kindergarten have taken some lessons from Florida's experience about the importance of building quality standards in from the start, even if it takes longer to expand to serve all children. Libby Doggett of Pre-K Now commented in 2006 on "the difficulty of trying to fix a program that is offered to lots of kids but is not the high quality that you want."[42] Steve Barnett of NIEER observed that high-quality targeted programs may offer a better alternative than low-quality universal ones:

> West Virginia and Tennessee both have committed to serve all four-year-olds as fast as they can without sacrificing quality, whereas Florida basically took the opposite approach: "Let's get all the kids in and we'll look at quality later." I would hope no one else would follow the Florida model.[43]

Indeed, as an adviser to Democratic Kansas governor Kathleen Sebelius worked on a pre-kindergarten plan for her state in 2006, she commented on Florida's example: "From where I sit, what unfolded is really trying to do pre-K on the cheap. Because of both the low per-child funding and the real absence of standards for high quality, Florida became the model of exactly what we didn't want to do."[44]

Looking beyond Florida to other states, we see that universality is not a predictor of program quality. When NIEER measured state program standards against ten quality benchmarks in 2006, targeted programs in Alabama and North Carolina were the only ones to meet all ten benchmarks; targeted programs in Arkansas, New Jersey, South Carolina, New Mexico, and Tennessee met nine out of ten benchmarks, as did universal programs in Oklahoma and Illinois. New York's targeted program (Experimental Pre-Kindergarten) met eight of the benchmarks, while its universal program met only six. Nor was universality a predictor of greater funding: the ten states with the highest per-child funding amounts for state pre-kindergarten in 2006–7 all had targeted programs.[45]

EXPANDING INCREMENTALLY

While public pre-kindergarten in the states has grown significantly since 2001, much of that growth has come from increases in programs targeted to low-income children, as well as in universal programs. Indeed, targeted programs seem to be growing faster, in many cases with stronger political support, higher funding levels, and higher standards. Rather than launching new initiatives to provide "preschool for all," many states are pursuing an incremental approach to expanding access to preschool.

Total state spending on pre-kindergarten climbed significantly in the five years between 2001–2 and 2005–6, creating an increase of more than 40 percent in the enrollment of four-year-olds.[46] Legislative action in 2006 and 2007 added to this upward trend, with an overall spending increase of 12 percent each year. Growth has been particularly strong in southern states, which lead the nation in enrollment in public pre-kindergarten. (One out of three four-year-olds in the South attended a public pre-kindergarten program last year, compared with one out of five nationally.)[47] Between 2004 and 2007, only two states—Illinois and Iowa—committed themselves to providing universal pre-kindergarten. But the number of states that increased funding for pre-kindergarten grew from fourteen in 2004 to thirty-six in 2007. As a result, total funding grew from $2.9 billion in 2004 to $4.8 billion in 2007.[48]

Some of these increases represented a concerted plan to expand preschool for a targeted population. For instance, between 2004 and early 2006, Arkansas added $60 million to an existing $11 million budget to expand the Arkansas Better Chance program for low-income children, which had some of the highest quality standards in the country. In 2007, the legislature added another $40 million, allowing the program to serve all three- and four-year-olds in the state from families with incomes up to 200 percent of the federal poverty line.[49] Similarly, Louisiana increased funding to its pre-kindergarten programs in 2007, aiming to serve all eligible children (again, these low-income children make up a significant part of the state's population.) Rates of increase in other state programs were also significant: in 2007, Alabama and Ohio each nearly doubled their pre-kindergarten funding, Pennsylvania increased its funding by 135 percent, and Tennessee built on its recent dramatic growth, increasing funding by 45 percent. While other states were expanding their own preschool programs, advocates in Oregon decided to focus on increasing Head Start enrollment for children in poverty, as only 60 percent of the eligible children in the state were being served. Rather than pushing for universal preschool, Annette Dicker, who works at a Head Start center near Portland, said: "We've got to get to 100 percent for low-income kids first. Those kids are most at risk."[50]

Another type of incremental expansion was in Texas, which in 2006 changed the eligibility rules for its long-standing pre-kindergarten program to include children with parents on active military duty, killed or wounded in action, or in an activated reserve unit. An effort led by the United Ways of Texas and the Military Child Education Coalition brought together some of the state's most liberal and most conservative legislators. Military officials testified before the legislature about the benefits of pre-kindergarten and the educational needs of military families, who often struggle with frequent relocation and poverty. Advocates saw this change as a way of benefiting these families while adding to the targeted program's constituency, ultimately building support for more expansion. One of the legislative leaders explained in a Pre-K Now conference: "If we limit pre-K to kids who are at risk, it will always just be those kids...it needs to be everybody's kids." She noted that advocates might move next to expand eligibility to the children of police officers, first responders, and public school teachers.[51] In practice, however, the next step was to make another group of particularly disadvantaged children—those in the foster care system—eligible for the program.

The lines distinguishing universal from targeted approaches to preschool turn out to be quite fuzzy in practice. A state may expand a targeted program, as in Tennessee or Illinois, hoping to lay the groundwork for a universal program. Conversely, among the states that have made a commitment to "universal" pre-kindergarten, most do not have the funding to actually provide universal coverage. They are more likely to follow New York's or Illinois's path of developing a program that aspires to universality but gives priority to lower-income children since it does not have enough funding to offer access to all.

Furthermore, the differences in enrollment between targeted and universal programs are not as great as might be imagined, especially in states with high poverty rates and substantial funding for targeted programs. For instance, half the children in Arkansas are eligible for the state's pre-kindergarten program, which targets families with incomes up to 200 percent of the federal poverty line. Only Georgia, Florida, and Oklahoma served more than 50 percent of their four-year-olds in 2006–7, but ten other states served a significant proportion of their four-year-olds. Targeted programs in Texas, Vermont, Maryland, Wisconsin, South Carolina, Kentucky, and New Jersey served between a quarter and a half of those states' four-year-olds. Some targeted programs actually served a higher proportion of four-year-olds than did "universal" programs in New York and Illinois.

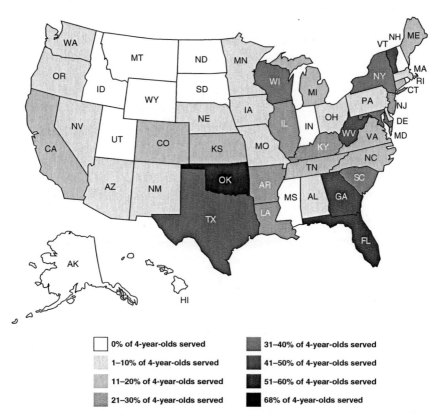

Figure 6.2 Percentage of 4-year-olds served in State Pre-K, 2006
Source: Reprinted with permission from the National Institute for Early Education Research, Rutgers University, New Brunswick, NJ.

Watching the incremental expansion of targeted programs, as well as the difficulties faced by some universal programs, may have influenced leaders at Pew and elsewhere to readjust their strategy. In reporting on the first five years of Pew's pre-kindergarten initiative, Urahn and her colleague Watson downplayed the importance of creating universal programs, explaining that their goal was for states to set universal access as a goal, though they might begin by serving disadvantaged children and expand to serve others over time.[52] As a result, the goal of achieving "preschool for all" has transformed into a more pragmatic approach, with the aim of expanding programs one step at a time up the socioeconomic ladder.

The political ramifications of universal and targeted programs were also on the minds of those who sought to influence preschool policy on a national level. In 2007, the Washington-based think tank Education Sector proposed a plan for preschool as one of its eight "Education Ideas for the Next President." Rather than calling for universal preschool, the group recommended providing it to four-year-olds with family incomes below $50,000, noting that the defeat of the California preschool initiative showed that "many Americans seem wary of demands by some for universal access to preschool for all 4-year-olds regardless of income." The proposed plan targeting preschool to low-income families would avoid "the universal approach's biggest political vulnerabilities: it is far cheaper and far more efficient than universal preschool; and it recognizes that voters without young children may be willing to support preschool programs to help the disadvantaged but do not want to pay for the education of rich people's children."[53] Pre-K Now's Libby Doggett disagreed with this assessment, writing: "History has proven that targeted pre-kindergarten programs are more vulnerable to chronic underfunding and political attacks," pointing to the challenges faced over time by Head Start, and to the success of universal pre-kindergarten in states like Georgia and Oklahoma.[54] In the run-up to the 2008 presidential election, the most detailed preschool plan advanced by any of the major candidates was New York Democratic senator Hillary Clinton's proposal to serve families with incomes under 200 percent of the federal poverty line. In formulating her proposal, Clinton favored the targeted approach suggested by Education Sector rather than embracing a universal approach.

THE PROMISE OF UNIVERSALITY

How can we explain the disjuncture between a historical and political analysis that calls for universal programs and the mixed experiences of states that have tried to implement the idea? The idea that universal programs generate more political support—an argument that many advocates, foundations, and policymakers have embraced wholeheartedly—is not a simple or straightforward proposition. It requires a long-term historical perspective, and recognizing the complexity of how social programs fare over time.

While history offers strong evidence of the value of a universal approach, it also reminds us that building broad political support for public spending has often taken decades, and has been influenced by different factors. Looking at the history of Social Security and public K–12 schools, we see that these programs' universality was not an instant guarantee that they would become popular, permanent, and well funded. Rather, public attachment to these social programs was a gradual process, shaped over time as much by the ideas that made them appealing and legitimate public endeavors as by the fact that they were universal. The way the programs were structured and financed also played a key role in how they fared over time. For instance, programs like Civil War veterans' pensions or Social Security were strong, Skocpol noted, not only because they were universal but also because they were set up as ongoing "entitlements" rather than subject to yearly appropriations.[55]

What we now refer to as Social Security—the Old Age Insurance program that was part of the original Social Security Act of 1935—was not particularly popular when it was first passed, despite being universal. The new taxes on workers and employers it created took a toll on the nation's struggling economy; some even called the economic downturn of 1937 the "Social Security recession." Worse, because the first payments were not to be made for seven years, the federal government was collecting payroll taxes and accumulating an unheard-of amount of money in federal treasuries while no one was receiving any benefits. The pensions workers could eventually expect to receive were small and excluded many categories of workers. For all these reasons, many members of Congress and the public were much more interested in increasing state welfare grants for the elderly than in this new social insurance fund. Amendments passed in 1939 helped boost Social Security's attraction by adding benefits for wives and widows and extra insurance to those with young children who survived them, reinforcing the program's appeal to male heads of household concerned about protecting their dependents.

The Social Security Board also launched a public relations campaign to sell Old Age Insurance "as an honored citizenship entitlement." Rather than an additional burden, the message went, the payroll tax was a prudent form of savings that workers could collect in their old age—as opposed to the indignities of receiving "welfare." Skocpol writes: "Through a clever and widely disseminated public metaphor, Americans were told that their 'contributions' insured that each wage earner would be entitled in old age to collect benefits that he or she had 'individually earned.' Actually, benefits are paid out of a common fund."[56] The fact the worker contributed from his paycheck made the benefit a "right," not a matter of welfare or need, and thus sustained the worker's dignity. This dignity was thought to be important especially for white men; female and African-American workers were largely excluded from the original legislation. In a nation that prized economic independence and feared reliance on government, linking jobs to social benefits preserved an ideology of individual responsibility and work while also providing some mechanisms for economic security. One architect of the Old Age Insurance program testified before Congress in 1939 that while welfare involved "mounting dependency," Social Security was a uniquely American program emphasizing "thrift and self-reliance" and thereby retaining individual dignity. Despite the improvements of the 1939 amendments, however, historian Edward Berkowitz argues that Social Security was still "small, inconsequential, and vulnerable to attack" in the 1940s. It was only following the 1950 amendments, which increased the size of the benefit and included more categories of workers, that the program became the nation's largest and most important social welfare program.[57]

Similarly, in nineteenth-century America, the creation of common schools open to all children was a process that took several decades and engendered some significant opposition. Indeed, the history of creating common schools has many parallels with today's efforts to provide preschool for all. Schooling in the early nineteenth century was, in the words of historian Carl Kaestle, "plentiful but disorganized," with parents purchasing education from schoolmasters who offered everything "from the alphabet to astronomy, for children of all ages, at all times of day. Schooling arrangements were haphazard and temporary; people in all ranks of society gained their education in a patchwork, rather than a pattern, of teachers and experiences."[58] This patchwork included charity schools, pay schools, district schools, dame schools, church schools, elite boarding schools, and private tutoring. School reformers saw this existing approach to schooling as a source of disorder and inequality and sought instead to create a single system, supported and controlled by the public, to educate all children. This was not always a popular idea.

While most people supported the creation of charity schools for the poor in the young nation's cities, the idea of providing free public education for children whose parents could afford to pay part of the cost was controversial. Provision for education had traditionally been a private duty, not a public one, and some communities were reluctant to use local property taxes to end parent tuition payments. Historian William Reese explains that in the 1840s, "the great educational question of the day was whether citizens would rally around the fledgling public system to enable all children and not just the poor to receive a free education." For reformers like Horace Mann, the challenge was making the schools "good enough for the richest, open to the poorest."[59] In Baltimore, opponents argued that public schools were not necessary, as the rich could afford to pay for their children's education, while church-based charity schools were available to serve the poor. Supporters argued that charity schools carried a social stigma and did not fulfill the goal of common education: "We do not want charity schools—we do not want free schools—we want schools for freemen; such schools as the honest and independent mechanic and merchants of this city will send their children to." An 1825 bill establishing public education failed to pass the state legislature, and when a different bill was ultimately successful, the public schools that were created suffered from neglect and lack of funding for a period of years.[60] In New York state, the question of free public schooling was in doubt for twenty years; when the legislature passed a provision requiring free schooling for all in 1849, opponents argued that this authorized people "to put their hands into their neighbors' pockets," while others called the tax "unconstitutional, arbitrary, and unjust"; the law was repealed the following year.[61] In most southern states, resistance to common schooling was stronger, and public money only supported education for poor whites; other white families fended for themselves with fee payments, and slaves were denied education altogether.

Reformers, sharing a strong commitment to advancing the nation by bringing together all (white) children into a uniform system of education and imparting a common set of moral values and opportunities, were ultimately able to win over those who opposed providing a universal system of public education. By the 1870s, the last of the northern states abolished the practice of charging parents fees for their children's schooling. Proponents of "common schools" drew on widely held social beliefs about the power of education to shape individual morality and the virtue of the republic, and to unify the nation's diverse population. Education was seen as a solution to the specter of crime and social disorder in the nation's expanding cities. A school proponent in Baltimore wrote: "one consideration alone is sufficient to justify it…and that is that ignorance is a great cause of crime, and therefore, it is the part of wisdom as well as humanity to provide means of education adequate to its removal."[62] The power of these ideas, which appealed simultaneously to religious, democratic, and assimilationist values, helped build support for the idea of universal education.

In the case of common schools, of course, universality was not only a feature that helped gain broad public support but also an essential goal in itself. Reformers saw the coming together of children from different social classes in the same schools as instrumental to their mission of social cohesion and good citizenship. As one reformer wrote in 1839, teaching students "in the same house, the same class, and out of the same book, and by the same teacher" reflected the best in republican values, countering social divisions that might threaten the nation.[63] "It has been justly noted," education proponents in Baltimore wrote in 1825,

> that one of the most beautiful and republican features of this system is its bringing our youth of the higher as well as the lower classes to know and respect one another's rights at a tender age…and to teach them…that rich and poor must submit alike to the wholesome disciplines of the laws.[64]

Moreover, proponents thought that public commitment to (and investment in) a system of public schools would be greater if families of all social classes relied on it for their own children. If wealthier families used private schools, reformers argued, the public system would suffer. Massachusetts school reformer James Carter claimed in 1826: "every private establishment...detaches a portion of the community from the great mass, and weakens or destroys their interest in those means of education which are common to the whole people."[65] When high schools were created, though they served only a small fraction of the population, it was hoped they would draw the "respectable classes" into the emerging public education system. The support of the middle class, Reese writes, was "essential to uplifting and maintaining the status of the public system."[66]

More recent generations of education reformers have also prized the public schools' ability to bring together students from different backgrounds, promoting equal opportunity for students as well as socioeconomic and racial integration. In addition to the social and civic values engendered by educating children of all backgrounds together, researchers in recent decades have also contended that disadvantaged children learn better when they are in mixed classrooms. The well-known Coleman Report of 1966 found that economically disadvantaged students had higher achievement when they were in classrooms with middle-class children; another body of research found that children with disabilities learned more in "mainstream" classrooms than in segregated ones. Such "peer effects" may be even greater in preschool classrooms, where there is more interaction between children than in older grades. Educational reformers, whether in the nineteenth century or today, thus have two different kinds of reasons to pursue a universal approach: to build broad public support and to promote positive interaction among children in the classroom, which may both benefit them academically and serve broader social goals.

The histories of public education and Social Security demonstrate that while universal programs do have a greater chance of building broad political support over time, simply making a program universal is no guarantee of its fate. Social Security and public education took decades to develop their reputations and constituencies as broad-based social entitlements. Moreover, these reputations were strongly shaped by the ideological framework within which these policies were understood. Social Security, historian Alice Kessler-Harris writes, was part of a response to the Great Depression that reaffirmed America's sense of itself as a "predominantly individualistic nation" of economically self-sufficient male providers.[67] The genius of Social Security lay in its ability to provide economic security to many American workers within an existing ideological framework that prized economic self-sufficiency and limited government. It was ultimately the program's appeal to commonly held values of individualism,

private ownership, and thrift—as well as the way benefits were structured—
that made it popular and successful. Similarly, advocates of common schools in
the nineteenth century built on widespread beliefs about the importance of
individual virtue and self-discipline to the future of the republic, as well as on
democratic values about providing the same education to children of different
social class backgrounds. The appeal of these ideas allowed reformers to system-
atize public schooling across the northern and midwestern states, defining free
schooling not as a charity provided to the needy but as a right of citizenship
enshrined in state constitutions.

What can preschool advocates take from this history about the promise of
universality? Universal programs do, over time, have the potential to create
broad political support, establishing a system in which many different citizens
have a stake, and which can make a bigger difference than a small program that
only seeks to serve those most "in need." However, there is no immediate or
simple relationship between a program's universality and its political stability
or longevity. Many other factors—especially the fit between the way the program is understood and popular ideas about social values—come into play.
History thus confirms the importance of considering how programs are connected to broader social values and of framing programs for young children in
terms of education and equal opportunity. Furthermore, it matters greatly how
government programs are structured and administered, so linking preschool to
public education (with its own budget lines and administrative infrastructure)
is an important way for preschool advocates to seek greater stability as well as
legitimacy for these programs.

CONCLUSION

Preschool advocates and policymakers have embraced the idea that universal
programs can create stronger political support, leading to better funding and
higher program quality down the road. However, in the short run at least, they
are finding that a universal approach is no guarantee of either political support
or higher quality. While "preschool for all" carries the promise of broader political support and cross-class alliances in the long run, it also carries a much higher
price tag and often generates opposition from those who do not want to subsidize more affluent families. Targeting programs to disadvantaged or at-risk children fits more neatly with the research evidence and is an easier "sell" to
policymakers, both fiscally and ideologically. Advocates must be aware that

generating public support for any universal social program is a long-term process. In the meantime, they have to consider the political and educational context of their own states to decide whether to push for "preschool for all" or preschool for the needy. The trend in the states in the past few years points to an incremental strategy of building programs for disadvantaged children and gradually opening them up to others. It may be that building support for "preschool for some" provides a foundation for ultimately arriving at "preschool for all."

CHAPTER 7

Mixed Blessings

Delivering Preschool Inside and Outside the "Education Tent"

Today's preschool movement is marked not only by a shift to a universal approach but also by a close relationship between preschool and K–12 public education. Since the late 1980s, reformers like Yale psychologist Ed Zigler, frustrated with the limitations of existing provision for young children, had been urging preschool advocates to "climb into the education tent," linking preschool to the goals and structures of public education. As they pioneered universal preschool in the 1990s, as we have seen, Oklahoma, New York, and New Jersey cast preschool as a part of K–12 education reform and put school districts in charge of programs. Building on these experiences, the recent preschool movement as a whole has sought to ally its cause with that of public education.

Reformers in the 1990s hoped to use the logic of public education to transform the terms on which early childhood programs operated and were understood. They believed that this redefinition would bring both concrete benefits—more stable funding, better trained teachers—and symbolic ones: legitimizing early childhood programs as part of the institution of public education, made available to all children and funded by taxpayers for the common good. Bringing preschool into the education tent promised to reframe the issue of public support for young children's development and place it on more solid ground. By attaching itself to the more established sector of public schools, early education could share in the schools' organizational legitimacy as well as some of its structures and practices. As Zigler argued, the school "is the only universal entitlement children in America have, no other, none. And we never have to worry, will the schools open in the fall? They're always going to open."[1] While child care was seen as a private concern governed largely by how much parents could afford to pay, and Head Start was seen as an instance of federal largesse on behalf of poor children, K–12 education was a public institution with established structures of funding, governance, and staffing. By the late twentieth century, it was widely held that children had a *right* to education, whereas they had only a *need* for child care. Since early childhood programs served both ends, reformers just needed to shift their emphasis to education. Given the dismal state of child care across the country, climbing into the education tent rather than continuing to try to build a separate system for young children on the fragile foundation of private providers, struggling nonprofit agencies, and parent fees seemed to be a wise strategy.

Yet moving preschool into the education tent was not a simple matter, for that tent was crowded and under stress. Moreover, public preschool emerged in a landscape already populated by private and community-based providers, who were not eager to have public schools take over their domain. In shaping new preschool programs, then, policymakers have had to reckon with the legacy of previous policy decisions. Rooted in private firms and nonprofit community agencies, both child care and Head Start had generated a great diversity of program approaches and creative efforts to meet the needs of children and families. But both also suffered from unstable and inadequate funding, insufficiently training and poorly compensation for teachers, and a weak infrastructure. This mixed historical legacy continues to shape decisions about preschool education today.

Rather than extending or replicating the K–12 system for preschoolers, several states have opted to build on the patchwork of existing programs, allowing private and community-based providers as well as schools to deliver pre-kindergarten. Universal programs in Georgia, New York, New Jersey, Florida, and Los Angeles County rely on multiple providers to serve large numbers of children. Policymakers in these states have looked for ways to combine, through a mixed public-private system, the best of both worlds: the universal access, stable funding, and educational standards of public schools and the flexibility, diversity, and responsiveness to families of existing early childhood programs. However, weaving together these different strands of the early childhood world is a complicated task, requiring that those who shape and implement policy pay careful attention to the details that can strengthen the patchwork on which they rely.

HITCHING THE PRE-K WAGON TO THE SCHOOLS?

Basing public pre-kindergarten in the schools has some distinct advantages. School-based systems of preschool can guarantee a certain level of quality by standardizing teacher qualifications, compensation, curriculum, and funding. When they operate preschool programs, school districts tend to hire teachers with bachelor's degrees and certification and to compensate them better than do most private preschools or child care centers. School-based programs can more easily make preschoolers part of the elementary school, ensuring that learning goals and curriculum are aligned with those of the early elementary grades. Programs also benefit from the larger infrastructure of the public schools, from facilities to professional development. Schools are also more likely to be able to serve children with special needs and less likely to turn away children who have behavior problems or other difficulties. Because of these advantages, studies of child care quality have often found that public schools provide higher quality programs on average than do private providers. Teachers' unions (an influential voice in state legislatures) and other education groups tend to support school-based systems, and administrators hoping to boost test scores with early education often want to have programs under their jurisdiction. For all of these reasons, public pre-kindergarten as a whole tends to be school based, with about 70 percent of children nationwide being served in school settings.

In some contexts, school funding mechanisms make it relatively easy to expand preschool within the K–12 system. We have seen how Oklahoma's high-quality program grew once it was included in the school aid formula, and how advocates in New York pushed for inclusion in the state aid formula, defining pre-kindergarten as part of a "sound basic education." West Virginia's preschool program grew in part as a means of stopping the decline in school funding as K–12 enrollment decreased. Proponents noted that including preschoolers in the school funding formula would funnel money back into the school system, preventing school closings and teacher layoffs. Because overall enrollment continued to drop, lawmakers did not see education costs soaring as a result of adding preschool to the school system. Indeed, the provision for universal pre-kindergarten (which came as a surprise to many early childhood leaders and advocates in the state) was included in a bill passed on the last day of the 2002 legislative session, entitled "Increasing Salaries for Teachers and Service Personnel."[2] Borrowing from the organizational structure and logic of public education, a few states have actually made preschool an entitlement: Kentucky districts must offer preschool to each eligible child, Texas school districts are required to offer a pre-kindergarten program if they have fifteen eligible children, and New Jersey *Abbott* districts are required by court mandate to offer preschool to all children in the district.

For Ruby Takanishi, director of the Foundation for Child Development, the most logical course for expanding access to preschool was simply to make it the beginning grade for public elementary schools. In advocating for universal preschool, she commented:

> I think we have really...hitched our wagon to the public education system, with all of its inequities and flaws, and also improvement, clearly it's going through a lot of change...but you know, it's sort of like living in an imperfect world, if you don't hitch your wagon to that, what are you going to hitch it to?

She saw her efforts as part of

> a whole idea of trying to redefine and reframe when publicly supported education in the United States should begin....Given what we know about [young children's] development, given the huge achievement gaps that occur at the kindergarten door, why, given current knowledge and changing work patterns of families and so on, why shouldn't education, publicly supported education, begin at least at three?

Similarly, Zigler observed, "Ideally, if you were going to have preschool education in this country, you'd probably just lower, you'd have schools take it on to age 3," as in his Schools of the Twenty-First Century. In a 1998 commentary, he called for public education to begin at age three, as in France and Italy, with additional child care hours offered to working parents for a fee. Such a plan, he wrote, "would guarantee equal access to both quality preschool and child care to children of all income levels."[3] More recently, the New Commission on the Skills of the American Workforce came to a similar conclusion, recommending that in restructuring American schools to compete in the global economy, the last two years of high school should be eliminated and some of the money used to provide early childhood education to three- and four-year-olds.[4]

To ensure that early education is well integrated with the years of schooling that follow, Takanishi's foundation advocates restructuring elementary schools to focus on the education of children aged three to eight. These "Pre-K to 3" schools would offer universal access to both preschool and full-day kindergarten and would focus on curricular alignment to make sure that children are building up to reading and other crucial skills by the end of third grade. Fourth and fifth grades would be treated as a separate unit of elementary education, possibly housed in a different building. In 2005, the National Association of Elementary Principals embraced the idea of making pre-kindergarten the beginning of a restructured school system, urging principals to support a continuum of learning from age three through the primary grades and putting forward profiles of schools that fulfilled this ideal.[5] As a demonstration, the University of North Carolina's child development institute began to create a model of what it calls "First School" in several communities. Director Richard Clifford wrote: "Eventually, public school will begin for most children at age three or four.... We want to do all we can to ensure that new programs are the best they can be."[6]

Even as some reformers sought to hitch the pre-kindergarten wagon to the public schools, they recognized that the road ahead looked bumpy. While preschool advocates were trying to make early education more public, different sets of reformers were simultaneously trying to remake K–12 public education. One group sought to push public schools toward privatization, through decentralizing reforms such as vouchers, parental choice measures, and charter schools. These reformers, convinced that the large-scale bureaucracies of public schools were not the best mechanism for creating quality education for all, wanted schools to have the choice, flexibility, and innovation that they associated with private markets. A second movement sought to improve K–12 schools through increased school accountability measures linked to common standards and assessment. This movement, strengthened by the 2001 federal No Child Left Behind legislation, intensified the sense that public schools were themselves in need of reform and restructuring. In this policy environment, with its skepticism about public schools and faith in market-based solutions, the idea of expanding preschool by simply extending public schools downward is a difficult sell. For instance, one business leader told the Pew Trusts' Sarah Watson: "As business leaders who have been really discouraged about K–12, when you say what we want to do is create K–12 but for 4-year-olds, that makes us not really want to participate."[7] Writing in opposition to the idea of universal preschool, the president of the free-market-oriented Commonwealth Foundation in Pennsylvania asked:

> Would you hire a carpenter to remodel the first floor of your home if he was already working on the second and third floors and doing a poor job? Would you expect the results on the second and third floors to improve just because the carpenter was also remodeling the first floor?[8]

Community-based private and nonprofit child care providers, for their part, continued to be reluctant about handing over preschool to the schools. Education journalist Gene Maeroff writes that one of the main obstacles to creating universal pre-kindergarten through the public schools is "the existence of thousands of centers, churches, storefronts in strip malls, and other sites— mostly nonprofit but for-profit as well—that now serve preschoolers, mostly with child care.... This powerful lobby will seek to protect private providers."[9] Similarly, Zigler noted that while the ideal solution might be to simply extend the public schools downward, the opposition of private providers has been a powerful force: "you have all these private providers out there, there's all these small businesses, and some are big businesses.... They have a lot of wallop with the state legislature.... They're going to fight tooth and nail against giving this to the schools."[10] Decisions made in the 1970s to rely on the private market for child care needs had created a "path dependency"—reinforced by an active constituency of private providers—that was difficult to overcome.

Beyond protecting their turf, community providers and early educators also raised larger questions about what would be lost if preschool moved into the public schools. Providers (including nonprofit programs, Head Start, YMCAs, churches, large for-profit franchises, and small proprietary nursery schools and day-care centers) argued that they were more responsive to families and their diverse offerings were more welcoming to children with different ethnic, religious, and linguistic backgrounds. They claimed to be more likely to take a developmentally appropriate, whole-child approach, rather than "pushing down" an overly academic curriculum aimed at older children. Moreover, parents may place greater trust in local, community agencies that cultivate parent involvement than they do in public school districts that hold parents at arm's length. Researcher Bruce Fuller argued that the diverse range of preschool provision is an important part of the richness of American civil society, with roots in neighborhoods, ethnic organizations, and community action. He contended that young children should learn in these settings that families have helped shape rather than in "already overburdened" public schools.[11]

Even advocates of expanding preschool worried that a system of early education based only in the public schools could mean sacrificing the child-centered classrooms, diverse approaches, and openness to parents that community-based programs had developed over the years. At a national forum in 2002, Karen Hill-Scott, a child development and public policy expert who led the planning for Los Angeles' universal pre-kindergarten initiative, commented on the tension in the field between the school-based and community-based approaches.

> For those who are in early education, there's this dialectic that goes on where early education people want to have conferred on their profession the legitimacy of the mantle of public education. But at the same time, they are very conflicted about losing their developmental touch. Losing their child-centered approach, having to become more bureaucratic, more tied to many of the things people associate with the negativity of public schooling and public institutions in general.[12]

In reality, parents' experiences with preschool offered outside the schools—whether by for-profit chains, religious congregations, nonprofit community agencies, or individual providers—could be as varied as their experiences with different public schools. But the claims made by private-sector providers carried significant weight as policymakers looked for ways to expand preschool.

SEEKING THE BEST OF BOTH WORLDS IN "MIXED SYSTEMS"

At the same conference where Hill-Scott raised these concerns, Massachusetts advocate Margaret Blood explained another alternative: incorporating community-based providers into a publicly funded network of preschools. "We don't want to replicate K–12 for pre-K," she declared. "We want to embrace the diversity and the strengths of what we already have investments in. It's pragmatic; it's more cost effective; it's what research shows us parents want—that choice. And it appeals."[13] Combining public and private programs helped solve both political and logistical problems in expanding pre-kindergarten—defusing opposition from private and community-based providers and proponents of parental choice while expanding the number of children that could be served by going beyond the walls of the public schools. Creating mixed systems for pre-kindergarten also offers opportunities to raise the quality of existing early childhood programs overall, by requiring high quality standards and providing public funding for improvements. But mixing school and community-based early childhood programs together in a way that overcomes their deficits and brings forth the best of each is a tremendous policy challenge, requiring careful attention to the details of policy choices and implementation.

On a practical level, making use of nonschool providers allows states to implement pre-kindergarten without investing large amounts of money in building new facilities. It also allows states to take advantage of staff, enrollment, and organizational structures that are already in place. Relying on the existing infrastructure is especially important when programs need to be launched quickly and when there is little available space in the schools. When Governor Zell Miller decided to make Georgia's pre-kindergarten program universal, for example, the K–12 school population was already "bursting out of the buildings," but he wanted to get the program launched very quickly. So administrators decided to use private child care centers in order to accommodate large numbers of children rather than using state money for constructing new facilities. By 1999, Georgia's pre-kindergarten program had become "one of the nation's most extensive public-private education ventures," serving 57 percent of its students in non-public-school settings.[14] New York City experienced an even greater challenge, expecting immediate implementation within a school system that was already short 80,000 seats. In 1999, the city's Independent Budget Office estimated that in order to house even one-quarter of the city's eligible pre-kindergarten students in public school facilities, along with implementing reduced class sizes, the city would need 1,800 new classrooms.[15] Challenged by that daunting task, city school officials had a strong motivation to turn to private and community-based providers; by 2006, the city was working with 600 different ones.[16] Similarly, in New Jersey, the court's mandate that a preschool program be launched immediately to serve all preschool children in the *Abbott* districts was the key reason for including community providers. The state has relied on community-based providers to meet its ambitious goal of providing preschool slots to all children in these needy school districts. Seventy percent of children attending *Abbott* preschools are housed in community-based programs rather than schools.

Working with private providers (both for-profit and nonprofit) enables public programs to serve more children, especially those who need a full day of care. Most public pre-kindergarten programs are only part-day, lasting as little as two and a half hours; working parents who want their children to have the benefit of pre-kindergarten must typically cobble together a day of care, arranging for children to be shuttled from one setting to another. Including child care centers in a state pre-kindergarten system allows many more children to participate—including those in low-income working families who stand to benefit the most from pre-kindergarten.[17] Embedding pre-kindergarten in a child care center allows public and private funds to be combined, so that parents pay for the "child care" part of the day, but the "pre-K" part of the day is offered without charge. From a policymakers' perspective, these arrangements are desirable because they preserve the private investments parents and others are already making in early childhood programs but add public funding to broaden access to more families and improve program quality. Combining different streams of public and private funding represents an appealing way to stretch public dollars.

Indeed, even states whose pre-kindergarten programs have been oriented largely toward the public schools are turning to community-based programs in order to serve more children. As Oklahoma schools filled up the classroom space they had available, they sought out partnerships with child care centers, Head Start programs, churches, and other organizations. Head Start programs also initiated collaborations with school districts as they realized they were competing for some of the same children that schools were interested in serving. Education official Ramona Paul encouraged district officials to think creatively in order to accommodate more children and find ways to meet parents' needs for child care. For instance, the town of Norman added forty-five slots for four-year-olds by cooperating with three local day-care centers. Putnam City (which had already used up available school space for pre-kindergarten) made arrangements with the local United Methodist Church's preschool and day-care program to provide a certified teacher for the class, taking the program where the children already were. In the town of Jenks, a private assisted living facility was designed with an early childhood program in the building's center, allowing elderly residents to take part in some of the children's activities.[18] Similarly, school-based programs in Wisconsin, Tennessee, and Texas are encouraging districts to partner with community-based preschool and child care centers in order to expand slots and give parents the option of having wraparound child care.[19]

In addition to solving logistical challenges, public-private partnerships can help gain political support from private and community-based providers. Florida's pre-kindergarten program offered parents vouchers to use at their choice of private child care centers, in part because the state's Association of Child Care Management lobbied vigorously to ensure that its members would figure prominently in the program.[20] This arrangement also brought support from those who favored parental choice in public education more generally. In Georgia, gaining the support of private providers was essential for the political success of pre-kindergarten initiatives. The private child care industry, a powerful lobby in the state, "would have tried to kill the program if they had not been allowed to participate," according to Georgia Child Care Council president Susan Maxwell. Administrators also faced opposition from Head Start providers, who were still smarting from losing five-year-olds to the public school system when the state started funding kindergarten in the 1980s, and now feared they would lose their four-year-olds as well.[21] Similar concerns also spurred officials in West Virginia to include a requirement that 50 percent of each school district's pre-kindergarten program be in collaborative settings. Kathy Jones of the state education department explained:

> I really went out on a limb in putting the 50 percent level in the policy; I did it in order to get buy in from Head Start and child care. When we put kindergarten in place, it did a lot of damage to child care and Head Start, and hard feelings still existed.[22]

New York was the first state to mandate that schools collaborate with community agencies, requiring that districts contract at least 10 percent of their funds to local community-based providers that met state standards.[23] This requirement not only earned support from early childhood providers but also mobilized them to help make the contracting system work. Their involvement was crucial to the successful implementation of the UPK program in the state, and the program quickly surpassed the legislation's mandate for collaboration between schools and community-based providers. By 2005, 60 percent of the children statewide attended programs in community settings, with higher percentages in New York City.[24]

In Los Angeles County, the nation's most populous metropolitan area, a diverse array of providers, neighborhood activists, and parents helped to press for a broad approach to determining who would deliver pre-kindergarten. Indeed, policy analyst Bruce Fuller writes, no one in the pluralistic political culture of Los Angeles seriously advocated a school-run system. Lead planner Karen Hill-Scott (a former UCLA professor and founder of a community agency in South Central Los Angeles) explained: "I thought you couldn't have a school district just sweep in and take over....It doesn't make it responsive, culturally sensitive." The county ended up taking the most inclusive approach of any pre-kindergarten program in the nation, incorporating family child care homes as well as community-based centers and schools. One of the local child care activists who pushed for this approach noted: "In terms of facilities...there's no way under God's green earth that you can get every kid in L.A. into a school-based center. These ladies [running family child care homes] really need help and resources." Hill-Scott knew that this broad-based neighborhood approach might have its risks, saying: "people around the country thought I was crazy...but it's all a big experiment."[25]

ENSURING QUALITY AND "LIFTING ALL BOATS"

Beyond the immediate benefits of serving more children, addressing families' child care needs, and securing the political support of community-based providers, advocates of "mixed systems" for pre-kindergarten have broader aspirations as well. They believe that publicly funded programs for preschoolers could "lift all boats" within the early childhood sea by infusing it with new funding, high program standards, and support for achieving high expectations. Janet Hansen of the Committee for Economic Development explained in a 2003 interview that as she worked on pre-kindergarten,

> I really personally became convinced that this was a wedge that could have important impact on improving child care, that had been harder to accomplish with a head-on attack. Especially if you had a system where you were using a multiplicity of providers, including the traditional child care providers, that this was a way

that would give them access to resources, training, and other things that would help improve the quality of child care, which has been a really hard issue.[26]

Speaking of New York's requirement that schools work with community-based providers in their UPK programs, Karen Schimke explained,

> Most of us were child care advocates. And for us, it seemed to us that kind of recasting child care in an educational way caused the potential to raise all boats. We hope to see the quality improve in child care generally because of this, and I think it has.[27]

In states like New York, New Jersey, and Georgia, where pre-kindergarten systems were built with attention to policies that would strengthen the existing infrastructure of providers, this promise has been at least partially fulfilled. In these states, community-based programs can use the pre-kindergarten funds they receive to improve the quality of their educational services—by extending the length of their program day, hiring a more highly qualified teacher, providing training for staff, buying additional equipment or materials, or "whatever it takes to get that quality."[28] In New York, child care center directors reported making changes that included staff development and training, hiring of teachers, and improvement of facilities, in order to take part in UPK. They were able to increase teachers' salaries, enhance educational programming, and reduce parent fees.[29] One commented: "It's been a shot in the arm, because it's so well-resourced. They have equipment, they have money, there's supplies, and the training that's available to their staff because they're UPK sites...resources like psychologists being available." Another commented: "We've gone from programs where literally there wasn't a toy in the classroom, and there were like long wood planks for these three-year-old boys, to rooms now that have learning centers."[30] Such quality enhancements could also help private programs attract more families. Some providers noted that being linked to the public school enhanced their image among parents and potential staff members: one compared it to "the value of a trademark or brand name."[31] When pre-kindergarten programs require participating child care centers to hire more highly trained teachers, this can also have a positive effect on the other staff. Officials in Oklahoma have found that when a school district places a certified early childhood teacher in a child care center, that teacher can serve as a model for the rest of the child care staff. Directors in New York agreed, saying: "having certified teachers in a day care center definitely raises the bar."[32]

While mixed systems for pre-kindergarten have the potential to create positive change by "lifting all boats," this can only happen if states *both* establish high standards (especially for teacher training and curriculum) *and* find ways to help programs to achieve them. Without high standards, pre-kindergarten will simply replicate the weaknesses of the existing system, with insufficient teacher training, inadequate compensation for staff, weak or inappropriate curricula, and lack of learning materials and technical assistance. For example, Florida's low program standards means that the state runs the risk of putting more children into the same kind of leaky boats rather than raising all boats to a higher level. Another example is Texas, which has no limit on class size or staff-to-child ratio, leading to overcrowded classrooms in which the aims of pre-kindergarten cannot really be met (some principals report classes with as many as forty four-year-olds).[33] One key national advocate said: "You can't just change child care's name, you need to change the system, how you do it, which is what pre-K is about."[34] But high standards are not enough, without support and incentives that enable providers and teachers to reach them.

Given the fragility of the systems on which they build, policymakers need to find ways of strengthening the infrastructure of early childhood programs even as they use it to provide pre-kindergarten to a wider range of children. For instance, rather than just raising requirements for teachers, New Jersey poured resources into helping ensure that teachers in child care centers would become certified, providing scholarships, salary enhancement, and grants to institutions of higher education to help develop new training programs. In Georgia, state officials worked to raise standards overall by providing training to all child care center staff, not just to the pre-kindergarten teachers. The state allowed all child care centers to participate in an initiative that provides training and technical assistance, grants to improve classroom quality, and recognition (including a higher subsidy reimbursement rate) when centers receive a specific score on classroom quality evaluation scales.[35] Such examples of deliberate efforts to strengthen the infrastructure of private-sector providers are rare, unfortunately, but they are essential if state pre-kindergarten programs are to achieve the aim of lifting all boats in the early childhood sea.

While the idea of bringing together public schools and private, community-based providers may be appealing, it is not an easy task. Indeed, researcher Anthony Raden concluded from his study in Georgia that integrating private providers into a public program is "one of the toughest challenges of universal Pre-K." In implementing pre-kindergarten, the state department of education's early childhood staff wrangled with providers over guidelines for developmentally appropriate practices, enrollment policies, monitoring, and auditing financial records. One staff member recalled tense, complex interactions with associations representing the for-profit child care industry. "The private for-profit providers really...just wanted the money to be sent to them and [had a] 'leave me alone and let me do my job' kind of attitude. They didn't want oversight, no curriculum.... They wanted to be able to make a profit." Private providers, for their part, were offended by the department staff's mistrust and the assumption that "people are in the business for the money and only for the money." Providers felt that the department's efforts to monitor programs and enforce standards were rigidly bureaucratic, and some became wary and defensive, seeing monitoring as punitive rather than supportive. In some communities, the local coordinating councils that were meant to bring together all the different programs involved in the initiative became embroiled in conflict. The initial mistrust between state pre-kindergarten administrators and private providers was never completely resolved, although some conflict was defused when the new leadership of the program adopted a less regulatory, more consultative relationship with the private providers.[36]

Collaboration was particularly challenging in New Jersey. The state mandated collaboration with child care providers when it rejected many school districts' plans for preschool, so superintendents did not have a choice about working with community agencies. Some clearly would have preferred to keep the programs in their own schools, where they could monitor and influence them more easily. In this context, advocate Cynthia Rice observed, collaboration was "more like a shotgun wedding than a marriage made from love." While community-based providers often felt they were already providing a high-quality educational program, school officials did not agree. Rice believed that while providers did need to improve their programs' educational quality, school officials also needed to learn that a high-quality preschool classroom looks quite different from a second- or third-grade classroom.[37] Few districts had extensive experience with preschool; only 6 percent of children in these districts were already being served by district-run preschools before the *Abbott* mandate, and district leaders were often skeptical about working with the private providers and community agencies that ran programs in their area.[38] To promote smoother collaboration, Rice's organization, the Association for Children of New Jersey, helped develop a working group of child advocates, researchers, child care providers, Head Start staff, school district officials, college and university faculty, unions, business people, and foundations. This coalition was able to agree on quality standards and to influence the court's subsequent rulings on the implementation of the *Abbott* preschools. Agreeing on standards for teachers was particularly difficult. While the majority of members supported requiring a bachelor's degree, some of the child care representatives thought this was "extreme and unrealistic." It took a formal vote for the group to settle on the bachelor's degree, with the child care community putting aside "a significant self-interest to support the coalition." Rice noted later: "Even though everyone agreed that teachers needed to be back in school, there was no 'Kumbaya' being sung; it was very difficult for many teachers and providers."[39]

In New York, bringing together schools, private providers, and Head Start programs meant creating partnerships "among multiple provider systems that have little knowledge of how each other operate." In some cases, public school officials and early childhood educators had never met before or thought about how they might work together. There was distrust on both sides—school district staff tended to doubt that private providers were offering high-quality programs, whereas private providers feared that the schools would take away "their" four-year-olds, driving them out of business.[40] Head Start directors shared these fears and worried that collaboration would mean that Head Start's focus on services such as health, nutrition, and family support would get pushed aside in favor of more academic school-readiness skills. One child care director in New York wrote about a sense of

> frustration over the fact that the government had now come up with this wonderful new program for four-year-olds and it's going to be the best program there is and they're going to dump all of this money into it...and what about us little tiny child care centers that are striving to make it every day, who are providing quality services to four-year-olds? Why not dump all that money in what's already there?[41]

To try to build effective partnerships, several states created community advisory boards to plan and implement pre-kindergarten programs. In New York, advisory boards in many communities helped to guide program implementation, providing a consistent structure to enable parents and professionals from child care centers and the public schools to plan together, and giving local communities "ownership" of the program. Working on such advisory boards and in direct partnerships with private providers has increased school administrators' awareness of the importance of early childhood programs in their communities. A school official in Syracuse noted: "Those programs just weren't in my line of vision. Now I see that all children come to me eventually, so I must pay attention to what happens in all settings."[42] Consultant Anne Mitchell noted that as a result of the collaboration for UPK, some school principals in New York "see pre-K places as their feeder schools now" and are happy to have some role to play in talking with pre-kindergarten directors about curriculum, teacher training, and professional development, whereas before they had no incentive to have that relationship.[43] Connecticut's School Readiness Councils were required to develop a five-year plan for ensuring that programs provided all the quality components envisioned in the legislation, and these councils could make key decisions about how the program would operate in their community.[44]

Other states have focused more on collaboration at the state level for coordinating pre-kindergarten programs with other early childhood initiatives. Ramona Paul emphasizes that in Oklahoma, the education department, child care staff, and Head Start worked together from the beginning of the pre-kindergarten program to write standards, trying to always pick the highest standard when choosing among the different rules that applied to these programs. She met with state agency representatives responsible for child care and Head Start every month in order to iron out difficulties that arose in trying to combine the three funding streams, modeling at the state level the kind of collaboration she hoped for at the local level. Formal state structures such as interagency cabinets, councils, and workgroups have been formed to address concerns that arise in coordinating state programs, such as setting core standards that apply to different programs or creating common structures for professional development. Georgia, Massachusetts, and Washington have recently created independent state agencies to focus on early childhood education, in the effort to bring together related programs that are spread across separate systems of education and welfare. Although Head Start is funded and administered at the federal level, each state has a Head Start Collaboration Office to help promote connections between Head Start and state initiatives in education and child care. Unfortunately, RAND researchers concluded in a 2005 study, collaboration is often stymied, especially in periods of budget crisis, when funding sources are jealously guarded and competition among different agencies can be intense. One respondent explained: "People have to still stand up for their individual programs, but we're trying to create a system." Rivalries among different programs—about who offers the highest quality program, who really meets the needs of working parents—as well as substantive differences in these programs "make meaningful coordination difficult."[45]

At the local level, program directors often struggle to blend (or "braid") together multiple funding streams with different standards, regulations, reimbursement rates, and reporting requirements. For instance, providers in New York faced an array of complications in bringing together UPK with other funding streams. The length of the program day and year (and thus the funding available per child) was different for UPK than for publicly funded child care, Head Start, and preschool special education programs. Eligibility was also determined differently among the three programs, as was a preference for enrolling children who lived in variously defined catchment areas. Some school districts allowed UPK children to be grouped with children in other programs, whereas others required a self-contained classroom. Moreover, programs

blending funding from different agencies could expect to be separately moni-
tored and assessed by each of the agencies, in a way that might vary from school
district to school district.[46] In New Jersey, about 450 small businesses and nonprofit groups run preschool programs for the state's *Abbott* preschool program,
reporting to both the Department of Education and the Department of Human
Services. The challenge of the bookkeeping involved in reporting *Abbott* and
non-*Abbott* funds was a contributing factor in fiscal and management problems turned up by investigators in 2005.[47] Assistance on how to combine different sources of funding and manage complex accounting and reporting
requirements could help providers meet some of these challenges. For instance,
a child care center in the Bronx relied on help from the local school district to
sort out accounting practices and access to teacher training when it sought to
combine funding from employer benefits, public child care subsidies, preschool
special education funding, and UPK funding. This enabled the center to offer
pre-kindergarten in a setting with extended hours and enabled children who
had already been at the center for several years to have the continuity of familiar teachers, classmates, and routines and to be close to younger siblings who
also attended.[48]

As this example suggests, schools can play a key role in providing assistance
and monitoring to private and community-based pre-kindergarten programs.
In New York, state officials believed that putting districts in charge of their
pre-kindergarten programs would help build these supportive relationships.
One official said: "The contracts [between the school district and the community provider] are the lever of change," helping ensure that community programs meet high standards for educational quality.[49] In Oklahoma, when
school districts contract with community agencies to provide the four-year-
olds program, they play a fairly active role in supervising the program and
may provide professional development, curriculum support, and other
resources, making it clear that pre-kindergarten is part of the school, even if it
is located elsewhere.

In practice, however, not every school district is willing or able to develop
a strong relationship with community-based pre-kindergarten providers.
Relying on school districts to monitor and support "their" pre-kindergarten
programs may mean leaving many programs without support. In New York,
Anne Mitchell notes, some districts essentially "hand over the money and say,
'You're on your own.'" Others view the pre-kindergarten programs as part of
their system, speak of pre-kindergarten programs as their "feeder schools,"
and offer these programs the same supports—staff development, curriculum
frameworks, child study teams, assessment systems, and technical assistance
services—they offer to their other schools.[50] Such districts are fulfilling the

promise of integrating community providers into the supportive infrastructure of the K–12 system. On the other hand, districts or local councils may simply not have the capacity to monitor and provide support. In Florida's Voluntary Pre-Kindergarten program, monitoring is the responsibility of fifty local Early Learning Coalitions, which administer pre-kindergarten programs in their regions. But advocate Roy Miller of the Florida Children's Campaign said in 2006 that these coalitions have been too "strapped to get out into the field and monitor." State official Gladys Wilson explained: "A lot of parents think we're already making sure they're good centers. We're not." Given the sparse monitoring built into the system, the state was considering adding a voluntary quality rating system to help guide parents in choosing programs.[51] At a national event on pre-kindergarten programs, Pre-K Now's Libby Doggett urged "every advocate to go out and work on a monitoring system, because it is not in place in most places.... Get school principals involved to make sure that the quality is there."[52] A different model for providing monitoring and support locates this responsibility at the state level rather than with the school. States like Georgia and Massachusetts contract directly with community providers, monitoring and supporting the pre-kindergarten program through the state agency.

States tend to rely primarily on local districts and the autonomous professional judgments of teachers and principals to ensure quality in pre-kindergarten classrooms. One state education official contended that having "that early childhood teacher who knows what they're doing" alleviates some of the need for monitoring that is such a concern in Head Start and child care. In response to questions about monitoring,

> I say, 'First of all, who monitors the chemistry teacher? Who monitors the English teacher?' Well, the principal does, and so forth and so on. But you know what, they're professionals, they know what they're supposed to do.... You don't have this huge gap in there that you do when you're running programs with not professionally trained teachers.[53]

This hands-off approach borrowed from K–12 schools, however, may not be sufficient for pre-kindergarten programs, especially when they are combining different school- and community-based classrooms. Once again, New Jersey's *Abbott* program was exceptional in requiring frequent site visits from "master" teachers to coach less experienced staff, providing districts with tools to conduct their own assessments, using university researchers to assess classroom quality, and tracking the effects of preschool on students entering kindergarten.[54]

CONCLUSION

Capitalizing on the K–12 education reform movement, reformers since the 1990s have sought to bring preschool "into the education tent" in order to secure better trained teachers, more stable funding, and greater access to high-quality preschool. Pre-kindergarten has become recognized as part of public education in many states and has benefited from becoming part of that larger system. At the same time, both general skepticism about the effectiveness of the K-12 education system and the existence of a strong sector of providers outside the public schools have worked against simply adding preschool as another grade of public school. The historical strength of private and community-based programs has complicated efforts to expand publicly funded preschool but also has created opportunities to do so in more creative and responsive ways, by creating "mixed systems" for delivering pre-kindergarten. Offering pre-kindergarten through mixed systems holds the promise of serving more children in a diversity of programs, meeting child care needs, and improving quality in early childhood programs across the board. This promise, however, can only be met if policymakers and practitioners deliberately work to strengthen the system of private and community-based provision for young children, even as they use it to expand access to quality pre-kindergarten.

CHAPTER 8

Putting the Promise of Preschool into Practice

The movement to expand pre-kindergarten has already had significant success, and it is clear that many states are moving toward providing "preschool for all." As policymakers seek to create structures to offer preschool education to more children, they need to be aware of the complex relationships among schools, private providers, and families that mark this arena. Because of the history traced in earlier chapters, preschool today straddles the world of public schools and the world of early childhood. As was pointed out in chapter 7, even as preschool advocates work to bring preschool into the "education tent," they need to cooperate with private child care providers and Head Start programs in order to deliver pre-kindergarten to the largest number of children. Yet this chronically underfunded patchwork of providers needs bolstering in order to sustain high-quality programs that will make a difference in children's education. As Gordon McInness, who led New Jersey's *Abbott* program, writes, "preschool without quality is just high-cost day care. It is not a simple matter of buying colorful alphabetic rugs, supplying age-appropriate toys, and finding two adults to supervise play."[1] To put the promise of preschool into practice, those charged with making and implementing policy need to pay careful attention to quality issues such as teacher training and compensation, curriculum, and parent involvement.

At the same time, as preschool moves from its roots outside schools into the "education tent," it risks leaving behind some of the strengths of the best private and community-based programs: a child-centered curriculum with a diversity of approaches, in an atmosphere that is welcoming to families. Skeptics point to the historical example of how kindergarten changed when it was integrated into elementary schools at the turn of the twentieth century: the curriculum became more academic, and teachers devoted less time to interacting with families and the community, focusing instead on preparing children for first grade. Advocates need to consider how we might learn from this history in order to preserve some of the traditional strengths of early childhood programs as they become more widespread and more integrated into public education.

WHO SHOULD TEACH PRESCHOOL?

Developing the teacher workforce is one of the greatest challenges facing policymakers who wish to fulfill the promise of preschool. Young children's learning is deeply shaped by their relationships with supportive adults, and researchers agree that teachers need training to create a high-quality learning environment. It is no accident that the model programs such as Perry Preschool and the Abecedarian Project, whose successes inspired the growth of public pre-kindergarten, were staffed by highly trained teachers. Yet there is a large gap between the type and number of preschool teachers that are needed and the workforce that currently exists. Overall, the early childhood workforce has low levels of formal education and notoriously low wages, rooted in the long-standing assumption that caring for young children does not take special training or deserve substantial compensation. State regulation has set low standards for child care staff: forty states require no formal credential at all beyond a high school diploma, and virtually none require that child care teachers have a bachelor's degree. Child care workers earn less than almost any other occupation, averaging just above $8 an hour, and typically do not receive benefits. Low wages lead to high turnover rates, creating emotional disruptions for children. Preschool teachers—who are better off than child care workers in general—average less than half the salary of their elementary school counterparts.[2] Furthermore, meaningful career ladders with salary increases for additional training and experience are rare.

These problems have their roots in the way early childhood programs have developed over time, as priorities such as serving more children and keeping programs affordable for families have outweighed recruiting highly trained teachers. In the early years of Head Start, for example, hiring poor parents and community residents to staff programs was more important than having teachers with formal training in early childhood education. Faced with the prospect of a dramatic expansion of child care services and Head Start in the early 1970s, Edward Zigler helped create the CDA credential, which required far less training than what was expected for K–12 teachers. The CDA was designed to provide a basic standard for people working with young children, not to create a high bar for professional teacher training. Still in use in both Head Start and child care centers, it is based on competencies rather than formal educational credentials, and requires the equivalent of about a year of postsecondary training.

The rapid expansion of early childhood programs made it difficult for teachers to follow the routes to professionalization that K–12 teachers had traveled over the course of the twentieth century: credentialing and unionization.

Committed to openness and inclusivity, early education as a field has been ambivalent about defining specific credentials and a body of knowledge that one must master in order to be an effective early childhood professional. One indicator of this ambivalence is that while professional organizations in nursing and social work restrict membership to those who hold professional credentials in their areas, membership in the National Association for the Education of Young Children is open to anyone.[3]

As the early childhood field has tripled in size from the late 1970s to the present, teacher compensation has remained stagnant, and the education level of the early education workforce (outside of school settings) declined, going against an overall trend in the workforce toward higher education levels. As college-educated women found other career paths open to them, some other traditionally female occupations, such as nursing, have raised wages in order to keep attracting workers. Early childhood programs, on the other hand, have shifted toward a workforce with less formal education in order to meet the growing demand for child care slots at rates families can afford and that the federal government is willing to subsidize. As a result, the percentage of center-based teachers and administrators with a four-year degree dropped from 43 percent in 1983 to 30 percent by 2004.[4] Nor was this less-educated workforce protected by unionization; only about 3 percent of child care workers were in a union or covered by a union contract in 2004.[5]

Child care workers called attention to their perennially low wages and the need for a more stable workforce in a variety of ways. In the early 1990s, "Worthy Wages" campaigns in dozens of cities made the cause visible with parades and demonstrations. Although these campaigns brought together a wide range of child care providers and helped raise public awareness, organizers had difficulty harnessing their momentum to bring about concrete change. The 1990 federal child care legislation addressed some teacher training concerns by setting aside quality improvement funds for states, and initiatives such as the scholarship program offered by Teacher Education and Compensation Helps (TEACH) supported training for child care teachers. But since the number of children in child care, especially with home-based providers, was growing during the 1990s due to welfare reform, such efforts did not result in significant change in teachers' training and compensation.[6] Congress also raised standards for teacher training in Head Start in 1998, requiring that at least half of all lead teachers have a two-year associate's degree. While teachers met this requirement, it has not made a big difference in compensation: the average annual salary for a Head Start teacher with a bachelor's degree was $26,500 in 2007, compared to an average kindergarten teacher's salary of $45,250.[7]

Linking preschool to the public schools was another strategy for improving the training and compensation of early childhood teachers. If preschool was part of public education, advocates argued, preschool teachers should have similar training and compensation as K–12 teachers. For instance, Ellen Frede, who directed the preschool effort in New Jersey's *Abbott* districts, said: "This [preschool] is public school. Why would we think it's OK for teachers who teach three-year-olds not to have the same qualifications as someone who teaches second grade?"[8] Getting better trained teachers seemed to be an element of K–12 schools well worth imitating. It held the promise of improving teachers' ability to promote children's learning while also creating a more professionalized and decently compensated workforce that would have parity with K–12 teachers. Requiring higher standards for teachers could also help convince legislators and the public that pre-kindergarten is not "just babysitting" but an important element of education. (For instance, Tennessee governor Phil Bredesen said in 2007 that requiring certified teachers with bachelor's degrees was keeping the state's program "very sound and very blue chip.")[9] Advocates also argued that requiring a bachelor's degree—a requirement for an increasing number of jobs in the U.S. economy—is a reasonable minimum for someone in the teaching profession and one that can affect a teacher's ability to operate as a professional.

Requiring that pre-kindergarten teachers have bachelor's degrees (preferably in early childhood education), whether they are teaching in a community-based setting or a school, has thus become a goal for advocates. The National Research Council in 2000 called for teachers to have a four-year bachelor's degree, including specific training in child development; researchers at the NIEER used the same qualifications when they created benchmarks to judge quality standards in state pre-kindergarten programs. The 2007 reauthorization of Head Start requires that half of all teachers have bachelor's degrees by 2013, building on earlier efforts to increase teachers' educational level.

Meeting this standard is a daunting task. Only about a third of preschool teachers in the country currently have a bachelor's degree, with important regional variations. States may face a "crisis of credentialing" if they decide to set a high requirement, especially if their institutions of higher education do not have sufficient training programs for early childhood teachers. Nationally, less than a third of institutions of higher education offer an early childhood education program, and less than half of these offer a bachelor's degree in the field. Given this level of access to training, it would take ten years to produce enough teachers with bachelor's degrees in early childhood to meet the current demand on a national level, without addressing any needs for expansion. In Massachusetts, advocates estimate it would take twenty years to ensure that every preschool classroom in the state had at least one teacher with a bachelor's degree. To meet these needs, early educators will need both to recruit new students into teacher preparation programs and to upgrade the training of those already in the field.[10]

Raising requirements for teacher training may have other costs as well, including a narrowing of the diversity of the early childhood workforce, which is currently much greater than in the K–12 workforce. (For instance, in Los Angeles, more than half of all preschool teachers were nonwhite, compared with a quarter of K–12 teachers.) Researcher Marcy Whitebook noted:

> We don't want the workforce to look linguistically and culturally like K–12 education, which is predominantly white and monolingual English-speaking, but we want the workforce to reflect the diversity of the children and families we're serving, and in many ways the early care and education workforce now has that diversity.[11]

Immigrants and minorities are statistically less likely to complete a bachelor's degree than are whites, so requiring a four-year degree could sacrifice bilingualism and cultural diversity at a time when it is most needed.

While requiring the bachelor's degree may be a good strategy for professionalizing the workforce, increasing compensation, and creating parity between early education and the K–12 system, experts disagree about its actual impact on children. Those who favor the move point to research conducted in child care centers showing that teachers' educational levels are strongly linked to the kind of positive interactions with children that promote learning. Teachers with bachelor's degrees had more constructive interactions with children and richer classroom environments; as a result, they elicited more language activity and higher levels of complex play from the children, who developed stronger language skills.[12] Those who question the need for teachers with bachelor's degrees look at research focused specifically on pre-kindergarten classrooms, where several studies have found little difference between teachers with a bachelor's degree and those with a two-year degree plus early childhood training.[13]

On the whole, it seems that preschool teachers have trouble finding ways to integrate academic skills with playful, child-directed activities and the kinds of meaningful adult-child interactions that nurture and support learning. Children's learning is spurred when adults are involved in their activities, helping them understand concepts and starting conversations that encourage more advanced thinking. For instance, a skillful teacher might ask a child engaged with building a block tower how she might make the tower grow higher and higher, or help her create a story about the tower that could be written down, embellished, and read back. But University of North Carolina researchers found that in the public pre-kindergarten classrooms they observed, these kinds of interactions were limited; children spent the largest chunks of their days in routine, maintenance activities such as cleaning up, eating, washing hands, or standing in line. Even in whole group time, teachers' conversations with children were minimal, consisting of giving instructions, asking simple questions, or answering questions without elaborating. A researcher hypothesized that early childhood teachers had not been taught how to move from rote activities such as counting and recitation to higher level learning.[14] Researcher Robert Pianta concluded from a larger study of classroom quality in preschool and early elementary grades that only about a quarter of these classrooms provided students with the kind of high-quality teaching that could make a difference in closing the achievement gap.[15] Recent preschool research echoes research in elementary grades showing little correlation between teacher credentials and classroom quality. The debate over the bachelor's degree for preschool teachers, Pianta noted, "is symptomatic of this larger issue of how we ensure that what we are doing in teacher education contributes to teachers' effectiveness in the classroom."[16]

In the meantime, states wanting to expand access to pre-kindergarten programs have to decide how high to set the bar on teacher qualifications. There is a trend toward requiring that teachers have bachelor's degrees and teaching certification, but states often relax these rules in order to include community-based providers in their pre-kindergarten programs. States that treat their pre-kindergarten programs as part of the public education system (such as Oklahoma or Tennessee) are most likely to require teachers to meet the same requirements as their K–12 counterparts, while those that rely heavily on community providers (such as Georgia or Florida) tend to have lower requirements.

A significant number of states have sought to accommodate private child care and Head Start providers by allowing different standards for these settings than for school-based programs. New York requires that pre-kindergarten teachers be certified but allows some community sites to hire teachers without college degrees if they are supervised by a certified teacher. In West Virginia, school district programs must have teachers who are certified in early childhood education, but teachers in community programs can work toward certification over five years. In Florida, teachers in community sites need only have a high school diploma and a CDA, and are not required to work on upgrading their credentials. When Florida legislators were debating requirements for teachers, some argued that requiring certified teachers was a "Mercedes-Benz" design for a preschool program. Steve Barnett of NIEER countered that voters may not have expected a "Cadillac pre-K system" but wanted "a car with wheels

Table 8.1 Teacher Requirements in States Enrolling at Least 10% of 4-Year-Olds in State-funded Pre-kindergarten[1]

States Requiring BA + Certification in Early Childhood for Lead Teachers

Oklahoma	BA + certification in early childhood education
South Carolina	BA + early childhood certification
Kentucky	BA (for teachers hired after 2004) + Birth-Kindergarten certificate
Louisiana (LA4)	BA + certification in Nursery, Kindergarten, Pre-K to 3, or Early Intervention
Tennessee	BA + pre-K endorsement
North Carolina	BA + Birth-K license or pre-K add-on
Illinois	BA + Birth-8 certification
Wisconsin	BA + Birth-8 license
New Jersey (*Abbott*)	BA + Pre-K-grade 3 certification
Texas	BA + generalist (early childhood-grade 4) teaching certificate

States Requiring BA + General Certification for Lead Teachers

Maine	BA + early childhood or elementary certification
Kansas	BA + elementary certificate + elementary or early childhood license
Maryland	BA in early childhood + certification in N-3, N-6, or N-8

States Requiring Less than a BA for Lead Teachers

Georgia	AA in early childhood
Colorado	CDA
Head Start	*50% of teachers must have AA*

(continued)

Table 8.1 (Continued)

States with Varied Requirements for Different Settings

Vermont	*School settings*: BA + license in early childhood
	Community settings: BA in early childhood
New York	*School settings*: BA + Birth-grade 2 certification (requires MA degree)
	Community settings: 9 credits toward CDA if supervised by certified teacher
Michigan	*School settings*: BA + elementary certificate and early childhood endorsement
	Community settings: BA + elementary certificate and CDA, or degree in child development
Virginia	*School settings*: BA + license + certification in preK-grade 3 or preK-grade 6
	Community settings: CDA
West Virginia	*School settings*: BA + certification in early childhood, preschool special needs, or elementary education with a pre-K/kindergarten endorsement
	Community settings: AA in early childhood + work toward certification over 5 years
Arkansas	*Single classroom sites*: BA in early childhood + Birth-grade 4 license
	Multiple classroom sites: AA in early childhood, if one teacher per every three classrooms has higher qualifications above
Connecticut	*School settings*: BA or CDA + 12 credits in early childhood + certification in elementary education with Pre-K, Nursery-Kindergarten, or SpEd endorsement
	Community settings: CDA + 12 credits in early childhood
Florida	*School settings*: BA + any certification, or BA in early childhood, primary or preschool education, family and consumer science, or elementary education
	Community settings: CDA or equivalent + training in emergent literacy

W. Steven Barnett, Jason Hustedt, Laura Hawkinson, and Kenneth Robin, *The State of Preschool 2006: State Preschool Yearbook* (New Brunswick, N.J.: National Institute for Early Education Research, 2006), 12, 18.

and tires." Without standards for teachers, the legislature was giving the voters a "car...that doesn't even have an engine."[17]

Policymakers' choices can make an important difference in encouraging community programs to hire certified teachers. In Florida, legislators expressed the "intent of the legislature" that teachers would obtain associate's and bachelor's degrees over the next several years, but provided no mechanism to encourage them to do so. By contrast, although Georgia initially set a similarly low standard for teachers (a high school diploma and a CDA), it used incentives to encourage grantees to hire more qualified teachers and later raised the requirement to at least a two-year degree in early childhood education. By 2004, most lead teachers had four-year degrees, and more than half were certified.[18]

Establishing requirements for teachers to meet is, in a sense, the easy part of securing a trained and stable teaching workforce. Only a few states have gone beyond this to help teachers overcome barriers they face in completing a four-year degree or to address the crucial question of teacher compensation. States may help teachers complete college degrees by providing supports such as scholarships, extra academic advising, a variety of class locations and scheduling, and articulation agreements that allow students to apply credits from a two-year institution toward a four-year degree. This type of support can be particularly important in helping to maintain the diversity of the early childhood workforce while upgrading teachers' credentials. In New Jersey, the *Abbott* program created a system for upgrading the early childhood education workforce, helping teachers in community-based settings reach the court's requirement of a bachelor's degree and early childhood certification. Early childhood experts created a new early childhood teaching certificate, and institutions of higher education responded with new training programs. Colleges and universities offered classes at child care centers, at satellite facilities, and online in order to make programs accessible to teachers; some also offered mentoring assistance and allowed students to complete their student teaching requirements at their place of employment.[19] State funds provided scholarships to teachers to enroll in college courses and offered grants to colleges and universities to expand programs and faculties. The state also funded release time and higher compensation for participating teachers. As a result of these efforts, the percentage of certified teachers with bachelor's degrees in community-based child care programs rose dramatically, from 35 percent in 1998 to 99 percent by 2005. The average starting state salary for a preschool teacher also grew significantly, from $18,000 to $40,000.[20] New Jersey's efforts, however, were the exception rather than the rule. Because the *Abbott* pre-kindergarten program was mandated by the court, much greater funding has been made available than in other states; indeed, New Jersey spends more per pupil on its pre-kindergarten program than any state in the country.

While many states are moving toward requiring teachers to have higher credentials, few address the equally vital issue of teacher compensation. Teacher salaries are one of the most robust predictors of the overall quality of the classroom learning environment, even after controlling for teacher education and training, staff-to-child ratio, and group size. Edward Zigler and Walter Gilliam write: "In a nutshell, higher wages allow directors to staff their programs with higher-skilled teachers and improve work force stability."[21] On average, preschool teachers are not well paid; 13.9 percent of teachers in publicly funded pre-kindergarten classrooms reported an annual salary below federal poverty guidelines, and 70.9 percent qualified as "low-income."[22] Teacher turnover and migration to K–12 teaching jobs are thus major issues for the early childhood field. When states require pre-kindergarten teachers to have bachelor's degrees and teaching certification but do not pay them at a rate similar to that earned by teachers of older children, teachers are much more likely to leave preschool teaching for better paying positions in the elementary grades. Researcher Marcy Whitebook commented on this Catch-22: unless compensation is increased, requiring more education is essentially "training people to go work with older children, because people aren't going to invest in a college degree and then be satisfied with an early child care salary." On the other hand, she noted: "the only way we're ever going to really pull the salaries up is if we make it clear that what it takes to work with young children is comparable to what it takes to work with older children, and people have the same qualifications."[23]

Failing to address teacher compensation has a major impact on mixed delivery systems for pre-kindergarten. A substantial salary gap between K–12 and community-based child care positions makes it very difficult for community-based programs to attract well-qualified teachers. The Center for the Child Care Workforce warned in 2002 that an unequal, "two-tier system of pre-kindergarten education" was taking shape. Teachers in school-based programs more closely resembled their colleagues teaching at the K–12 level, receiving higher pay and benefits and enjoying greater job stability. (For example, in New York, school-based programs paid teachers an average of $10,000 more than community sites, were more likely to have certified teachers, and had low teacher turnover rates.)[24] Those teaching preschool in community-based programs, on the other hand, shared in the lower pay and qualifications of the child care workforce as a whole. As a result, even when state requirements for teacher qualifications were the same, school-based pre-kindergarten programs could attract teachers with higher qualifications than those in other settings. In California, more than 80 percent of teachers in school settings exceeded the state's requirement for training, while only 8 percent of those in community settings did; a less dramatic but similar pattern obtained in other states.[25]

Given this disparity between school-based and community-based programs, teachers tended to leave the community programs as soon as they could, treating them as "training grounds for the public schools."[26] Only a few states, including Oklahoma and New Jersey, have directly addressed the issue of equal compensation across settings; advocates in New York are testing the idea of a teacher equity compensation fund that districts could draw on to help equalize resources between community sites and schools.[27] Even with efforts to equalize compensation, teachers are likely to gravitate to school-based programs. New Jersey's efforts to achieve salary parity between public and nonpublic preschool providers slowed down the "exodus" of teachers but could not put community-based programs on an equal footing with the schools for benefits and pension plans.[28] While incentives to promote teacher stability (such as bonuses to qualified teachers who pledge to remain at their jobs for a certain period of time) may help address this problem, they cannot overcome the discrepancy between schools and community sites that decades of history have created.[29]

Indeed, the history of early childhood programs has created a difficult legacy for those who now seek a professionally trained and decently compensated workforce for pre-kindergarten. In raising standards for pre-kindergarten teachers, states with "mixed systems" have sought to include community-based providers by allowing different standards for teachers in these programs. If states do not address the issue of compensation across different settings, however, their efforts may end up simply accelerating the migration of trained teachers from community-based programs to schools rather than strengthening the skills of the workforce overall. As RAND researchers cautioned, little progress will be made if pre-kindergarten teachers improve their status at a cost to other early childhood programs, especially when these other programs are part of the network for delivering pre-kindergarten education.[30] This problem reminds us that even as advocates have sought to move preschool into the realm of K–12 education, it remains intertwined with other early childhood programs, making it necessary to consider how to "lift all boats" simultaneously.

WHAT SHOULD CHILDREN LEARN IN PRESCHOOL?

The question of what we should expect children to learn in preschool is, of course, paramount in designing high-quality preschool programs. Excellent preschool teaching requires the ability to integrate preacademic skills and social skills into children's imaginative play and chosen activities through extensive interaction and conversation as well as to construct a stimulating classroom environment. Teachers lead activities designed to foster children's language and other skills but also converse with children engaged in their own play and conversations to add new ideas, enrich vocabulary, and enhance learning. Skilled teachers can weave early literacy and math skills, along with crucial social and emotional skills, into a child-oriented, holistic approach to learning. Deborah Stipek, dean of Stanford University's School of Education, wrote in 2004: "The good news is that children can be taught basic academic skills in the context of playful activities that exploit rather than destroy their natural desire to learn." For instance, conversations, storytelling, and labeling games can all teach vocabulary and oral language skills; songs and rhyming games can help with phonemic awareness, and writing and math skills can be integrated into daily activities and pretend play such as running a restaurant or a post office.[31] The bad news is that this is hard to do, and we have seen that pre-kindergarten teachers often struggle to strike the right balance.

Early childhood educators generally believe that preschool should attend to multiple domains of development rather than focusing primarily on academic skills. Indeed, they have traditionally been concerned especially with nurturing social-emotional skills such as independence, self-confidence, self-control, and cooperation, seeing these as crucial to later success in school and life. "Learning through play" with a range of materials that promotes social interaction, language development, and fine and gross motor skills has been the cornerstone of mainstream early education philosophy. At the same time, there is a growing consensus that young children are capable of learning more than has traditionally been assumed. In its 2000 publication *Eager to Learn: Educating Our Preschoolers*, the National Research Council pointed to "unexpected competencies in young children." Researchers were concluding that children have a natural proclivity to learn, experiment with, and explore language, numbers, and science that can be nurtured and extended through a variety of activities. Preschool, these experts concluded, should thus focus not only on socialization but also on children's emerging cognitive skills, which are more complex than traditional early childhood programs, relying on theorists like Piaget, imagined.[32] Furthermore, school administrators, under pressure to improve overall student achievement, may press preschool programs to stress preacademic skills and to get children used to classroom behaviors such as sitting still and waiting in line.

Indeed, the early childhood orthodoxy of "learning through play" is increasingly on the defensive. As preschool becomes more closely integrated with K–12 schools that are intently focused on raising student achievement on mandated tests, there is a real danger of narrowing the curriculum to emphasize preacademic knowledge rather than taking a more developmentally appropriate approach. In Tulsa, Oklahoma, Bruce Fuller notes:

> School principals and district officials live under stiff pressure to raise test scores and to reduce the count of "failing schools" as defined by NCLB [No Child Left Behind]....Because of this, school authorities are, quite rationally, attempting to pull the new preschool teachers into line, synchronizing what four-year-olds are to learn with what's covered on standardized tests in first and second grade.

One observer noted that teachers often feel "caught in the middle of what you know about...developmentally appropriate practices" and the district officials' expectations. For instance, the district had recently capped at one hour per day the time that children would be allowed to explore classroom learning centers, long the centerpiece of early childhood classrooms. The "growth inventory" checklist that teachers were to complete for each of their students included only four items related to social-emotional growth, compared to seventy-eight items related to vocabulary, colors, phonemes, reading numbers, and counting. A school administrator in Los Angeles explained: "Thinking of No Child Left Behind, even though it doesn't apply [to preschools]...we want to align teachers (and curricular practices) to it."[33]

In this context, children's play—a crucial component in children's linguistic, social, and cognitive development—is often seen as dispensable. For instance, a teacher in a West Coast preschool classroom commented on the importance of learning specific academic skills, saying: "They won't be able to just sit there and play with blocks all day." Another explained:

> The kindergarten teacher tells us that they have to know these things:...they write their name, they know their home address...their phone numbers, and 1 to 20, and the alphabet. So we are doing this the whole year. And that's why I tell you we have to sit down with them. That's the way they'll learn these things.

Parents—especially those from immigrant backgrounds—often echoed this idea that preschool should be more like school. One mother said: "They should write a little more and play less. They should have a little more pressure to learn the letters." Another mother explained: "I would like it if they would make them work more, in things like the alphabet, their name or how to write it, because almost all the time I see them, they have their activities that they do, or play, but they should have some time to study."[34] This dichotomy between "work" and "play" ignores the important role of imaginative play in developing children's language, ideas, and social interaction and of the ways a skilled teacher can integrate reading, writing, and math skills and concepts into children's play. Concerned that play was endangered by an emphasis on teaching preacademic skills, Zigler edited a book of essays in 2004 that he called *Children's Play: The Roots of Reading.*

These issues of finding the right balance between child-directed exploration and teacher-driven instruction in specific academic skills have become a focus of debate over assessing preschoolers' learning. In 2003, the George W. Bush administration introduced a standardized assessment of letter, number, and word recognition, that was to be given to all Head Start students twice a year. This was the largest standardized testing of such young children ever conducted in the United States and aroused criticism from early childhood experts, who contended that the test was not an appropriate tool and that the difficulties of assessing preschoolers would make the data of limited use. The test violated what professional early educators considered to be important guidelines for assessing the development of young children, such as developmental appropriateness, use of multiple measures based on observation of daily activities, and ability to capture preschool children's rapid and uneven growth.[35] After some public outcry, Congress ultimately halted the test in 2007 and asked the National Research Council to provide guidance on appropriate assessments for early childhood programs.[36]

In addition to requiring testing in Head Start, the Bush administration's early childhood initiative also required states to create early learning standards for young children. These standards—patterned on state standards that were part of K–12 testing and accountability systems—were meant to provide guidance about what young children should know and be able to do, and be linked to K–12 standards. A comprehensive study of emerging state standards in 2003 found that some emphasized academic content (specifying facts or knowledge that young children should learn—such as naming body parts, recognizing letters, or classifying materials according to criteria such as length or color) whereas others were primarily developmental (such as "a growing ability" to coordinate fine and gross motor movements or to use language to express emotions). Overall, state standards tended to emphasize language and cognition over other areas. Researchers were concerned about the lack of attention to social-emotional development and motivation to learn, which are considered vital to children's later development and learning. Two major professional associations in early childhood education cautioned that standards should not be simplified versions of K–12 standards but should be specifically tailored to the way young children learn, and should include the multiple domains of children's development: social, emotional, cognitive, language, and physical. Similarly, researchers at the NIEER wrote in 2004 that standards addressing social-emotional development, approaches to learning, and physical health need to have "as much emphasis and specificity as those that address cognitive and language development." Foundational skills such as the ability to listen, pay attention, and regulate emotions needed to be emphasized rather than focusing mainly on academic content, as do standards for older students.[37]

As state pre-kindergarten programs expand and become part of public education, leaders must decide how much these programs will look like K–12 schools, and to what degree they will draw on the more holistic approach of early childhood education. Writing in 2005 about pressure to prepare children for standardized testing, Deborah Stipek worried that preschools were coming to look too much like elementary schools. "Instead of the early elementary grades becoming more child centered and family friendly (more like preschool), preschools are likely to become more like elementary school, with formal, scripted instruction and less emphasis on student-centered approaches and family involvement."[38] This may be another good reason to develop preschool systems that include community-based providers, who are less likely to feel pressure to prepare children for standardized testing, are more likely to preserve a child-centered approach, and may be more responsive to family and community desires for what children should learn. In this context, bringing together the best of both school and community-based worlds means having programs that focus on all developmental domains, where teachers know how to help children learn academic and social skills through carefully directed play and hands-on experiences, and where appropriate assessment practices are designed to be part of a thoughtful curriculum.

WHAT ROLE SHOULD PARENTS PLAY IN PRESCHOOL?

As preschool climbs into the education tent, we also need to be sure that parents are not left behind. Strong connections between families and school are particularly important as young children begin to navigate a wider world; parents and teachers need trust, easy communication, and a sense of shared commitment to children's growth. Historically, early childhood programs developed outside of schools have tended to be more effective at welcoming and working with parents than have K–12 schools, and policymakers need to consider what steps they can take to make this a deliberate focus of the pre-kindergarten systems they are creating.

Since its inception, Head Start has had a particularly strong commitment to promoting parent involvement, empowerment, and education. Parent involvement is built into the structure of the program, which requires that an advisory council of parents plays a role in governing each program, encourages the hiring of Head Start parents as staff members, and includes home visits, parent education sessions, and family support services. The program encourages parents to develop skills to increase their participation and advocate for their children as they move through their school years. In the recent large study of Head Start families, more than 70 percent of parents reported they had volunteered in the classroom in the past year, while between 75–90 percent reported talking with their children about school and playing educational (i.e., counting) games at home on a regular basis.[39] The substance of this parent involvement varies from program to program as well as over time, and does not always live up to all its goals, especially for parent participation in governing programs.[40] Nevertheless, parents typically found that Head Start programs welcomed their involvement and respected their efforts, and the program provided a space (literally and figuratively) for strengthening ties with other parents. The social networks developed in the program in earlier decades, writes Joshua Kagan, empowered mothers "to demand a greater voice in and in behalf of the program," while the encouragement to volunteer in the program boosted mothers' confidence in their parenting skills. These types of experiences, along with the concrete help Head Start staff tried to provide to families, helped produce strong parent support for the program, which has endured over the years.

Another important model for parent engagement is the Chicago Child-Parent Centers, which provided extensive parental outreach and support to the families of the low-income children it targeted in the 1980s. A full-time staff member coordinated the family support aspect of the program, and parents were expected to spend a day a week volunteering in the classroom, in the parent room, or participating in other program activities.[41] (Arthur Reynolds, who has conducted longitudinal studies showing long-term benefits for this program, estimates that the increase in parental participation, home visits, and training accounts for about one-quarter of the program's effects).[42] Parents who participated in the preschool program were more likely to be involved in their children's schooling as they moved into elementary school. In addition to encouraging parents to spend as much as time possible in their children's classrooms, the centers, still in operation, have parent rooms and offer GED and other classes as well as parenting programs.

Private and community-based child care and preschools also tend to encourage parent involvement, albeit not as deliberately. Tuition-based providers depend on parent satisfaction for their bottom line, and small nonprofit agencies also seek to be responsive to parents, on whom they often rely for various kinds of support. The very diversity of community-based child care, from family home providers to church-based and ethnically identified programs, can also encourage parents to find a place where they feel comfortable. Moreover, fostering parent involvement is a value in the field overall. For instance, to become accredited by the National Association for the Education of Young Children, programs must meet standards that include "Knowing and Understanding the Program's Families," "Nurturing Families as Advocates for Their Children," and "Sharing Information Between Staff and Families." These require that teachers learn about families' backgrounds and preferred child-rearing practices, "foster strong reciprocal relationships with families," allow parents to visit at any time, and personally communicate with parents regularly about their children's activities.[43]

On the other hand, K–12 schools often struggle to encourage meaningful parental involvement. Although educators recognize that parental involvement can increase educational achievement, they also expect parents to defer to their professional expertise and are not accustomed to giving parents a role in governing programs or to welcoming them routinely into classrooms. Rather, they tend to seek a limited kind of parental involvement: sending children to school on time, helping with homework, reinforcing academics at home, and supporting the school through fundraising and other ancillary activities.[44] As a result, they often find it difficult to bridge the barriers that separate parents and schools. Working-class and poor parents in particular face both practical difficulties (inflexible work schedules, lack of transportation) and other barriers to meaningful interaction with their child's public school. Sociologists have found that working-class parents tend to see education as the job of the school and to defer to teachers as professionals who know more than they do, despite schools' stated desires to create "partnership" between school and home. Professional middle-class parents, on the other hand, are more likely to actively involve themselves in their children's schooling, helping with academic work at home, monitoring their children's progress, and communicating frequently with teachers.[45] If preschool is going to make a big difference in the lives of poor and working-class children, it is particularly important that parents be encouraged at every step to be actively involved in their children's education and to help bridge the worlds of home and school. If we use K–12 schools as our only model, as Bruce Fuller warns, we may "replicate in preschool the yawning distance that has opened up between teachers and parents in so many public schools."[46]

Again, the historical example of the kindergarten is relevant. Late nineteenth-century kindergartens were agents of social reform and Americanization in poor city neighborhoods. Teachers often spent their mornings teaching children and their afternoons visiting their families, meeting with mothers and making connections between the kindergarten and the community. The directors of kindergartens in New York City's schools in the 1910s declared that the kindergarten teacher was "not only a teacher, but a social worker."[47] As the kindergarten became more fully absorbed into public school systems, this family involvement role faded away and was replaced by an emphasis on enrolling more children and preparing them for first grade.

Among the reformers calling for universal pre-kindergarten today, fostering parent involvement has not been a high priority. Rather, advocates have stressed the importance of hiring professionally trained teachers, creating curricular standards, and reaching more children. In documents created to guide policymakers, and in pre-kindergarten legislation, parent involvement is rarely emphasized or elaborated. Structures such as parent advisory boards, parent rooms, and parent education programs are not highlighted as key features for programs to emulate; home visits are sometimes referred to as a supplemental service that programs can offer families but not as something that would strengthen the program itself. The NIEER's checklist of standards for state programs does not emphasize parent involvement, nor does the Policy Framework of the National Pre-Kindergarten Center at the University of North Carolina. Pre-K Now goes further, including in its virtual tour of an ideal preschool classroom descriptions such as "families receive frequent invitations to participate in classroom activities, contribute to studies, and accompany the class on field trips; home visits are conducted at least once a year"; "families are encouraged to visit the classroom at any time; and the program links families to needed services—health, social services, or parenting classes."[48] Even this more detailed description aims at a one-way type of parent involvement rather than the two-way vision of programs like Head Start, in which parents learn from program staff but the program also changes in response to parents' needs and decisions. This description also does not address the need to consider cultural differences between families and the preschool or the need to seek input from parents about what is most important to them in their children's learning and overall development.[49]

In drawing on public schools as a model for preschool, reformers may be gaining greater professionalism and stability but losing an emphasis on parents. Community-based providers may have more strengths to draw on in creating pre-kindergarten programs that welcome and build strong relationships with families. This is another good reason for policymakers to incorporate community-based providers and Head Start programs into pre-kindergarten. To preserve the "family friendly" ethos of early education, directors and teachers in school-based programs will have to focus on deliberately seeking ways to encourage parents to participate in their children's early education.

CONCLUSION

We have seen that in the past decade, preschool advocates have scored impressive victories in expanding publicly funded preschool. They have done so by pursuing a strategy of separating preschool from child care and defining preschool as part of education. In following this strategy, the more pre-kindergarten looks like school—with certified teachers, formalized curriculum focused on academic skills, and funding coming through state aid formulas—the better. When pre-kindergarten looks like K–12 schooling, it is easier to convince legislators and the public that it deserves public funding, and it is easier to manage it with existing administrative structures. By borrowing the practices of K–12 schooling, pre-kindergarten advocates hope to gain higher quality classrooms, trained and well-compensated teachers, stable funding, and access for more children.

However, good strategy is not always the same as good policy. Looking beyond getting pre-kindergarten legislation passed to building effective systems for pre-kindergarten education, we see that "climbing into the education tent" is not as simple as it sounds. States may require that pre-kindergarten teachers have the same credentials as K–12 teachers, but states still need to address broader issues of teacher quality and compensation across the early education field. Inside the education tent, pressure to improve student achievement in reading and math may make it difficult for a balanced, child-centered curriculum to flourish, and parent involvement may be a lower priority. Putting the promise of preschool into practice requires attention not only to securing for preschool the professionalism and stability that schools can offer but also to sustaining the strengths of early childhood programs that have grown up outside schools.

Conclusion

History Lessons for Preschool Advocates

In our politically polarized nation, "universal pre-K" now enjoys nearly universal support. Notably, Barack Obama campaigned on a platform that included a strong focus on early childhood education. During presidential debates in the fall of 2008, he pointed to early childhood as one of the strategic investments that would remain a priority for his administration, despite the nation's deepening economic crisis. His commitment to the issue may have been inspired by his relationship with Chicago philanthropist Irving Harris, who founded the Ounce of Prevention Fund to focus on early childhood development and backed Obama's campaigns for Illinois state senate. The Fund's director recalled that in 2001, Obama was the only legislator to show up for a reception held in Springfield to discuss pre-kindergarten issues. Following his election, one advocate described the elation of those working in the early childhood field: "People are absolutely ecstatic. Some people seem to think the Great Society is upon us again."[1] Obama's secretary of education, Arne Duncan, shared this commitment to early education. During his Senate confirmation hearing in January 2009, he pledged to make early education a priority, saying: "There's nothing more important that we can do to get our children off to a great start in their life."[2] As president, Obama outlined an education agenda whose first pillar was early education, stressing the importance of quality standards and seamless "Zero to Five" state systems; the stimulus package he championed in the early months of his presidency included $2 billion for Early Head Start and Head Start.[3] His first budget included new investments in Title I grants for pre-kindergarten, home visiting programs for at-risk families, and Early Leaning Challenge grants to help states improve quality in early childhood programs.

President Obama is likely to find considerable support for a new national commitment to early childhood programs. As a centrist idea for improving education and reducing the achievement gap between poor and affluent children, pre-kindergarten has wide appeal. Obama was not alone in talking about early childhood education during the 2008 campaign; endorsements also came from candidates Hillary Clinton (a liberal Democrat who proposed pre-kindergarten legislation in the Senate) and Mike Huckabee (a conservative Republican who had supported its growth as governor of Arkansas). Governors, philanthropists, and business leaders had also come to see pre-kindergarten as an important cause. When asked why he pushed so hard for pre-kindergarten in Tennessee, Governor Phil Bredesen said he wanted to be remembered for education. "What are the things you can do in education that will make a difference? There does not seem to be a better place to go than pre-K; it has a fundamental effect on our educational system." Furthermore, his commissioner of education noted, expanding pre-kindergarten was "something a lot of people could agree on."[4] Pre-kindergarten was also common ground in South Carolina, where researchers conducted thousands of hours of interviews with educators, parents, students, and business leaders to garner their opinions about what should be done to improve K–12 education. Making high-quality early education available in all schools was one of three steps that all these stakeholders thought most important to pursue.[5] For the members of the New Commission on the Skills of the American Workforce, in restructuring American education, it was "patently obvious to everybody that early childhood education was the best investment that could be made." They recommended using the money saved by eliminating the last two years of high school to provide all four-year-olds (as well as low-income three-year-olds) with high-quality, full-day pre-kindergarten.[6]

Preschool is of particular interest to reformers concerned about the achievement gap between poor and affluent children. Discussing his 2005 book on educational inequality, Jonathan Kozol called expanding preschool the "easy" part of delivering equal education to every child in America. Kozol would "immediately create universal, full-day, richly developmental preschool, starting at the age of two and a half, for every low-income kid in America. This nation can easily afford to do that. You could probably do that with the money spent in a few months of the Iraqi war." In his 2004 book *Class and Schools*, Richard Rothstein argued that the educational achievement gap would not disappear without intervention into poverty. He recommended language-rich early childhood programs for disadvantaged children starting at the age of six months, as well as full-day, year-round preschool for three- and four-year-olds.[7]

Awareness of the promise of preschool goes beyond education reform circles. A 2007 *New York Times* article about how the $1.2 trillion spent on the Iraq war could have been spent differently featured universal preschool for three- and four-year-olds as one desirable social policy that might have been pursued (along with implementing national security recommendations, reconstructing New Orleans, doubling cancer research, and funding a global immunization campaign).[8] The *Wall Street Journal* also called attention to pre-kindergarten, noting in a front-page article in 2007 that it represented a historic expansion of public education, driven by politicians looking for "relatively inexpensive ways to tackle the growing rich-poor gap in the U.S."[9]

For some, pre-kindergarten even seemed to hold the promise of restoring Americans' faith in government. David Kirp wrote in 2007 that pre-kindergarten was an example of "kids-first politics," showing that politicians could gain support across the ideological spectrum by addressing the needs of children. He pointed out that in a time of skepticism about the effectiveness of public programs, pre-kindergarten is "a rare example of an expanding public square." Similarly, *Washington Post* columnist E. J. Dionne observed in 2006 that Rob Reiner's advocacy of universal preschool in California could make the broader point that government programs can be effective: "He thinks that California, which started the tax revolt in the late 1970s, could inaugurate a new era of public investment in things that matter."[10] As the Obama administration seeks to restore the public's faith in government—asking (as Obama put it in his Inaugural Address) "not whether our government is too big or too small, but whether it works"—preschool's record of effectiveness will also draw attention.

This growing consensus around preschool should not mask the fact that today's preschool movement is not monolithic: it includes different opinions about how public money for preschool should be spent, who should be responsible for preschool, how to ensure its quality, and what to expect of teachers, children, and parents. These questions—rooted in understandings of the past as well as visions of the future—need to be fully debated as the nation moves toward building a stronger system of preschool education.

Indeed, as more people climb on the pre-kindergarten bandwagon and as we anticipate a renewed federal interest in early childhood programs, it is important to understand what legacies we have inherited from the past, and what lessons we might learn from it. This book has traced the emergence of preschool as a question of public policy, from the creation of Head Start in 1965 through efforts to craft a child care system in the 1970s and 1980s, and the recent campaign to expand public pre-kindergarten programs. We have seen that visions of the promise of preschool in each time period were shaped by available knowledge, a sense of what was politically possible, and an understanding of what had gone before. The legacies of policy decisions made in the 1960s and 1970s—notably the creation of Head Start for poor children and the failure of universal child care legislation—shaped the terrain that advocates and policymakers faced in the 1980s and 1990s. Dissatisfied with the path that policy had taken, children's advocates tried to shift course, using their under-standing of history's "lessons" to devise strategies that would work in a new context shaped by concern about K–12 education reform, debate about gov-ernment's responsibility for families, and knowledge about the promise of pre-school. These strategies, in turn, shaped the way they approached preschool and the promises they made for it. Yet the lessons that advocates have learned—that preschool should be framed in terms of education, provided to all chil-dren, and attached to K–12 education—are not the only lessons to be learned from the history of public policy for young children. Our close examination of this history in this book suggests more nuanced lessons as well.

Lesson 1: Frame preschool in terms of education, not in terms of child care, but be aware that separating the two issues completely is counterproductive.

Frustrated with a lack of progress on securing support for quality child care, some advocates in the 1980s and 1990s sought to "climb into the education tent," making preschool part of public education. A movement for K–12 educa-tion reform drew attention to the promise of quality preschool for improving children's success in school, and provided an opportunity to expand educa-tional programs for young children. At the same time, debates over federal child care legislation in the late 1980s showed the difficulties of regulating child care, which was seen as a private family need best addressed by the diverse mar-ket of providers.

Advocates deliberately sought to reframe the issue away from care and toward education, which typically was at the top of a list of voters' concerns. When the Committee for Economic Development consulted experts in the early childhood field, one of the strongest conclusions that emerged across the board was "the pragmatic belief that a lot of constituencies were sort of recep-tive to, and ready to move on education issues, framed as education issues, and that there was not the same consensus yet around things called child care."[11] The Benton Foundation, based in Washington, D.C., urged advocates to shift from focusing on child care as custodial "child storage" to a framework that highlighted young children's education, emphasizing the fact that the early years of life are a time of intense learning. "Don't refer to 'day care,'" they coun-seled. "Do refer to 'early education.'"[12]

This lesson shaped the pre-kindergarten advocacy efforts supported by Pew and others in the past decade. Casting preschool in terms of education shaped the language that proponents used, the alliances they built, and the quality standards they set for programs. In promoting the educational promise of pre-school, advocates were quick to distinguish the programs they were promoting from child care, stressing the importance of trained teachers and academic skills and insisting that preschool was not "just babysitting." Indeed, some deliberately chose the name "pre-kindergarten" to differentiate their programs from more general "early childhood" or "child care" programs. Pre-K Now explained on its website that "Pre-K" is a better term than "preschool" because it "is more readily associated with the K–12 system" and clearly denotes an educational program that will help children succeed in later schooling.[13]

Today's advocates have recognized the importance of framing preschool in terms of education in order to garner support for expanding these programs. But this choice may also have consequences to which we should pay attention. For instance, boosting preschool by saying that it is not "just babysitting" reinforces the idea that the work of caring for children is unimportant and unskilled, strengthening false barriers between "education" and "care." Children need both care and education to thrive, and families need good child care as well as education for their children. Advocates must be careful that in making the case for preschool, they do not denigrate the very child care providers they need in order to deliver pre-kindergarten successfully. In order to make pre-kindergarten work for most families, states need a strong network of child care providers who can combine pre-kindergarten (typically offered only for a few hours a day) with child care services. Meanwhile, within pre-kindergarten classrooms themselves, teachers must find the right balance between emphasizing "education" and "care"; many worry that a preschool concerned only with "education" will not meet all the needs of young children.

The movement for universal pre-kindergarten represents a strategic decision to focus on education for four-year-olds (and sometimes three-year-olds) rather than pushing to improve child care in general. This is not because the needs of younger children are less striking—in fact most studies show that child care for infants and toddlers is scarcer and of lower quality than that offered for preschoolers—but because the cause of preschool education seems more winnable. Lois Salisbury of the Packard Foundation explained: "Preschool is a strategic choice, informed by twenty years of doing it the other way"—that is, trying to improve child care in general. "To improve kids' opportunities you need to start with four-year-olds, and work down, rather than diluting the effort and being unsuccessful, as we've always been."[14] Pre-kindergarten, former CDF lobbyist Helen Blank noted, was an easier issue to "sell" to the public, because it was easier to understand and to organize than child care.

> You can put pre-K in a box, you tie it up, and you put the bow on it. Child care is birth to thirteen. It's pretty messy. It's neighbors...it's people working off hours...it's everything. With pre-K you can really feel good. You get the four-year-olds, they're in their classes, and you did it—education. They're all going to grow up successful.[15]

When Pew was gathering information in advance of its decision to make pre-kindergarten a major priority, some children's advocates said it was a mistake to split off a campaign for preschool from the needs of younger children. Since preschool is only one of many things that young children need, they argued, making it the centerpiece of advocacy for children risked ignoring other crucial issues. But as Susan Urahn at Pew explained, preschool was the "piece of this agenda that we can move forward on." An Arkansas legislator, responding to a 2006 essay in *Education Week* that argued that the needs of infants and toddlers needed to be taken as seriously as those of preschoolers, stressed "the strategic political value of starting where we can win." In Arkansas, a statewide campaign for pre-kindergarten "grabbed the interest of people across the state in a way that a broader agenda never could have." Recognizing that pre-kindergarten did not solve the whole problem, he wrote that it was nevertheless "a bigger win than we've seen in a long time in the children's arena."[16]

Organizations concerned with the needs of infants and toddlers fear that the considerable attention paid to expanding and implementing pre-kindergarten may take focus away from programs for younger children. New resources for pre-kindergarten may also end up drawing the most qualified teachers away from infant/toddler programs. This would ultimately be damaging to the cause of school readiness, given the importance of children's early development. In 2003, the Ounce of Prevention Fund declared that to ensure "long-term, far-reaching outcomes, especially for those children most at-risk of school failure," programs for infants and toddlers should be given equal weight with programs for preschoolers.[17]

A campaign for universal preschool *can* help draw attention to the needs of younger children, if it is carefully structured with this goal in mind. In Illinois, advocates and policymakers have been particularly conscious of the need to strengthen all early childhood programs. When pushing for early childhood funding in the mid-1990s, key organizations such as the Ounce of Prevention Fund and Voices for Illinois Children supported setting aside a percentage of funding (first 8, then 11 percent) to programs for infants and toddlers. The rapid increase in funding for child care and pre-kindergarten since 1997 thus led to funding increases from $3 million to $20 million for infants and toddlers. One pre-kindergarten advocate said: "The pre-kindergarten community actu-ally supports this set-aside. Pre-kindergarten teachers understand the link and know that they need the birth-to-three programs to help children get ready for school." In New York, the early childhood organizations that came together to implement UPK were also inspired to look at the early childhood landscape as a whole and spent several years developing a blueprint for an expanded early childhood system in the state.[18]

Lesson 2: Aim for "preschool for all," not just for the disadvantaged, but recognize that universal programs do not lead automatically to greater political support.

Concluding from Head Start's history that programs for America's most disadvantaged children would inevitably fail to secure adequate political support, advocates shifted course to push for "preschool for all." For instance, Graciela Italiano-Thomas, who spent ten years working in Head Start before directing Los Angeles' universal preschool effort, commented in 2006: "When you only aim at those in greatest need, history tells us that the programs lose the political support they need to survive, and therefore those in greatest need don't benefit."[19] Susan Urahn of the Pew Charitable Trusts and Head Start champion Ed Zigler gave similar explanations, pointing to Head Start's failure to secure adequate political support over the years. Inspired by the success of Georgia's universal pre-kindergarten program and informed by scholars who argued that universal social programs (like Social Security and public education) ultimately build a stronger base of support than do those targeted to the poor, advocates decided instead to push for universal preschool. In addition to securing broader political support, advocates also believed that universal programs with a middle-class clientele would ultimately produce higher quality than programs aimed only at the poor. They picked up a discussion that had been going on since the 1960s about who needed preschool, and whether it was more effective to aim at serving all children, like the public schools, or to restrict public funds to the poorest children. The potential for building cross-class alliances around preschool intrigued politicians and advocates looking for ways to garner support for young children. Providing "preschool for all" could benefit families across the socioeconomic spectrum and was attractive to politicians across the ideological spectrum.

But, as we saw in chapter 6, the idea that a universal approach would be more politically popular and result in higher quality programs was not a useful guide in the short term. Attempts to enact universal pre-kindergarten in California and several other states ran into opposition precisely because the idea of providing "preschool for all" seemed a questionable use of public dollars and was not as clearly justified by research evidence as were programs restricted to the poor. Nor were the universal programs that states enacted necessarily of higher quality, as advocates had hoped. Preschool advocates themselves were divided on the question of whether new funds for preschool should be targeted to the poor—or provided to all. Looking more closely at the historical arguments for universal social programs, we saw that building public support is by no means an automatic process but one that can take years and that depends on the way a program is perceived and structured as much as on whom it benefits.

In each state, preschool advocates have had to weigh the question of whether to aim for a universal program or take a more incremental approach to expanding publicly funded preschool. A structure such as that proposed by economist Greg Duncan and his colleagues in 2007, which would provide an intensive, two-year preschool program with sliding scale fees (offered without charge to poor families and with a varied amount of subsidy for others), is one answer.[20] While decisions about what to push for in the short term vary, the idea that universal pre-kindergarten should be the ultimate goal has firmly taken root in many states, and will shape future efforts. There are good reasons to pursue a universal approach, but advocates and policymakers should weigh these thoughtfully, rather than taking it as a historical given that universal programs will automatically prosper more than targeted ones.

Lesson 3: Research on preschool's long-term effects can build strong support for expanding public pre-kindergarten. Yet the case for preschool should not rest solely on research on experimental preschool programs, which may raise unrealistic expectations for large-scale public programs.

From the creation of Head Start in 1965 to today's push for expanding pre-kindergarten, research has played an unusually strong role in shaping early childhood policy. Perhaps because providing educational programs for preschoolers is not a traditional function of government, research about preschool's effectiveness has helped to establish the legitimacy of public spending in this area. Conversely, research that cast doubt on preschool's long-term impact could be used to curtail programs for young children. Research studies in the early 1960s established the promise of preschool, inspiring the creation of Head Start. When the 1969 Westinghouse study cast doubt on Head Start's long-term impact on IQ and school achievement, the program suffered. But in the late 1970s and early 1980s, the CLS's finding that model preschool programs affected important long-term factors like grade retention and dropout rates helped create a new wave of public preschool programs. The cost-benefit analysis of the Perry Preschool project in particular was so widely reported that it has become part of common knowledge about the benefits of early education. In the 1990s, neuroscience research on brain development drew unprecedented public attention to young children, and advocates built on this interest to push for expanding early childhood programs. Longitudinal studies of programs like the Abecedarian Project and the Chicago Child-Parent Centers also helped build the case that high-quality preschool could produce significant benefits for poor children in the long run. This body of research helped convince courts in New Jersey's *Abbott* case and elsewhere that high-quality preschool is so essential for low-income children that it is part of a constitutionally guaranteed public education. This research also inspired economists and business leaders as well as educators and policymakers to argue that expanding high-quality preschool was not only a good thing to do for children but a crucial investment in society's future economic development.

Preschool advocates have clearly learned lessons about how positive research findings can be mobilized to call attention to the promise of preschool, gaining support from business leaders, educators, and policymakers who might not otherwise be receptive to increasing public spending on children. However, the history of Head Start should lead us to be careful about the research-based promises we make. There are limits to building a case for preschool based on research on the long-term effects of model programs. Neither Head Start nor most publicly funded programs approximate the level of resources and intensive planning that went into these model programs. If the entire case for preschool rests on research findings that are found not to be replicable in large-scale public programs, public support may evaporate. Furthermore, while long-term cost-benefit analyses of programs like Perry Preschool have generated enormous publicity for the preschool cause, they can also raise unrealistic expectations. The authors of the National Research Council's report *From Neurons to Neighborhoods* cautioned in 2000 that measuring impacts through the adult years is a "complex and highly speculative venture" that may be unreliable and may also end up downplaying the short-term value of intervention. It would be more useful, they concluded, to devise "the standard of proof that must be met in order to endorse a program as effective," based on immediate and short-term benefits.[21]

One effect of relying on these research findings has been to emphasize preschool's long-term benefits to society rather than its intrinsic value, or even its short-term benefits to children. Edith Grotberg, who commissioned the CLS study in the early 1970s, noted later that unlike preschool, "no other program in the history of education, health, or welfare had ever been required before to justify its existence by long-term benefits."[22] Edward Zigler and Sally Styfco wrote in 1993 that the findings of Head Start's short-term effects "are so plentiful and strong that it is perplexing" why social scientists got caught up in looking for long-term effects. Psychologist Craig Ramey contends that the political pressure to produce hard evidence on "something everyone thought was a good idea" pushed early intervention research "prematurely into looking at long-term consequences."[23] Economist Janet Currie argued that the short- and medium-term benefits of Head Start could pay back much of the program's cost, even without trying to estimate long-term benefits. While there was not enough evidence to conclusively identify an optimal age for intervention, she wrote, "we should be wary of claims that a short intervention delivered at any particular age is a 'magic bullet' that can greatly reduce the effects of a lifetime of deprivation."[24] In a 2003 article entitled "Do You Believe in Magic?" psychologist Jeanne Brooks-Gunn argued that it was unrealistic to expect the benefits of short-term early interventions to last indefinitely, especially given the difficult school and neighborhood environments that shaped poor children's development. "If the sum of the largest effects in the educational literature is not large enough," Brooks-Gunn wrote, "what do we want?"[25] Scholars and policymakers need to consider what kinds of benefits can reasonably be expected from early education programs, and how to define a program's social value. This is a question that should be informed by research but really requires public debate about priorities.

Lesson 4: Preschool needs to be part of a larger system, rather than standing alone. But as we attach pre-kindergarten to the system of public education, we can build on the existing patchwork of public and private child care, Head Start, and preschool providers.

Another lesson preschool advocates have learned from Head Start is that it matters how public programs are funded and organized. When Head Start was created, it was part of a new commitment from the federal government to fight poverty and promote equal educational opportunity for all children. When that context changed, however, Head Start was subject to the winds of political change in Washington, as a federal program that required yearly appropriations and regular reauthorizations. Furthermore, Head Start often stood alone, as its creators had intentionally kept it autonomous from the public schools, which were often seen as hostile to minority and poor children and parents. In the long run, this meant that rather than relying on the existing infrastructure of local school districts and state departments of education, Head Start developed its own separate systems for administering programs, creating quality standards, and providing monitoring and technical assistance. Head Start maintained its autonomy as a federal program, and never—for good or for ill—became fully integrated with the public education system. Its location outside the structure of the public schools allowed great creativity and flexibility in addressing the needs of poor children and their families, in spurring organizing in poor communities, and in employing poor parents but also made it vulnerable politically and isolated it from the schools for which it was supposed to be preparing children.

The current campaign for pre-kindergarten takes the opposite approach, aiming to make preschool part of the existing K–12 education system. By linking preschool to public education, reformers hoped to benefit from the K–12 system's infrastructure, relatively stable funding, and professional standards and compensation for teachers. The state pre-kindergarten programs that have grown during the past twenty years are almost all administered by state departments of education and school districts and connected more tightly to public schools than is Head Start. Foundation director Ruby Takanishi, who was involved with Head Start from the beginning of her career in child development, now advocates preschool as part of a public education system beginning at age three. While she recognized that "hitching our wagon to the public education system, with all of its inequities and flaws" carried some risks, she also believed that an effective system of early childhood education had to be connected to a broader system: "if you don't hitch your wagon to that, what are you going to hitch it to? There's nothing to hitch to."[26]

State programs reflect this desire to "hitch to" the public education system. In Oklahoma, pre-kindergarten is treated as part of public education: it is funded through the state aid formula, administered by school districts (although classes may also be located in community settings), and taught by certified teachers who are paid at the same rate as teachers in other grades. We saw in Chapter 4 that over time, Oklahoma essentially added pre-kindergarten as a grade to its public education system—albeit one that remains optional for both families and districts. New York's UPK program, launched in 1997, also reflects a desire to integrate preschool into public education. Local school districts administer the programs, which were designed to ensure that all children would be "ready" for school on kindergarten entry. The standards set for teachers and curriculum were similar to those for K–12 education, as the measure sought to raise the educational level of preschool to match that of the regular schools. The program was to be universal like public education, not restricted to the poor. When Governor Pataki proposed eliminating the program as part of a package of drastic budget cuts in education in 2003, advocates found that fighting for the program's life helped intensify its connection to the public schools. Indeed, the program's fortunes have risen and fallen with those of K–12 education in the state more generally. Advocates successfully argued—as had plaintiffs in New Jersey's *Abbott* case—that quality preschool was an important part of a constitutionally guaranteed public education, and sought to include pre-kindergarten in the school funding formula.

Even as they sought to attach preschool to the system of public K–12 education, however, some state policymakers also realized that organizations and providers outside the schools could play a significant role in delivering pre-kindergarten. One of the important legacies of earlier policy decisions was that preschool programs—whether in publicly funded Head Start or private-market child care—grew outside the domain of the public schools, taking root instead in community agencies and for-profit centers. While Head Start was designed to bypass the public schools, child care was largely left to the private market, following failure of efforts to create a public system through federal legislation in the early 1970s. As the demand for child care and preschool education exploded in the 1970s and 1980s, it was met by a complex array of providers: nonprofit agencies, churches, for-profit centers, private schools, and family child care homes. This patchwork of provision for children was uneven in quality and coverage, but providers grew into a constituency to be reckoned with when questions about public funding for young children moved onto federal and state agendas. Furthermore, the role of the private market came to seem natural, reinforcing itself over time. Disagreement over who should control preschool programs divided advocates during the 1970s and 1980s, undermining efforts to pass child care legislation and to expand public funding for preschool. Rather than continuing to struggle over whether schools or other providers would control funds for preschool, in recent years leaders in some states decided to combine the two in their pre-kindergarten programs, allowing community-based and private providers to deliver pre-kindergarten paid for with public funds. Even as preschool becomes a part of public education, then, its history means that it will be delivered in a much more varied range of public and private settings than is K–12 education.

Lesson 5: Pay attention to preserving the traditional strengths of early childhood education as preschool becomes more integrated into K–12 schooling.

Wherever preschool is delivered, it is worth focusing on how to preserve some of the traditional strengths of early childhood education programs, especially its child-centered curricula and family-friendly atmosphere. History offers the parallel of the creation of public school kindergartens about a century ago. Like preschool, nineteenth-century kindergartens were initially sponsored by agencies and individuals outside the public schools, and had a variety of aims, including reforming and assisting poor families as well as preparing children for school through a child-centered, hands-on approach. Historian Larry Cuban writes: "The appeal of the kindergarten with its focus on learning through doing, learning from and with others, and learning through play" and through songs, art, and group work "drew together educators and reformers who wanted to find a permanent home for this promising new approach in the public schools." When kindergartens became part of urban school systems in the 1900s and 1910s, however, the emphasis on home visiting and outreach to families diminished, as kindergarten teachers were required to teach double sessions and to focus more on preparing children for first grade.[27] Public school kindergarten teachers were often supervised by their male school principals rather than by female kindergarten directors with a background in teaching young children, and teachers' own training shifted to resemble what elementary teachers received. Worksheets and "reading readiness" assignments became more prevalent, reducing the amount of time available for play and raising the fear that kindergarten would become "the new first grade." But even as kindergarten became more like first or second grade in some respects, teachers preserved elements of its child-centered approach, blending free play and creative activities with teacher-directed activities such as letter, shape, and number recognition and seasonal theme-based units. The kindergarten's approach also influenced the lower elementary grades, where teachers borrowed its emphasis on using art, song, manipulative materials, and learning through doing.[28]

The history of the kindergarten's incorporation into the schools in the early decades of the twentieth century has long been a cautionary tale for early childhood educators, who feared that preschool would lose its developmental focus and creativity if it were to follow the same path. Certainly, the increasingly academic emphasis of kindergarten in recent years gives cause for concern about how preschool, once "hitched" to the public school wagon, can retain its holistic and developmental approach, as well as its tradition of close relationships with parents. Keeping this question in mind, advocates and policymakers should give special attention to structuring pre-kindergarten in ways that help to preserve a developmentally sound approach. One answer may be to create schools or units that focus on preschool and early elementary grades (as in the "PK–3" approach advocated by the Foundation for Child Development), headed by a principal with early childhood experience. Another is to build well-designed collaborations between schools and other early childhood providers in a mixed delivery system, preserving the traditional strengths of diverse early childhood programs while expanding them to serve more children. As we saw in chapter 7, however, these mixed delivery systems often need significant bolstering in order to "lift all boats" and ensure quality.

PROMISES WE CAN KEEP

One of the problematic legacies of the past is a tendency to make inflated promises for what preschool will accomplish. This is part of a broader American tendency, shared by liberals and conservatives alike, to see education as "an almost magical mechanism for equalizing opportunities between individuals."[29] Edward Zigler has written extensively about the problems that inflated promises for Head Start caused in the 1970s and 1980s, and the mistaken tendency to see it as an inoculation against the social ills of poverty. (For instance, he noted with concern Governor Neil Goldschmidt of Oregon's 1990 claim that expanding Head Start would be "the most significant—and most effective— anti-drug, anti-crime, pro-education strategy" in America.)[30] Yet today, some preschool advocates seem to be repeating this pattern, presenting pre-kindergarten as a vaccine against a range of social ills. For instance, California's state superintendent of education talked about how the research findings on preschool motivated her to try to build a universal preschool system in 1998. "It's like finding out there's an effective polio vaccine. Once you've seen the research, the evidence of what preschool can do for children, it becomes almost obscene not to call for universal preschool." Similarly, decrying budget cuts to Texas's pre-kindergarten program in 2007, a San Antonio newspaper columnist wrote: "Pre-K programs are intellectual vaccinations against the ills of illiteracy, ignorance, apathy, substance abuse and gangs." In 2006, California advocate Rob Reiner declared "preschool is the answer" to the educational problems the state faced, including 50 percent of fourth-graders not reading and a higher than 50 percent dropout rate.[31]

In reality, preschool is only one part of the answer to the serious problems of poverty and the challenges of educating all children. In presenting its prekindergarten initiative to the state legislature in 2006, staff from the Tennessee Department of Education stressed the idea that quality preschool was only one component of a good education: "In the same way we would not expect one year of exercise to maintain a lifetime of physical fitness, one year of quality instruction cannot be held responsible for producing lifelong academic gains."[32] This common-sense perspective has often eluded advocates and policymakers who want to gain attention and support for preschool programs. High-quality preschool can make a difference in school readiness, reducing the gap among children from different backgrounds while also improving the educational value of the settings where most young children spend at least part of their preschool years. Achieving the kind of quality that can make a significant difference for children educationally, however, is a complex task, requiring careful attention to teacher training, appropriate curricula, and ongoing mentoring, as well as to meaningful parental involvement and engagement. Achieving this level of quality also requires significant investment, beyond that which most states have made in their pre-kindergarten programs to date.

Pre-kindergarten is also only one piece of what is needed to ensure that children start school "ready to learn." Children's needs start at birth and include health care, nutrition, and strong family relationships as well as quality care and education. Although pre-kindergarten promises to have a significant impact on its own, its potential is even greater when it is linked to other supports to young children and their families. Rather than focus on pre-kindergarten as a single solution, communication strategist Susan Bales of the Frameworks Institute believes in laying the groundwork for a range of supportive policies by educating the public about how young children grow and develop.[33] Harvard's

Center for the Developing Child, established in 2006, has taken up this approach as it draws on neuroscience, public health, and economic research about children, aiming to close the gap between "what we know and what we do." The center's summary of policy recommendations proclaims: "Young children need positive relationships, rich learning opportunities, and safe environments, not quick fixes or magic bullets." Rather than focusing on a single service like preschool, this statement stresses the range of public policies that need to be put in place in order to ensure children's healthy development: prenatal and health care, regulation of environmental hazards, parental leave, and early intervention for children in need, as well as high-quality child care and preschool.[34] Most preschool advocates would be the first to agree with the idea that preschool is just one of the things that children need but believe that a strategically focused campaign is more effective than a general approach to children's needs. For instance, David Kirp writes that the movement for pre-kindergarten could be a first step toward a new "kids-first" politics, and he salutes activists for "building the house of children's entitlements, brick by brick."[35]

It matters a great deal, then, whether preschool is seen as a stand-alone solution to educational and social problems or as the first step toward changing the systems that help to shape children's lives. Preschool is situated at the juncture of K–12 schooling and child care. To fulfill preschool's promise, we need not only to make sure it is of the highest quality but also to make it part of reforming both early elementary education and child care.

On the one hand, pre-kindergarten can become part of restructured elementary schools that focus intensively on the first years of schooling in a developmentally appropriate manner, with learning goals aligned across these years and resources focused on giving children a strong start over a period of years. Separating out these years of early schooling from the upper elementary grades may help to retain a focus on young children's development, especially if school leaders have a background in early childhood education. By ensuring that children have access not only to pre-kindergarten but also to high-quality kindergarten and early elementary grades, this approach looks at the continuum of learning experiences that build up to competence during these years rather than simply adding a year of preschool to the existing arrangement. This "PK-3" approach has the promise of pre-kindergarten's benefits being sustained across early elementary grades rather than dissipating when children enter low-resource elementary schools, although this promise has yet to be proven. Creating an effective PK-3 structure, of course, is not easy; the experience of New Jersey *Abbott* districts that tried to build strong connections between preschool and early elementary grades shows the difficulty of the task.[36] The more school leaders see pre-kindergarten (wherever it is located) as the beginning of public education, the greater are the chances of achieving an integrated approach to early learning. For instance, in 2006, a superintendent in the Bronx pointed to pre-kindergarten student work on one wall and high school work on the other, saying, "What you are looking at is the new continuum of public education. It starts with pre-K and continues right on through to 12th grade."[37]

On the other hand, preschool is also part of a world of early care and education for infants, toddlers, and preschoolers that has evolved historically outside public schools. We have seen that some advocates focused on preschool as a means of improving the quality of child care and that some states have used high standards for pre-kindergarten to help "lift all boats" in the early childhood sea. By using community sites that meet quality standards to deliver pre-kindergarten and by making available resources such as teacher training to a wide range of community sites, these states try to improve the existing supply of child care even as they make use of it. Indeed, if pre-kindergarten is to serve a large number of children, partnerships with child care and Head Start providers will continue to be essential. This means that policymakers need to consider strengthening Head Start and child care programs in order to make them viable partners for delivering pre-kindergarten. In order to do this, they will need to conceive of different early education programs as parts of a whole rather than as separate items vying for the same scarce legislative dollars.

In addition to creating new pre-kindergarten programs, we also need to continue efforts to strengthen and improve child care as a whole. Part-day programs for four-year-olds only help families meet some of their child care needs and do not work at all for the significant proportion of parents who work during nonstandard hours, so we continue to need a broader approach to addressing child care. In several European countries, preschool systems are part of a wider commitment to help parents combine work and child-rearing, through parental leave policies, care for younger children, and flexible work hours. Preschool activists in the United States should remain connected with those who are pushing for such policies, ensuring that preschool remains part of efforts to support parents in both educating and caring for their children.

Preschool now plays a much larger role in the lives of families, and in our national debates about education and social policy, than it did when Head Start first drew national attention to the promise of preschool nearly forty-five years ago. The idea that "history tells us" what course to pursue in the present is simplistic; people may draw different legitimate conclusions from the same history and may disagree about how to adapt those lessons to the context in which they find themselves. History can, however, help us to know what questions to ask about current policy choices and to see the potential implications of the strategies that are shaping the current movement for universal pre-kindergarten. The developments traced in this book have left historical legacies that shape the terrain wherein we now approach questions about preschool. Understanding these legacies can help us to navigate that terrain, and to move through it with careful attention to the key questions that confront us: What should we expect from preschool? How do we build public support for spending on children? Whom should public programs serve? Who should control these programs? How should preschool be connected to the subsequent years of education? While history cannot dictate our answers to these questions, it can help us to understand what is at stake in devising thoughtful answers.

Appendix A Preschool Participation by Maternal Employment, 1967–2005
Source: Reprinted with permission from the National Institute for Early Education Research, Rutgers University, New Brunswick, NJ.

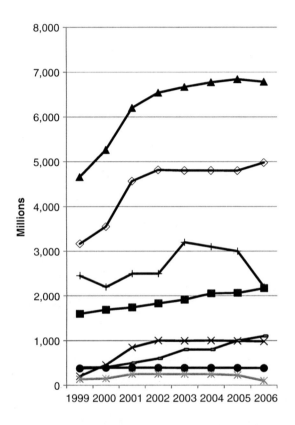

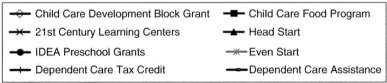

Appendix B Federal Spending on Selected Programs for Young Children, 1999–2006
Source: Melinda Gish, "Child Care Issues in the 108th Congress," CRS Report for Congress, updated April 10, 2003, www.law.maryland.edu/marsall/crsreports/crsdocuments/RL31817_04102003.pdf (accessed March 11, 2009); Melinda Gish and Gail McCallion, "Early Childhood Care and Education Programs in the 110th Congress: Background and Funding" (Congressional Research Service, 2007), http://assets.opencrs.com/rpts/RL33805_20070117.pdf (accessed March 11, 2009).

NOTES

Introduction

1. Valerie Polakow, *Who Cares for Our Children? The Child Care Crisis in the Other America* (New York: Teachers College Press, 2007), 72–77.

2. Ajay Chaudry, *Putting Children First: How Low-wage Working Mothers Manage Child Care* (New York: Russell Sage Foundation, 2004), 59, 174.

3. Chaudry, *Putting Children First,* 121.

4. Dana Hull, "Many Kids Priced out of Preschool," *San Jose Mercury News* (March 8, 2006).

5. "Why Jack Grubman Was So Keen to Get His Kids into the Y," *Wall Street Journal* (November 15, 2002), A1; "Private Preschool Admissions," *New York Times* (November 16, 2002), B1.

6. W. Steven Barnett and Donald Yarosz, "Who Goes to Preschool and Why Does It Matter?" *NIEER Preschool Policy Matters,* no. 8 (August 2004), http://nieer.org (accessed January 11, 2005). Figures are based on the Current Population Survey, which asks parents if their children are enrolled in "school." Figures for the percentage of children cared for by someone other than their parents are higher.

7. Janet Gornick and Marcia Meyers, *Families That Work: Policies for Reconciling Parenthood and Employment* (New York: Russell Sage Foundation, 2003), 203–4; Sonya Michel and Rianne Mahon, *Child Care Policy at the Crossroads: Gender and Welfare State Restructuring* (New York: Routledge, 2002).

8. Miriam Cohen, "Reconsidering Schools and the American Welfare State," *History of Education Quarterly* 45, no. 4 (2005): 512–15.

9. W. Steven Barnett et al., *The State of Preschool 2007: State Preschool Yearbook* (New Brunswick, N.J.: National Institute for Early Education Research, Rutgers University, 2007), 4.

10. Richard Neustadt and Ernest May, *Thinking in Time: The Uses of History for Decision-Makers* (New York: Free Press, 1988), 106.

11. Paul Pierson, *Politics in Time: History, Institutions, and Social Analysis* (Princeton, N.J.: Princeton University Press, 2004); Kathleen Thelen, "Historical Institutionalism in Comparative Politics," *American Review of Political Science* 2, no. 1 (1999): 369–404.

12. Kimberly Morgan, *Working Mothers and the Welfare State: Religion and the Politics of Work-family Policies in Western Europe and the United States* (Stanford, Calif.: Stanford University Press, 2006), argues that such policies "reproduce" themselves over time.

Chapter 1

1. "Edward P. Morgan and the News," radio address, March 13, 1967, printed in *Congressional Record* (90th Cong., 1st sess.), vol. 113, pt. 6 (March 20, 1967): 7186; "Remarks of Mrs. Lyndon B. Johnson" and "Excerpts from the Remarks of Sargent Shriver," in *Congressional Record* (90th Cong., 1st sess.), vol. 113, pt. 5 (March 14, 1967): 6645.

2. "Pancho Goes to the White House," *Head Start Newsletter* 2, no. 4 (April 1967): 1.

3. Elizabeth Rose, "Poverty and Parenting: Transforming Early Education's Legacy in the 1960s," *History of Education Quarterly* 49, no. 2 (May 2009): 222–34.

4. Quoted in Maris Vinovskis, *The Birth of Head Start: The Growth of Preschool Education in the Kennedy and Johnson Administrations* (Chicago: University of Chicago Press, 2005), 10.

5. Susan Gray, Barbara Ramsey, and Rupert Klaus, *From 3 to 20: The Early Training Project* (Baltimore: University Park Press, 1982); Leonard Buder, "Preschool Help Planned in Slums," *New York Times* (June 16, 1962), 1; Martin Deutsch, "Facilitating Development in the Pre-school Child: Social and Psychological Perspectives," *Merrill-Palmer Quarterly* 10, no. 3 (1964): 252–62; David Weikart, *How High/Scope Grew: A Memoir* (Ypsilanti, Mich.: High/Scope Educational Research Foundation, 2004), 49, 55.

6. Sargent Shriver, "Head Start, A Retrospective View: The Founders," in *Project Head Start: A Legacy of the War on Poverty*, ed. Edward Zigler and Jeanette Valentine (New York: Free Press, 1979), 52.

7. Vinovskis, *Birth of Head Start*, 42–52.

8. Shriver, "Head Start," 52.

9. Scott Stossel, *Sarge: The Life and Times of Sargent Shriver* (Washington, D.C.: Smithsonian Books, 2004), 418.

10. Urie Bronfenbrenner, "Head Start, A Retrospective View: The Founders," in Zigler and Valentine, *Project Head Start*, 82; Vinovskis, *Birth of Head Start*, 25.

11. Stossel, *Sarge*, 422.

12. Edward Zigler and Susan Muenchow, *Head Start: The Inside Story of America's Most Successful Educational Experiment* (New York: Basic Books, 1992), 24; "Mrs. Johnson Urges Help for Children," *New York Times* (February 20, 1965), 11; "'Project Head Start' Due in Summer," *Charleston Gazette* (February 23, 1965), 7.

13. Sargent Shriver quoted in Michael Gillette, *Launching the War on Poverty: An Oral History* (New York: Twayne, 1996), 223; Zigler and Muenchow, *Head Start*, 34, 40.

14. Shriver, "Head Start," 56.

15. Polly Greenberg, *The Devil Has Slippery Shoes: A Biased Biography of the Child Development Group of Mississippi* (London: Macmillan, 1969), 40.

16. David Weikart, "Head Start and Evidence-based Educational Models," in *The Head Start Debates*, ed. Edward Zigler and Sally Styfco (Baltimore: Paul Brookes, 2004), 144.

17. Vinovskis, *Birth of Head Start*, 33.

18. Quoted in Zigler and Muenchow, *Head Start*, 44.

19. Sargent Shriver to Jack Valenti, May 6, 1965; Jack Valenti to Lyndon Johnson, April 30, 1965, in *The War on Poverty, 1964–1968*, pt. 1, *The White House Central Files* (Frederick, Md.: University Publications of America, 1986), microfilm reel 7, frame 356.

20. Lyndon B. Johnson, "Remarks on Project Head Start, May 18, 1965," in Zigler and Valentine, *Project Head Start*, 67–69; "Suggested Remarks of the President at Announcement of 2,000 Head Start Centers on May__1965," in *War on Poverty, 1964–1968*, reel 7, frame 348.

21. "Recommendations for Head Start Program by a Panel of Experts," quoted in Rebecca Schrag, Sally Styfco, and Edward Zigler, "Familiar Concept, New Name: Social Competence/ School Readiness as the Goal of Head Start," in Zigler and Styfco, *Head Start Debates*, 20.

22. Polly Greenberg, "The Origins of Head Start and the Two Versions of Parent Involvement," in *Critical Perspectives on Project Head Start*, ed. Jeanne Ellsworth and Lynda Ames (Albany: State University of New York Press, 1998), 50; Carolyn Harmon, "Was Head Start a Community Action Program? Another Look at an Old Debate," in Zigler and Styfco, *Head Start Debates*, 89.

23. "Head Start Policy Change," *Head Start Newsletter* 5, no. 5 (July 1970): 5.

24. Eveline Omwake, "Assessment of the Head Start Preschool Education Effort," in Zigler and Valentine, *Project Head Start*, 223.

25. James Hymes, "Head Start, A Retrospective View: The Founders," in Zigler and Valentine, *Project Head Start*, p. 97.

26. Shriver, "Head Start," 66, and Jule Sugarman, "Head Start," 115," 66, 115.

27. Zigler and Muenchow, *Head Start*, 174; Office of Child Development, *Project Head Start 1969–79: A Descriptive Report of Programs and Participants* (Washington, D.C.: U.S. Department of Health, and Welfare, 1972), 21.

28. U.S. Senate, Committee on Labor and Public Welfare, *Examination of the War on Poverty*, pt. 9 (Washington, D.C.: U.S. Government Printing Office, 1967), 2845.

29. Zigler and Muenchow, *Head Start*, 182.

30. Bill Crook to Bill Moyers, August 22, 1966, in *War on Poverty, 1964–1968*, reel 7, frame 304.

31. Jacqueline Wexler, "Head Start: A Retrospective View," in Zigler and Valentine, *Project Head Start*, 113, and Hymes, "Head Start: A Retrospective View," 97.

32. June Solnit Sale, "Implementation of a Head Start Preschool Education Program: Los Angeles, 1965–1967," in Zigler and Valentine, *Project Head Start*, 184–89.

33. Nedra Iliff, "What Is Head Start?" *Head Start Newsletter* 3, no. 7 (November 1968): 1–2.

34. "A Flying Adventure," *Head Start Newsletter* 3, no. 3 (June 1968): 2.

35. The TV spots are described in *Head Start Newsletter* 3, no. 4 (July 1968):7, and the poster is featured in *Head Start Newsletter* 4, no. 4 (June 1969).

36. Greenberg, *Devil Has Slippery Shoes*, 105.

37. Josh Kagan, "Empowerment and Education: Civil Rights, Expert Advocates, and Parent Politics in Head Start, 1965–1980," *Teachers College Record* 104, no. 3 (2002): 531; Greenberg, *Devil Has Slippery Shoes*, 63.

38. Christopher Jencks wrote in 1966 that CDGM was seen as the "residual legatee of 'the movement'" in Mississippi and was large enough to have a substantial impact. Jencks, "Accommodating Whites," *Nation* 154 (April 16, 1966): 20.

39. Shriver, "Head Start," 61–64.

40. "Group Acts to Aid Head Start Fund," *New York Times* (September 14, 1966), 39. The delegation included A. Philip Randolph, Kenneth Clark, Robert Coles, and others. The ad appeared in the *New York Times* (October 19, 1966), 35.

41. "Shriver Comes Across," *New Republic* 156 (January 7, 1967): 10.

42. Kirschner Associates, *A National Survey of the Impacts of Head Start Centers on Community Institutions* (Washington, D.C.: U.S. Department of Health, Education, and Welfare, 1970), 7, 9.

43. Jeanette Valentine and Evan Stark, "The Social Context of Parent Involvement in Head Start," in Zigler and Valentine, *Project Head Start*, 298.

44. "Parents Get to Work," *Head Start Newsletter* 2, no. 7 (July 1967).

45. *Head Start Newsletter* 1, no. 7 (November 1966): 6.

46. Kagan, "Empowerment and Education," 538.

47. Jack Gonzales, "Too Many Cooks?" *Head Start Newsletter* 2, no. 1 (January 1967): 1.

48. Project Head Start, *Head Start: Manual of Policies and Instructions* (Washington, D.C.: Office of Child Development, 1967), 11.

49. John Herbers, "Provocative Child Agency Head: Edward Frank Zigler," *New York Times* (June 27, 1970), 13; Richard Nixon, "Statement Announcing the Establishment of the Office of Child Development" (April 9, 1969), www.presidency.ucsb.edu/ws/index. php?pid=1991 (accessed February 13, 2009).

50. Richard Nixon, "Special Message to the Congress on the Nation's Antipoverty Programs" (February 19, 1969), www.presidency.ucsb.edu/ws/index.php?pid=2397&st =head+start&st1=, accessed December 18, 2007.

51. V. G. Cicirelli, *The Impact of Head Start: An Evaluation of the Effects of Head Start on Children's Cognitive and Affective Development,* report presented to the Office of Economic Opportunity by the Westinghouse Learning Corporation (Washington, D.C.: Clearinghouse for Federal Scientific and Technical Information, 1969); Zigler and Muenchow, *Head Start*, 68–70.

52. Zigler and Muenchow, *Head Start*, 61–63; Lois-ellin Datta, "The Impact of the Westinghouse/Ohio Evaluation on the Development of Project Head Start," in *The Evaluation of Social Programs*, ed. Clark Abt (Beverly Hills, Calif.: Sage, 1976), 133.

53. Zigler and Muenchow, *Head Start*, 51–53.

54. Edward Zigler and Karen Anderson, "An Idea Whose Time Had Come: The Intellectual and Political Climate of Head Start," in Zigler and Valentine, *Project Head Start*, 16.

55. Vinovskis, *Birth of Head Start*, 105.

56. Lois-ellin Datta, "Another Spring and Other Hopes: Some Findings from National Evaluations of Project Head Start," in Zigler and Valentine, *Project Head Start*, 405; Datta, "Impact of the Westinghouse/Ohio Evaluation," 160; James Coleman, *Equality of Educational Opportunity* (Washington, D.C.: U.S. Department of Health, Education, and Welfare, 1966).

57. Jeanne Ellsworth, "Inspiring Delusions: Reflections on Head Start's Enduring Popularity," in *Critical Perspectives on Project Head Start*, 329.

58. U.S. Senate Committee on Labor and Public Welfare, *Headstart Child Development Act: Hearings Before the Subcommittee on Employment, Manpower, and Poverty on S. 2060* (Washington: U.S. Government Printing Office, 1969), 357.

59. Zigler and Muenchow, *Head Start*, 75, 70; Datta, "Tale of Two Studies."

60. Jude Wanniski, "This Week in Washington: A Lagging Headstart," *Congressional Record* (91st Cong., 1st sess.), vol. 115, pt. 9 (May 12, 1969): 12180.

61. Datta, "Impact of the Westinghouse/Ohio Evaluation," 150; Zigler and Muenchow, *Head Start*, 92.

62. Zigler and Muenchow, *Head Start*, 150.

63. Carolyn Harmon and Edward Hanley, "Administrative Aspects of the Head Start Program," in Zigler and Valentine, *Project Head Start*, 390.

64. Zigler and Muenchow, *Head Start*, 111.

65. Elizabeth Cascio, "Schooling Attainment and the Introduction of Kindergartens in the South," unpublished paper in author's possession, Department of Economics, University of California, Berkeley, 2003; Larry Cuban, "Why Some Reforms Last: The Case of the Kindergarten," *American Journal of Education* 100, no. 2 (1992): 177; Kristen Dombkowski, "Will the Real Kindergarten Please Stand Up? Defining and Redefining the Twentieth-century U.S. Kindergarten," *History of Education* 30, no. 6 (2001): 535.

66. Jack Gonzales, "Person to Person," *Head Start Newsletter* 1, no. 7 (November 1966): 1.

67. "Irrational Backlash," *New York Times* (August 30, 1970), 136; M. A. Farber, "Now a Head Start for Everyone," *New York Times* (December 31, 1967).

68. These Title I kindergartens served a relatively small proportion of the nation's five-year-olds. Cascio, "Schooling Attainment," 10.

69. Laurel Tanner and Daniel Tanner, "Unanticipated Effects of Federal Policy: The Kindergarten," *Educational Leadership* 31, no. 1 (October 1973): 52.

70. Elizabeth Prescott, Cynthia Milich, and Elizabeth Jones, *"Politics" of Day Care* (Washington, D.C.: National Association for the Education of Young Children, 1972), 9; "Preschool Boom: Its Pressures and Rewards," *Newsweek* 67 (May 16, 1966), 109.

71. Educational Policies Commission, *Universal Opportunity for Early Childhood Education* (Washington, D.C.: National Education Association, 1966).

72. Gerald Grant, "Public Nursery Schools Are Urged by Educators," *Washington Post* (February 17, 1966), A2.

73. New York State Board of Regents, *Prekindergarten Education: A Statement of Policy and Proposed Action* (Albany: State Education Department, 1967), 10.

74. Gordon Ambach, telephone interview with author, March 4, 2004.

75. Quoted in Thomas Cook et al., *"Sesame Street" Revisited* (New York: Russell Sage Foundation, 1975), 30, 34.

76. Gerald Lesser, *Children and Television: Lessons from Sesame Street* (New York: Random House, 1974), 8, 13, 47.

77. Lesser, *Children and Television*, 208.

78. Lesser, *Children and Television*, 203–6.

79. Shalom Fisch and Rosemarie Truglio, eds., *"G" Is for Growing: Thirty Years of Research on Children and Sesame Street* (Mahwah, N.J.: Erlbaum, 2001), xvi.

80. Keith Mielke, "A Review of Research on the Educational and Social Impact of *Sesame Street*," in Fisch and Truglio, *"G" Is for Growing*, 87. The original studies are S. Ball and G. Bogatz, *The First Year of Sesame Street: An Evaluation* (Princeton, N.J.: Educational Testing Service, 1970); and G. Bogatz and S. Ball, *The Second Year of Sesame Street: A Continuing Evaluation* (Princeton, N.J.: Educational Testing Service, 1971).

81. Cook et al., *"Sesame Street" Revisited*, 37.

82. Andrew Malcolm, "'Sesame Street' Rated Excellent," *New York Times* (November 5, 1970), 55.

83. Zigler and Muenchow, *Head Start*, 165. The OCD contributed $300,000 to the Children's Television Workshop during fiscal years 1968–71. Cook et al., *"Sesame Street" Revisited*, 165.

84. Robert Fisher, "Project Slow Down: The Middle-Class Answer to Project Head Start," *School and Society* 98, no. 2327 (October 1970): 356–57.

85. Edward Zigler, Jeanette Valentine, and Deborah Stipek, "Project Head Start: A Critique of Theory and Practice," in Zigler and Valentine, *Project Head Start*, 479.

86. Susan Gray, Barbara Ramsey, and Rupert Klaus, *From 3 to 20: The Early Training Project* (Baltimore: University Park Press, 1982), 9.

Chapter 2

1. Kimberly Morgan, "A Child of the Sixties: The Great Society, the New Right, and the Politics of Federal Child Care," *Journal of Policy History* 13, no. 2 (2001): 215–50.

2. Elizabeth Rose, *A Mother's Job: The History of Day Care, 1890–1960* (New York: Oxford University Press, 1999), 168.

3. Rose, *Mother's Job*, 181–94; Emilie Stoltzfus, *Citizen, Mother, Worker: Debating Public Responsibility for Child Care After the Second World War* (Chapel Hill: University of North Carolina Press, 2003); Ellen Reese, "Maternalism and Political Mobilization: How California's Post-war Child Care Campaign Was Won," *Gender and Society* 10, no. 5 (October 1996): 556–89.

4. Elizabeth Prescott, Cynthia Milich, and Elizabeth Jones, *"Politics" of Day Care* (Washington, D.C.: National Association for the Education of Young Children, 1972), 44; Stoltzfus, *Citizen, Mother, Worker*, 199–215.

5. Sonya Michel, *Children's Interests/Mothers' Rights: The Shaping of America's Child Care Policy* (New Haven: Yale University Press, 1999), 205–34; Rose, *Mother's Job*, 199–212.

6. Stoltzfus, *Citizen, Mother, Worker,* 231–34. For instance, in New York, state education officials focused on using their pre-kindergarten funding in school-based child care programs, in order to attract these federal dollars. New York State Education Department, *Annual Report* 1971–72 (Albany: New York State Education Department, 1973), 6–7.

7. Michel, *Children's Interests/Mothers' Rights,* 245.

8. "Poll Supports Aid to Child Centers," *New York Times* (July 13, 1969), 32. Note that the wording of the question referred both to mothers "in poor areas" taking jobs and providing children with early education training; the question was: "Would you favor or oppose having the Federal Government provide funds to set up these centers in most communities?" This poll was cited by congressman John Brademas in introducing hearings on his 1970 bill, U.S. House Committee on Education and Labor, *Comprehensive Preschool Education and Child Day Care Act of 1969: Hearings Before the Select Subcommittee on Education on H.R. 13520,* 91st Cong., 1st and 2nd sess. (Washington, D.C.: U.S. Government Printing Office: 1970), 8.

9. Jill Quadagno, *The Color of Welfare: How Racism Undermined the War on Poverty* (New York: Oxford University Press: 1994), 149; Jo Freeman, *The Politics of Women's Liberation: A Case Study of an Emerging Social Movement and Its Relation to the Policy Process* (New York: David McKay, 1975), 202.

10. Michel, *Children's Interests/Mothers' Rights,* 242; Sally Cohen, *Championing Child Care* (New York: Columbia University Press, 2001), 27.

11. John Nelson, "The Politics of Federal Day Care Regulation," in *Day Care: Scientific and Social Policy Issues,* ed. Edward Zigler and Edmund Gordon (Boston: Auburn House, 1982), 274–76.

12. Nan Robertson, "Parley on Young Begins Its Work," *New York Times* (December 15, 1970), 57; *Report to the President: White House Conference on Children 1970* (Washington, D.C.: Government Printing Office, 1970), 423–28; Gilbert Steiner, *The Children's Cause* (Washington, D.C.: Brookings Institution, 1976), 124–30.

13. Marian Wright Edelman, interview by Rochelle Beck and John Butler, *Harvard Educational Review* 44 (1974): 68, 71.

14. Steiner, *Children's Cause,* 100.

15. U.S. House Committee on Education and Labor, *Comprehensive Child Development Act of 1971: Hearings before the Select Subcommittee on Education on H.R. 6748 and Related Bills,* 92nd Congress, 1st sess. (Washington, D.C.: U.S. Government Printing Office, 1971), 203.

16. Dorothy Sue Cobble, *The Other Women's Movement: Workplace Justice and Social Rights in Modern America* (Princeton, N.J.: Princeton University Press, 2004), 133, 197.

17. Lauri Umansky, *Motherhood Reconceived: Feminism and the Legacies of the Sixties* (New York: New York University Press, 1996), 49; Ros Baxandall, "Women's Liberation and the History and Politics of Day Care in New York City," Talking History Program (2005), www.albany.edu/talkinghistory/arch2005july december.html (accessed April 22, 2008).

18. Bureau of Child Development and Parent Education, *Designs for the 1970s: Planning for Educational Facilities in the Elementary School for Very Young Children* (Albany: New York State Education Department, 1970), 3.

19. Testimony of Bella Abzug, U.S. House Committee on Education and Labor, *Comprehensive Child Development Act of 1971*, 64–65.

20. Edelman, *Harvard Educational Review*, 69.

21. Steven Gillon, *The Democrats' Dilemma: Walter F. Mondale and the Liberal Legacy* (New York: Columbia University Press, 1992), 128.

22. Comments of Walter Mondale, *Congressional Record* (92nd Cong., 1st sess.), vol. 117, pt. 8 (April 6, 1971): 9869–72.

23. Cohen, *Championing Child Care*, 27; Comments of John Brademas, *Congressional Record* (92nd Cong., 1st sess.), vol. 117 (March 24, 1971): 7887.

24. Comments of John Brademas, U.S. House Committee on Education and Labor, *Comprehensive Preschool Education and Child Day Care Act of 1969*, 215.

25. Comments of Patsy Mink and John Brademas, U.S. House Committee on Education and Labor, *Comprehensive Preschool Education and Child Day Care Act of 1969*, 112, 825.

26. Comments of Milton Akers, Nancy Rambusch, John Brademas, and Jerome Bruner, U.S. House Committee on Education and Labor, *Comprehensive Preschool Education and Child Day Care Act of 1969*, 17, 739, 826.

27. *Washington Post* (August 4, 1971), reprinted in *Congressional Record* (92nd Cong., 1st sess., August 4, 1971: 29278.

28. Jack Rosenthal, "Vast Plan for Health, Educational and Social Service to Children Gains in Congress," *New York Times* (June 14, 1971), 22.

29. U.S. House Committee on Education and Labor, *Comprehensive Preschool Education and Child Day Care Act of 1969*, 293, 465, 649, 655.

30. For instance, testimony of Marjorie Grosett, New York Day Care Council, U.S. House Committee on Education and Labor, *Comprehensive Preschool Education and Child Day Care Act of 1969*, 697.

31. Testimony of Shirley Chisholm, U.S. House Committee on Education and Labor, *Comprehensive Child Development Act of 1971*, 75.

32. U.S. House Committee on Education and Labor, *Comprehensive Child Development Act of 1971*, 102; U.S. House Committee on Education and Labor, *Comprehensive Preschool Education and Child Day Care Act of 1969*, 728–29.

33. Statement of Marian Wright Edelman, U.S. House Committee on Education and Labor, *Comprehensive Child Development Act of 1971*, 407.

34. Steiner, *Children's Cause*, 106.

35. James Patterson, *America's Struggle Against Poverty, 1900–1980* (Cambridge, Mass.: Harvard University Press, 1981), 192; Daniel Moynihan, *The Politics of a Guaranteed Income: The Nixon Administration and the Family Assistance Plan* (New York: Random House, 1973).

36. Moynihan, *Politics of a Guaranteed Income*, 327–40; Felicia Kornbluh, *The Battle for Welfare Rights: Politics and Poverty in Modern America* (Philadelphia: University of Pennsylvania Press, 2007).

37. Stephen Ambrose, *Nixon*, vol. 2, *The Triumph of a Politician, 1962–1972* (New York: Simon and Schuster, 1989), 294.

38. Vincent Burke and Vee Burke, *Nixon's Good Deed: Welfare Reform* (New York: Columbia University Press, 1974), 165.

39. Quoted in Edward Zigler and Susan Muenchow, *Head Start: The Inside Story of America's Most Successful Educational Experiment* (New York: Basic Books: 1992), 129.

40. Quoted in Burke and Burke, *Nixon's Good Deed*, 90.

41. Testimony of Jule Sugarman, U.S. House Committee on Education and Labor, *Comprehensive Preschool Education and Child Day Care Act of 1969*, 93–95.

42. Zigler and Muenchow, *Head Start*, 140–42; testimony of Stephen Kurzman and Edward Zigler, U.S. Senate Committee on Labor and Public Welfare, *Comprehensive Child Development Act of 1971*, 758–61.

43. Morgan, "Child of the Sixties," 228.

44. Statement from Marian Wright Edelman, U.S. House Committee on Education and Labor, *Comprehensive Child Development Act of 1971*, 404.

45. Testimony of Arch Moore, U.S. House Committee on Education and Labor, *Comprehensive Child Development Act of 1971*, 174–82.

46. *Congressional Record* (92nd Cong., 1st sess.), vol. 117 (September 30, 1971): 34284–90.

47. "Economic Opportunities Amendments of 1971—Conference Report," *Congressional Record* (92nd Cong., 1st sess.), vol. 117 (December 2, 1971): 44116.

48. "Views on Child Development Section of OEO Conference Report," *Congressional Record* (92nd Cong., 1st sess.), vol. 117 (December 1, 1971): 43903–5; Morgan, "Child of the Sixties," 231.

49. Statement of Howard Samuel, U.S. House Committee on Education and Labor, *Comprehensive Preschool Education and Child Day Care Act of 1969*, 438.

50. *Congressional Record* (92nd Cong., 1st sess.), vol. 117 (September 9, 1971): 31227.

51. U.S. House Committee on Education and Labor, *Comprehensive Preschool Education and Child Day Care Act of 1969*, 162, 544, 17.

52. *Congressional Record* (92nd Cong., 1st sess.), vol. 117 (September 9, 1971): 31227.

53. *Congressional Record* (92nd Cong., 1st sess.), vol. 117 (September 30, 1971): 34290, 34309.

54. William Steif, "Child Care Aid in a Squeeze," *Washington Daily News* (November 29, 1971), reprinted in *Congressional Record* (92nd Cong., 1st sess.), vol. 117 (December 2, 1971): 44156.

55. James Kilpatrick, "Child Development Act: To Sovietize Our Youth," *Seattle Times* (October 23, 1971), reprinted in *Congressional Record* (92nd Cong., 1st sess.), vol. 117 (October 28, 1971), [p. unclear].

56. Paul Weyrich, "Family Issues," in *The New Right at Harvard*, ed. Howard Phillips (Vienna, Va.: Conservative Caucus, 1983), 19; Edwin Feulner, *Conservatives Stalk the House: The Republican Study Committee, 1970–1982* (Ottawa, Ill.: Green Hill, 1983), 50–55.

57. *Congressional Record* (92nd Cong., 1st sess.), vol. 117 (November 16, 1971): 415 95–96; *Congressional Record* (92nd Cong., 1st sess.), vol. 117 (December 14, 1971): 46834.

58. *Congressional Record* (92nd Cong., 1st sess.). vol. 117 (December 2, 1971): 44124–25, 44139.

59. *Congressional Record* (92nd Cong., 1st sess.), vol. 117 (December 1, 1971): 43877, 46083; *Congressional Record* (92nd Cong., 1st sess.), vol. 117 (December 2, 1971): 44146, 44156.

60. Zigler and Muenchow, *Head Start*, 144.

61. Alice Rivlin, "A New Public Attention to Preschool Child Development," *Washington Post* (December 1, 1971), reprinted in *Congressional Record* (92nd Cong., 1st sess.), vol. 117 (December 2, 1971): 44148.

62. Morgan, "Child of the Sixties," 231–33.

63. Mary Frances Berry, *The Politics of Parenthood: Child Care, Women's Rights, and the Myth of the Good Mother* (New York: Viking: 1993), 138.

64. Buchanan memo cited in Cohen, *Championing Child Care*, 50.

65. Steiner, *Children's Cause*, 114; for the text of the veto message, see *Congressional Record (92nd Cong., 1st sess.)*, vol. 117 (December 10, 1971): 46057.

66. Steiner, *Children's Cause*, 114.

67. Editorial, *Washington Post* (December 11, 1971), reprinted in *Congressional Record* (92nd Cong., 1st sess.), vol. 117 (December 11, 1971): 46753; comments of Sen. Mondale and Sen. Moss, *Congressional Record* (92nd Cong., 1st sess.), vol. 117 (December 10, 1971): 46203, 46206.

68. Morgan, "Child of the Sixties," 233; Weyrich. "Family Issues," 19.

69. Cohen, *Championing Child Care*, 55–56. On the 1972 bill, see Senate Committee on Labor and Public Welfare, *Comprehensive Headstart, Child Development, and Family Services Act of 1972 Report*, 92nd Cong., 2nd sess. (Washington, D.C.: 1972).

70. Alan Stang, "The Child Care Bill," *American Opinion* (December 1975), reprinted in U.S. House Committee on Education and Labor, *Background Materials Concerning Child and Family Services Act*, 94th Cong., 2nd sess. (Washington, D.C.: U.S. Government Printing Office, 1976), 148.

71. U.S. House Committee on Education and Labor, *Background Materials*, 81.

72. Gene Maeroff, "Teachers Urging Preschool Plan: 2 Groups Call for a National Program for 3-Year-Olds," *New York Times* (July 14, 1975), 17.

73. Barbara Bowman and Eugenia Kemble, "Should the Public Schools Control Child Care Services?" in *Early Childhood Education: It's an Art? It's a Science?* ed. J. D. Andrews (Washington, D.C.: National Association for the Education of Young Children, 1976), 114–26.

74. American Federation of Teachers, *Putting Early Childhood and Day Care Services into the Public Schools* (Washington, D.C.: American Federation of Teachers, 1976), 106–7.

75. U.S. House Committee on Education and Labor and U.S. Senate Committee on Labor and Public Welfare, *Child and Family Services Act, 1975: Joint Hearings*, 94th Cong., 1st sess., pt. 7 (Washington, D.C.: U.S. Government Printing Office, 1976), 1202.

76. Steiner, *Children's Cause*, 92.

77. Morgan, "Child of the Sixties," 238.

78. Morgan, "Child of the Sixties," 239.

79. Mary Dublin Keyserling, *Windows on Day Care* (New York: National Council of Jewish Women, 1972), 10.

80. Prescott et al., *"Politics" of Day Care*.

81. Michel, *Children's Interests/Mothers' Rights*, 251–52; Nelson, "Politics of Federal Day Care Regulation," 283.

82. Nelson, " Politics of Federal Day Care Regulation"; Cohen, *Championing Child Care*, 64–67.

83. Julia Wrigley, "Different Care for Different Kids: Social Class and Child Care Policy," *Education Policy* 3, no. 4 (1989): 421–39.

Chapter 3

1. Alfred Kahn and Sheila Kammerman, *Child Care: Facing the Hard Choices* (Dover, Mass.: Auburn House, 1987), 4.

2. Abbie Gordon Klein, *The Debate over Child Care, 1969–1990: A Sociohistorical Analysis* (Albany: State University of New York Press, 1992), 143–44.

3. Testimony of Douglas Besharov, House Education and Labor Committee, *Child Care: Hearings Before the Subcommittee on Human Resources*, 100th Cong., 2nd sess. (Washington, D.C.: U.S. Government Printing Office, 1988), 135; Douglas Besharov and Paul Tamontozzi, "Child Care Subsidies: Mostly for the Middle Class," *Washington Post* (May 2, 1988), A21; Douglas Besharov and Paul Tramontozzi, "Federal Child Care Assistance: A Growing Middle-class Entitlement," *Journal of Policy Analysis and Management* 8, no. 2 (1989): 313–18. The child care deduction had changed to a tax credit in 1976, and income ceilings were removed, making it more appealing to upper-income workers.

4. Caroline Zinsser, *Raised in East Urban: Child Care Changes in a Working Class Community* (New York: Teachers College Press, 1991), 20.

5. Claudia Wallis, "The Child Care Dilemma," *Time* (June 22, 1987), 54–61.

6. David Finkelhor and Linda Meyer Williams, *Nursery Crimes: Sexual Abuse in Day Care* (Newbury Park, Calif.: Sage, 1988), 8.

7. Margaret Talbot, "The Devil in the Nursery," *New York Times Magazine* (January 7, 2001), 51.

8. Zinsser, *Raised in East Urban*, 142.

9. Sally Cohen, *Championing Child Care* (New York: Columbia University Press, 2001), 93–94.

10. Anne Mitchell, "Old Baggage, New Visions: Shaping Policy for Early Childhood Programs," *Phi Delta Kappan* 70, no. 9 (May 1989): 672.

11. Phyllis A. Rozanski, "Piecemeal Solution on Child Care," *St. Louis Post-Dispatch* (August 25, 1989), 3C.

12. Christopher Howard, *The Hidden Welfare State: Tax Expenditures and Social Policy in the United States* (Princeton, N.J.: Princeton University Press, 1997), 142.

13. Howard, *Hidden Welfare State*, 153.

14. Cohen, *Championing Child Care*, 101.

15. Testimony of Gordon Ambach, U.S. House of Representatives, Committee on Education and Labor, *Hearings on Child Care: Hearings Before the Committee on Education and Labor* 101st Cong., 1st sess. (Washington, D.C.: Government Printing Office, 1989), 168–82.

16. Comments of Rep. John Williams, U.S. House of Representatives, Committee on Education and Labor, *Hearings on Child Care*, 166.

17. Steven Holmes, "Veteran of Rights and Poverty Wars Tastes Bitter Fruit of Many Battles," *New York Times* (September 28, 1990), A12.

18. Cohen, *Championing Child Care*, 112–15; Howard, *Hidden Welfare State*, 155.

19. Judy Mann, "Congress Remembers the Children—Finally," *Washington Post* (November 2, 1990), D3.

20. Quoted in Cohen, *Championing Child Care*, 125.

21. Howard, *Hidden Welfare State*, 190–91.

22. Margaret Wolf Freivogel, "Advocates Cheer Funding for Care of Children," *St. Louis Post-Dispatch* (October 30, 1990), 1B.

23. Kimberly Morgan, *Working Mothers and the Welfare State: Religion and the Politics of Work-family Policies in Western Europe and the United States* (Stanford, Calif.: Stanford University Press, 2006), 150.

24. Klein, *Debate over Child Care*, 56–57; Frank Swoboda, "Congress Passes $22 Billion Child-care Package," *Washington Post* (October 28, 1990), A19; editorial, *Christian Science Monitor* (November 19, 1990), 20.

25. Cohen, *Championing Child Care*, 140–41.

26. Cohen, *Championing Child Care*, 160; Helen Blank, "Improving Child Care Quality and Supply: The Impact of the Child Care and Development Block Grant," *Young Children* 48, no. 6 (September 1993): 32–33.

27. Nancy Duff Campbell, Judith Appelbaum, Karin Martinson, and Emily Martin, *Be All That We Can Be: Lessons from the Military for Improving Our Nation's Child Care System* (Washington, D.C.: National Women's Law Center, 2000), www.nwlc.org (accessed July 27, 2000).

28. Edith Grotberg, "A Tribute to the Consortium," in *As the Twig Is Bent...Lasting Effects of Preschool Programs*, ed. Consortium for Longitudinal Studies(Hillsdale, N.J.: Erlbaum, 1983), xii.

29. Irving Lazar, "Discussion and Implications of the Findings," in Consortium for Longitudinal Studies, *As the Twig Is Bent*, 463. Some earlier studies of Head Start had suggested impact on special education placement and grade retention, but had not proved these conclusively.

30. Lois-ellin Datta, "Epilogue: We Never Promised You a Rose Garden, But One May Have Grown Anyhow," in Consortium for Longitudinal Studies, *As the Twig Is Bent*, 468; Lois-ellin Datta, "A Tale of Two Studies: The Westinghouse-Ohio Evaluation of Project Head Start and the Consortium for Longitudinal Studies Report," *Studies in Educational Evaluation* 8 (1983): 271–80.

31. Edward Zigler and Susan Muenchow, *Head Start: The Inside Story of America's Most Successful Educational Experiment* (New York: Basic Books, 1992), 170.

32. Datta, "Tale of Two Studies," 276–77; Lawrence Schweinhart, "How the High/Scope Perry Preschool Study Grew: A Researcher's Tale," *Phi Delta Kappa Center for Evaluation Research Bulletin* no. 32 (June 2002), www.highscope.org (accessed November 21, 2005); Carolyn Breedlove and Lawrence Schweinhart, "The Cost-effectiveness of High Quality Early Childhood Programs: A Report to the Southern Governors' Conference," report presented at the Southern Governors' Conference, Hilton Head, South Carolina, July 26, 1982.

33. John Berruetta-Clement et al., *Changed Lives: The Effects of the Perry Preschool Program on Youths Through Age 19* (Ypsilanti, Mich.: High Scope Press, 1984); L. Schweinhart, H. V. Barnes, and D. P. Weikart, *Significant Benefits: The High/Scope Perry Preschool Study Through Age 27* (Ypsilanti, Mich.: High Scope Press, 1993).

34. Lazar, "Discussion," in Consortium for Longitudinal Studies, *As The Twig Is Bent*, 463.

35. Martin Woodhead, "When Psychology Informs Public Policy: The Case of Early Childhood Intervention," *American Psychologist* 43, no. 6 (1988): 451; Edward Zigler and Sally Styfco, "The National Head Start Program for Disadvantaged Preschoolers," in *Head Start and Beyond: A National Plan for Extended Childhood Intervention*, ed. Edward Zigler and Sally Styfco (New Haven, Conn.: Yale University Press, 1993), 22–24.

36. Nancy Rubin, "Head Start Efforts Prove Their Value," *New York Times* (January 6, 1980), ED13; Joseph Michalak, "Head Start–type Programs Get a Second Look," *New York Times* (April 30, 1978), EDUC9; Woodhead, "When Psychology Informs Public Policy," 445–46.

37. Sandra Condry, "History and Background of Preschool Intervention Programs and the Consortium for Longitudinal Studies," in Consortium for Longitudinal Studies, *As the Twig Is Bent*, 27.

38. Datta, "Tale of Two Studies," 271.

39. Quoted in Maris Vinovskis, "The Carter Administration's Attempt to Transfer Head Start into the U.S. Department of Education in the Late 1970s," unpublished paper, University of Michigan Institute for Social Research, 2002, 128.

40. Vinovskis, "Carter Administration's Attempt," 47–50.

41. Edelman to Harrison Wellford, quoted in Vinovskis, "Carter Administration's Attempt," 56.

42. Zigler and Muenchow, *Head Start*, 185.

43. Datta, "Tale of Two Studies," 276.

44. Christopher Cross, *Political Education: National Policy Comes of Age* (New York: Teachers College Press, 2004), 77.

45. National Commission on Excellence in Education, *A Nation at Risk: The Imperative for Education Reform* (Washington, D.C.: U.S. Government Printing Office, 1983), 1; Phil Gailey, "Education Emerges as a Major Issue in 1984 Presidential Campaigning," *New York Times* (June 9, 1983), A1.

46. Thomas Toch, *In the Name of Excellence* (New York: Oxford University Press, 1991), 19; Susan Fuhrman, "Riding Waves, Trading Horses: The 20-Year Effort to Reform Education," in *A Nation Reformed? American Education 20 Years After A Nation at Risk*, ed. David Gordon (Cambridge, Mass.: Harvard Education Press, 2003), 8.

47. Task Force 2000, *Oklahoma's Public Education: A Blueprint for Excellence* (Oklahoma City: The Task Force, 1989), i–iii.

48. Robert Schwartz, "The Emerging State Leadership Role in Education Reform: Notes of a Participant-Observer," in Gordon, *Nation Reformed,* 133.

49. Toch, *In the Name of Excellence,* 37

50. National Governors Association, *Time for Results: The Governors' 1991 Report on Education* (Washington, D.C.: National Governors Association, 1986), 3, 97, 101.

51. Walt Haney, "The Myth of the Texas Miracle in Education," *Education Policy Analysis Archives* 8, no. 41 (2000). Pre-kindergarten programs were also part of larger education reform packages in Illinois, South Carolina, and Massachusetts.

52. Council of Chief State School Officers, *A Guide for State Action: Early Childhood and Family Education* (Washington, D.C.: Council of Chief State School Officers, 1988).

53. Southern Regional Education Board, *Goals for Education: Challenge 2000* (Atlanta: Southern Regional Education Board, 1988), cited in Maris Vinovskis, *The Road to Charlottesville: The 1989 Education Summit* (Washington, D.C.: National Education Goals Panel, 1999), 20.

54. Cross, *Political Education,* 99.

55. Rima Shore, *What Kids Need: Today's Best Ideas for Nurturing, Teaching, and Protecting Young Children* (Boston: Beacon Press, 2002), 129.

56. Evelyn Freeman, "Issues in Kindergarten Policy and Practice," *Young Children* 45, no. 4 (May 1990): 32; Education Commission of the States, *Full-day Kindergarten: A Study of State Policies in the United States* (2005), 2, www.ecs.org/clearinghouse/62/41/6241.pdf (accessed September 1, 2005). The Education Commission of the States also notes that in 1984 only North Carolina required districts to offer full-day kindergarten, while by 2005 eight other states had made this a requirement. After 1984, fourteen states raised the entrance age for kindergarten.

57. On rising academic demands in kindergarten, see Lorrie Shepard and M. L. Smith, "Escalating Academic Demand in Kindergarten: Counterproductive Policies," *Elementary School Journal* 89 (1988): 135–45; Lorrie Shepard and M. L. Smith, "Synthesis of Research on School Readiness and Kindergarten Retention," *Educational Leadership* 44, no. 3 (November 1986): 78–86; Nancy Karweit, "The Kindergarten Experience," *Educational Leadership* 49, no. 6 (March 1992): 82–87; Elizabeth Graue, *Ready for What? Constructing Meanings of Readiness for Kindergarten* (Albany: State University of New York Press, 1993); and Kristen Dombkowski, "Will the Real Kindergarten Please Stand Up? Defining and Redefining the Twentieth-century U.S. Kindergarten," *History of Education* 30, no. 6 (November 2001): 545.

58. National Association for the Education of Young Children, "Position Statement on Developmentally Appropriate Practice," *Young Children* 41, no. 6 (1986): 4–29.

59. Only New York, California, Pennsylvania, and New Jersey had programs in place before 1980. Anne Mitchell, Michelle Seligson, and Fern Marx, *Early Childhood Programs and the Public Schools* (Dover, Mass.: Auburn House, 1989), xix. See also Susan Trostle and Barbara Merrill, *Prekindergarten Programs in Public Schools: A National and State Review* (Charleston, W.V.: Appalachia Educational Laboratory, 1986), and W. Norton Grubb, *Young*

Children Face the States: Issues and Options for Early Childhood Programs (New Brunswick, N.J.: Center for Policy Research in Education, Rutgers University, 1987).

60. Mitchell et al., *Early Childhood Programs and the Public Schools,* 81.

61. Shirley Gatenio, *Taking a Giant Step: A Case Study of New York City's Efforts to Implement Universal Pre-kindergarten Services,* Foundation for Child Development (2002), www.ffcd.org (accessed September 17, 2003); Virginia Thompson and Janice Molnar, "Take a Giant Step: Toward Universal Education for Four-Year-Olds," *New York Affairs* 10, no. 1 (1987): 79–95.

62. Terry Gnezda, "Early Childhood Education: The Status of State Involvement," *State Legislative Reports* 13, no. 16 (June 1988).

63. Anne McGill-Franzen. "Literacy and Early Schooling: Recursive Questions of Child Development and Public Responsibility" (Ed.D. diss., State University of New York, Albany, 1988), 203.

64. Connie Leslie, "Everybody Likes Head Start," *Newsweek* (February 20, 1989), 49–50.

65. Kenneth Cooper, "Head Start Endures, Making a Difference," *Washington Post* (April 22, 1990); Julie Rovner, "Head Start Is One Program Everyone Wants to Help," *Congressional Quarterly Weekly* (April 21, 1990), 1191–95; Zigler and Muenchow, *Head Start,* 202, 209–10.

66. Interviewee who wished to remain anonymous, interview with author, February 19, 2004.

67. Bettye Caldwell, "Day Care and the Public Schools—Natural Allies, Natural Enemies," *Educational Leadership* 43, no. 5 (February 1986): 34–40; Bettye Caldwell, "Day Care and the Schools," *Theory into Practice* 20, no. 2 (1981): 121–29. She suggested the term "educare" in "Future Directions for Early Intervention," *Peabody Journal of Education* 65, no. 1 (autumn 1987): 33.

68. Nadine Brozan, "Mapping Future of Child Care," *New York Times* (October 5, 1987), C16. See also Edward Zigler and Pamela Ennis, "Child Care: A New Role for Tomorrow's Schools," *Principal* 68 (September 1988): 10–13; Matia Finn-Stevenson and Edward Zigler, *Schools of the Twenty-first Century: Linking Child Care and Education* (Boulder, Colo.: Westview Press, 1999).

69. Matia Finn-Stevenson, interview with author, New Haven, October 23, 2000; Ed Zigler, interview with author, New Haven, December 11, 2000.

70. Carol Hoffman, *Public Education and Day Care: One District's Story* (Lancaster, Pa.: Technomic, 1985).

71. Walter Gilliam and Edward Zigler, "A Critical Meta-analysis of All Evaluations of State-funded Preschool from 1977 to 1998: Implications for Policy, Service Delivery and Program Evaluation," *Early Childhood Research Quarterly* 15, no. 4 (winter 2000): 442.

72. Mitchell et al., *Early Childhood Programs and the Public Schools,* xxv, 52; Mitchell, "Old Baggage," 668.

73. Council of Chief State School Officers, *Early Childhood and Family Education— Foundations for Success* (1988), reprinted in U.S. House Committee on Education and Labor, *Hearings on Child Care,* 183–85.

74. National Association of State Boards of Education, *Right from the Start: The Report of the NASBE Task Force on Early Childhood Education* (Alexandria, Va.: National Association of State Boards of Education, 1988).

75. Committee for Economic Development, *Children in Need: Investment Strategies for the Educationally Disadvantaged* (New York: Committee for Economic Development, 1987).

76. Grubb, *Young Children Face the States.*

77. Edward Zigler, "Formal Schooling for Four-year-olds? No," in *Early Schooling: The National Debate*, ed. Sharon Lynn Kagan and Edward Zigler (New Haven, Conn.: Yale University Press, 1987), 40.

78. Mitchell et al., *Early Childhood Programs and the Public Schools*, 221.

Chapter 4

1. Anne Mitchell, interview with author, Climax, New York, February 12, 2004; Karen Schimke, telephone interview with author, January 9, 2004.

2. Edward Zigler, Matia Finn-Stevenson, and Nancy Hall, *The First Three Years and Beyond: Brain Development and Social Policy* (New Haven: Yale University Press, 2002), 5.

3. "Remarks by the President and the First Lady at White House Conference on Early Childhood Development and Learning," White House press release (April 17, 1997), www.ed.gov/PressReleases/04–1997/970417d.html (accessed October 12, 2007).

4. John Bruer, *The Myth of the First Three Years: A New Understanding of Early Brain Development and Lifelong Learning* (New York: Free Press, 1999), 41–51.

5. Scott Groginsky, *Early Childhood Initiatives in the States,: Translating Research into Policy* (Denver, Colo.: National Conference of State Legislatures, 1998), 2, 6.

6. Denise Urias Levy and Sonya Michel, "More Can Be Less: Child Care and Welfare Reform in the United States," in *Child Care Policy at the Crossroads*, ed. Sonya Michel and Rianne Mahon (New York: Routledge, 2002), 239–63.

7. Rima Shore, *What Kids Need: Today's Best Ideas for Nurturing, Teaching, and Protecting Young Children* (Boston: Beacon Press, 2002), 114.

8. On the Abecedarian study, see Francis Campbell and Craig Ramey, "Cognitive and School Outcomes for High-risk African-American Students in Middle Adolescence," *American Educational Research Journal* 32 (1995): 743–72. On the Chicago study, see Arthur Reynolds, "Effects of a Preschool plus Follow-on Intervention for Children at Risk," *Developmental Psychology* 30, no. 6 (November 1994): 787–804; Arthur Reynolds, Judy Temple, Dylan Robertson, and Emily Mann, "Age 21 Cost-benefit Analysis of the Title I Chicago Child-Parent Centers," *Educational Evaluation and Policy Analysis* 24, no. 4 (winter 2002): 267–303.

9. Janet Currie, *Early Childhood Intervention Programs: What Do We Know?* (Chicago: Joint Center for Poverty Research, 2000), 25; W. Steven Barnett, "Long-term Effects of Early Childhood Programs on Cognitive and School Outcomes," *Future of Children* 5, no. 3 (1995): 25–50; Lynn Karoly, Peter Greenwood, and Susan Everingham, *Investing in Our Children: What We Know and Don't Know About the Costs and Benefits of Early Childhood Interventions* (Santa Monica, Calif.: RAND Corporation, 1998).

10. Durwood McAlister, "Lottery Is Gov. Miller's Baby; He Needs to Watch It," *Atlanta Journal and Constitution* (January 29, 1991), A10.

11. Anthony Raden, "Universal Pre-kindergarten in Georgia: A Case Study of Georgia's Lottery-funded Pre-K Program," Foundation for Child Development (1999), 20, www.ffcd.org (accessed April 18, 2000).

12. Diane Loupe, "Pre-kindergarten Program Expanded: Income Limits Removed from Education Initiative," *Atlanta Journal and Constitution* (July 6, 1995), 1.

13. Raden, "Universal Pre-kindergarten in Georgia," 37.

14. Betsy White, "Logistics May Hinder Local Pre-K Expansion," *Atlanta Journal and Constitution* (January 12, 1996), 4C.

15. Raden, "Universal Pre-kindergarten in Georgia," 31.

16. Raden, "Universal Pre-kindergarten in Georgia," 30, 32.

17. Ken Foskett, "State Moves Closer to New Pre-K Agency," *Atlanta Journal and Constitution* (December 21, 1995), 1D; Doug Cumming, "Pre-K Proposal Surprises Advisory Panel," *Atlanta Journal and Constitution* (December 21, 1995), 8D.

18. Raden, "Universal Pre-kindergarten in Georgia," 67–68.

19. Jacqueline Salmon, "States Expect Early Education Benefits; Preschools for All, and the Public Pays," *Washington Post* (March 13, 2000), A5.

20. Duane Stanford, "Pre-K's True Story," *Atlanta Journal and Constitution* (February 23, 2000), 1B.

21. Laura Diamond, "Mary Lin Process Makes School Board Rethink Policy," *Atlanta Journal-Constitution* (May 2, 2008), D1.

22. Raden, "Universal Pre-kindergarten in Georgia," 62.

23. Linda Jacobson, "Miller: A Passion for Improving Schools in Ga.," *Education Week* (May 14, 1997); Kevin Sack, "Georgia's Chief Reveling in His Sky-high Ratings," *New York Times* (February 16, 1998), A9.

24. Quoted in Bruce Fuller, *Standardized Childhood: The Political and Cultural Struggle over Early Education* (Stanford, Calif.: Stanford University Press, 2007), 107–8; *Laws of the 37th Oklahoma Legislature, Second Regular Session—1980*, chap. 353 (p. 1066).

25. Nancy Mathis, "Oklahoma Teachers Threaten Statewide Strike in Fall," *Education Week* (April 26, 1989).

26. Nancy Mathis, "Session Called in Oklahoma to Debate Taxes for Schools," *Education Week* (August 2, 1989); Task Force 2000, *Oklahoma's Public Education: A Blueprint for Excellence* (Oklahoma City: Task Force 2000, November 1989), iii, 7.

27. Jim Killackey, "Educators Praise, Slam 1017 Results," *Oklahoma City Oklahoman* (September 25, 1994).

28. "School Reform and Tax Bill Passes," *Oklahoma City Oklahoman* (April 20, 1990), 1; Michael Newman, "Reform Bill Clears Its Final Legislative Hurdle in Oklahoma," *Education Week* (April 25, 1990).

29. Brian Ford, "Bomb Rips Anti-1017 Office in OC," *Tulsa World* (October 1, 1991).

30. William Gormley and Deborah Phillips, "The Effects of Universal Pre-k in Oklahoma: Research Highlights and Policy Implications," Georgetown University Center for Research on Children in the United States (2003), www.crocus.georgetown.edu/publications.html (accessed October 27, 2003).

31. David Kirp, "You're Doing Fine, Oklahoma!" *American Prospect* (November 1, 2004), A5.

32. National Center for Education Statistics, *Statistics in Brief: Overview of Public Elementary and Secondary Schools and Districts* (October 1998), www.nces.gov (accessed January 25, 2006).

33. Gov. Frank Keating, veto message, June 14, 1996, *Senate Journal, 45th Legislature of Oklahoma*, 2nd Session, 999; Paul English, and John Greiner, "Career Teacher Pay Hikes Draw Keating's Veto," *Oklahoma City Oklahoman* (June 15, 1996), 1; "Keating Veto Hits Teachers, Local Control," press release from Oklahoma State Senate (June 17, 1996), www.oksenate.gov/news/press_releases (accessed July 20, 2004); "Keating Spokesman Says Senator Should Stop Scaring Teachers," Office of Governor Frank Keating press release (June 17, 1996), www.state.ok.us/osfdocs.nr617a96.html (accessed June 22, 2004).

34. Kay Floyd, telephone interview with author, June 22, 2004.

35. Marcia Goff, telephone interview with author, June 17, 2004.

36. Kay Floyd, interview; Randall Raburn, telephone interview with author, July 30, 2004.

37. *Oklahoma Legislative Reporter* (May 7, 1998), 3.

38. Floyd Coppedge, telephone interview with author, July 20, 2004.

39. Quoted in Fuller, *Standardized Childhood,* 102.

40. Randall Raburn, interview, and Kay Floyd, interview.

41. At the time the bill was passed, overall education appropriations increased by 6.5 percent, while enrollments were declining through the 1990s. Gormley and Philips, "Effects of Universal Pre-K in Oklahoma," 4.

42. Bobby Anderson, "Schools See Fewer Students," *Oklahoma City Oklahoman* (October 28, 2002), 1; Oklahoma State Department of Education, "Oklahoma Schools Report Record Enrollment," press release (January 3, 2007), www.sde.state.ok.us/Services/News/2008/Enrollment.pdf (accessed March 18, 2009). Per-child funding figures are from W. Steven Barnett, Jason Hustedt, Kenneth Robin, and Karen Schulman, *The State of Preschool: 2004 State Preschool Yearbook* (New Brunswick, N.J.: National Institute for Early Education Research, Rutgers University, 2004).

43. Ryan McNeill, "Pre-kindergarten Offered," *Oklahoma City Oklahoman* (November 20, 2002), 1; Gregory Potts, "Schools Add Pre-kindergarten Programs," *Oklahoman* (February 10, 2003).

44. Barnett et al., *State of Preschool: 2004 State Preschool Yearbook*, 115.

45. Gina Adams and Jodi Sandfort, *First Steps, Promising Futures: State Pre-kindergarten Initiatives in the Early 1990s* (Washington, D.C.: Children's Defense Fund, 1994), 205; Karen Schulman, Helen Blank, and Danielle Ewen, *Seeds of Success: State Pre-kindergarten Initiatives, 1998–1999* (Washington, D.C.: Children's Defense Fund: 1999), 201; Kathryn Doherty, "Early Learning: State Policies" in *Education Week's Quality Counts 2002: Building Blocks for Success,* 58–59; W. Steven Barnett, Jason Hustedt, Alison Friedman, and Judi Stevenson Boyd, *The State of Preschool 2007: State Preschool Yearbook* (New Brunswick, N.J.: National Institute for Early Education Research, Rutgers University, 2007).

46. Kristina Dudley, "Tulsa Joins the Push for Early Education," *Tulsa World* (August 19, 1998).

47. Carrie Pagley, "Students Getting Younger," *Oklahoma City Oklahoman* (July 26, 1999); Bobby Anderson, "Enrollment Campouts Halted for Moore Pre-K," *Oklahoman* (May 3, 2003).

48. "Preschool Plan Fails in California," *Oklahoma City Oklahoman* (June 13, 2006).

49. William Gormley, Ted Gayer, Deborah Phillips, and Brittany Dawson, "The Effects of Universal Pre-K on Cognitive Development," *Developmental Psychology* 41, no. 6 (2005): 872–84.

50. Gormley et al., "Effects of Universal Pre-K on Cognitive Development," 882.

51. Anne Mitchell, interview.

52. Anne McGill-Franzen, "Literacy and Early Schooling: Recursive Questions of Child Development and Public Responsibility" (Ed.D. diss., State University of New York, Albany, 1988), 204.

53. "Announcement by the Governor of a New Experimental Pre-Kindergarten Program for Culturally Deprived Children" (January 15, 1966), in *Public Papers of Nelson A. Rockefeller* (Albany: State of New York, 1966), 764.

54. New York State Education Department, *Evaluation of the New York State Experimental Pre-kindergarten Program: Final Report* (Albany: State Education Department, 1982).

55. Betsy McCaughey Ross, *Preparing for Success: Expanding Pre-kindergarten and Educational Daycare* (Albany: Educational Excellence Project, 1996).

56. Kerry White, "Early Education on Legislative Docket in N.Y.," *Education Week* (December 11, 1996).

57. Anne Mitchell, "The State with Two Pre-kindergarten Programs: A Look at Pre-kindergarten Education in New York State, 1928–2003" (National Institute for Early Education Research, 2004), 11, http://nieer.org (accessed August 3, 2004); Karen Schimke, interview; Anne Mitchell, interview.

58. Susan Hicks, Kristi Lekies, and Mon Cochran, "Promising Practices: New York State Universal Pre-kindergarten," Cornell Early Childhood Program (1999), www.human.cornell.edu/hd/cecp (accessed January 7, 2002).

59. Anne Mitchell, interview.

60. Linda Jacobson, "Plans for 'Universal' Preschool Gain Ground in New York State," *Education Week* (October 25, 2000), 1.

61. Richard Perez-Pena, "Agreement at Last in Albany on $73 Billion Budget Plan," *New York Times* (July 17, 1999), B1.

62. Jessica Sandham, "N.Y. Legislature Passes Bare-bones Budget That Incenses Educators," *Education Week* (August 8, 2001), 30.

63. John Gehring, "New York Pre-K Program on Chopping Block," *Education Week* (April 9, 2003), 26.

64. Winnie Hu, "Speaker Wields Preschool Education as a Sword," *New York Times* (March 4, 2003), B5.

65. Jinhee Lee, "Early Childhood Care and Education in the Midst of State Fiscal Woes" Washington, D.C.: Council of Chief State School Officers (2003), www.ccsso.org (accessed October 4, 2003); "Little Red Wagons Bring Pre-K Petitions to Albany," Winning Beginning NY press release via email (April 15, 2003).

66. "Oxford School District Finds Recipe for Pre-K Success," *Winning Beginning* (newsletter), no. 2 (2003): 1–2.

67. Al Baker, "State Legislature Overrides Pataki on Budget Vetoes," *New York Times* (May 16, 2003), A1; James McKinley, "Pataki Admits He May Not Be Able to Head Off Legislature," *New York Times* (May 11, 2003), 1, 38; Al Baker, "Governor Vetoes Increase in Taxes," *New York Times* (May 15, 2003), A1.

68. Karen Schimke, interview.

69. Comments of Nancy Kolben, Marketplace of Ideas, October 30, 2006, transcript, Drum Major Institute (2006), 12, www.dmi.org (accessed October 17, 2007).

70. "The Battle to Save Universal Pre-kindergarten," *Schuyler Center for Analysis and Advocacy Annual Report* (Albany: Schuyler Center for Analysis and Advocacy, 2003), 2.

71. Testimony submitted by Karen Schimke, Schuyler Center for Analysis and Advocacy, to Joint Fiscal Committees, Elementary and Secondary Education Hearing (February 9, 2004), www.winningbeginningny.org/latestnews.html (accessed March 15, 2004).

72. Anne Mitchell, presentation to the annual meeting of the National Association for the Education of Young Children, New York City, November 20, 2002.

73. Molly Hennesy-Fiske, "The Chosen Few," *Syracuse Post-Standard* (May 8, 2005), A1.

74. New York State Board of Regents, "Policy Statement on Early Education for Student Achievement in a Global Community" (July 2005), www.regents.nysed. gov/2005Meetings/July2005/0705brd5.htm (accessed October 7, 2005).

75. Education Law Center, "History of the Education Law Center," www.edlawcenter. org (accessed March 17, 2006).

76. Douglas Reed, *On Equal Terms: The Constitutional Politics of Educational Opportunity* (Princeton, N.J.: Princeton University Press, 2001). Quotation from Gordon MacInnes, in Catherine Gewertz, "A Level Playing Field," in *Education Week's Quality Counts* 2005: *No Small Change* (January 5, 2005) www.edweek.org (accessed March 21, 2006).

77. Supreme Court of New Jersey, "Abbott v. Burke (a-155–97)," 1998, www.lawlibrary .rutgers.edu/courts (accessed April 6, 2006).

78. "Schools Agency Rejects Pre-kindergarten Plans," *New York Times* (February 12, 1999), B4; W. Steven Barnett, Julie Tarr, Cynthia Esposito Lamy, and Ellen Frede, "Fragile Lives, Shattered Dreams: A Report on Implementation of Preschool Education in New Jersey's *Abbott* Districts," National Institute for Early Education Research (2001), http:// nieer.org (accessed September 23, 2003).

79. Linda Jacobson, "Tensions Surface in Public-private Preschool Plans," *Education Week* (September 15, 1999), 1, 12–13.

80. Barnett et al., "Fragile Lives, Shattered Dreams."

81. Per-child spending in the *Abbott* program was $10,361 in 2005; this was less than the per-child spending for K–12, but it was a cost fully borne by the state, while the K–12

figure was split between state and local levels. W. Steven Barnett, Jason Hustedt, Kenneth Robin, and Karen Schulman, *State of Preschool: 2005 State Preschool Yearbook,* National Institute for Early Education Research, Rutgers University (2006), 22, 102–4.

82. Early Learning Improvement Consortium, "Inch by Inch, Row by Row, Gonna Make This Garden Grow: Classroom Quality and Language Skills in the Abbott Preschool Program," National Institute for Early Education Research, Rutgers University (2004), http://nieer.org (accessed August 16, 2004); Cynthia Esposito Lamy and Ellen Frede, "Giant Steps for the Littlest Children: Progress in the Sixth Year of the Abbott Preschool Program," New Jersey Department of Education (2005), www.state.nj.us/njded/ece/abbott/giantsteps/ (accessed May 26, 2005).

83. Ellen Frede, Kwanghee Jung, W. Steven Barnett, Cynthia Esposito Lamy, and Alexandra Figueras, "Abbott Preschool Program Longitudinal Effects Study: Interim Report," National Institute for Early Education Research, Rutgers University (2007), http://nieer.org (accessed September 10, 2007).

84. Catherine Gewertz, "N.J. State Board Backs Rewriting School Finance Formula," *Education Week* (January 11, 2006), 17. On the situation of non-*Abbott* districts, see Sherri Lauver, Gary Ritter, and Margaret Goertz, "Caught in the Middle: The Fate of the Non-urban Districts in the Wake of New Jersey's School Finance Litigation," *Journal of Education Finance* 26, no. 3 (winter 2001): 281–96.

85. David Kocieniewski, "Corzine Defies Liberal Expectations in Call to Freeze Aid to Needy Schools," *New York Times* (April 11, 2006), www.nytimes.com (accessed April 14, 2006); "Supreme Court Protects Education Rights of Poor and Minority Schoolchildren," Educational Law Center press release (May 10, 2006), www.edlawcenter.org (accessed September 1, 2006); Tom Hester, "Tax Panel Wants Change in School Funding," *Bergen County Record* (September 6, 2006).

86. David Chen, "New Jersey Revamps State Aid to Schools," *New York Times* (January 8, 2008), B4.

87. Gordon MacInnes, *In Plain Sight: Simple, Difficult Lessons from New Jersey's Expensive Effort to Close the Achievement Gap* (New York: Century Foundation Press, 2009), 106.

88. Paul Cox, "Court Rejects Corzine's Bid to End N.J. Schools Case," *Newark Star-Ledger* (November 18, 2008), www.nj.com/news/index.ssf/2008/11/njs_top_court_rejects_corzine.html (accessed November 25, 2008).

89. Starting at 3, "Case Law/Litigation," www.startingat3.org/case_law/overview.html (accessed October 26, 2007).

Chapter 5

1. Ruby Takanishi and Fasaha Traylor, interview with author, New York City, October 23, 2003.

2. John Merrow, "The 'Failure' of Head Start," *Education Week* (September 25, 2002), 52, 38.

3. Interviewee who wished to remain anonymous, interview with author, Washington, D.C. February 19, 2004.

4. Anne McGill-Franzen, "Literacy and Early Schooling: Recursive Questions of Child Development and Public Responsibility" (Ed.D. diss., State University of New York, Albany, 1988), 204.

5. Theda Skocpol, *Social Policy in the United States: Future Possibilities in Historical Perspective* (Princeton, N.J.: Princeton University Press, 1995), 259–67; William Julius Wilson, *The Truly Disadvantaged: The Inner City, the Underclass, and Public Policy* (Chicago: University of Chicago Press, 1987), 118–24, 152–55. Skocpol's work was specifically cited in W. Steven Barnett et al., "The Universal vs. Targeted Debate: Should the United States Have Preschool for All?" *Preschool Policy Matters (National Institute for Early Education Research)* 6 (April 2004): 12.

6. Kimberly Morgan, *Working Mothers and the Welfare State: Religion and the Politics of Work-family Policies in Western Europe and the United States* (Stanford, Calif.: Stanford University Press, 2006), 93.

7. Candy Cooper, *Ready to Learn: The French System of Early Education and Care Offers Lessons for the United States* (New York: French-American Foundation, 1999), 36.

8. Michelle Neuman and Shanny Peer, *Equal from the Start: Promoting Educational Opportunity for All Preschool Children—Learning from the French Experience*, French American Foundation (2002), www.frenchamerican.org (accessed July 30, 2003).

9. Carnegie Task Force on Learning in the Primary Grades, *Years of Promise: A Comprehensive Learning Strategy for America's Children* (New York: Carnegie Corporation, 1996), 4, 16, 54; "Earlier, and Better, Education," editorial, *New York Times* (October 2, 1996), A22.

10. Council of Chief State School Officers, "Early Childhood and Family Education: New Realities, New Opportunities—A Council Policy Statement" (1999), 8, www.ccsso.org (accessed June 9, 2003).

11. National Association of State Boards of Education, *From Planning to Practice: State Efforts to Improve Early Childhood Education* (Alexandria, Va.: National Association of State Boards of Educcation 2005); "NASBE Awarded Grant to Replicate Successful Early Childhood Learning Strategies," press release (March 13, 2006), www.nasbe.org (accessed March 14, 2006); Jessica Sandham, "Reporter's Notebook: States Urged to Invest in Children's Earliest Years," *Education Week* (August 8, 2001), 31.

12. American Federation of Teachers, "AFT President Calls for New Kindergarten-plus Initiative" July 15, 2002), www.aft.org/convention/speech_pr.html (accessed October 20, 2002); National Education Association, "NEA Delegates Call for Universal Pre-K and Full-day Kindergarten," press release (July 4, 2003), www.nea.org (accessed July 9, 2003).

13. Janet Hansen, telephone interview with author, September 9, 2003.

14. Committee for Economic Development, *Preschool for All: Investing in a Productive and Just Society* (New York: Committee for Economic Development, 2002).

15. Janet Hansen, interview.

16. Ruby Takanishi and Fasaha Traylor, interview; *Annual Report of the Foundation for Child Development* (New York: Foundation for Child Development, 1997–98), 13.

17. Ruby Takanishi, interview, and Fasaha Traylor, interview.

18. Pew Charitable Trusts, "Starting Early, Starting Strong: Investing in Early Education" (2002), www.pewtrusts.org (accessed October 2, 2002).

19. Ann Bradley, "Pew to Add $10.2 Million to Support Phila. Reforms," *Education Week* (June 17, 1992); Meg Sommerfeld, "$9.8 Million in Pew Grants to Support Phila. Reforms," *Education Week* (November 8, 1995).

20. Richard Lee Colvin, "A New Generation of Philanthropists and Their Great Ambitions," in *With the Best of Intentions: How Philanthropy Is Reshaping K–12 Education*, ed. Frederick Hess (Cambridge, Mass.: Harvard Education Press, 2005), 26. See also Ray Bacchetti and Thomas Ehrlich, eds., *Reconnecting Education and Foundations: Turning Good Intentions into Educational Capital* (San Francisco: Jossey-Bass, 2006), which talks about some of the largest foundations, especially Pew and Atlantic Philanthropies, turning away from traditional K–12 and especially from higher education.

21. Susan Urahn and Sara Watson, "The Trusts' Advancing Quality Pre-K for All Initiative: Building on Four Years of Progress," *Preschool Matters* 4, no. 1 (December–January 2006).

22. Deborah Cohen, "Demise of Pew Project Offers Lessons to Funders," *Education Week* (June 1, 1994).

23. Susan Urahn, interview; Dana Hull, "Should California Pay for Preschool?" *San Jose Mercury News* (February 12, 2006).

24. Susan Urahn, interview; Rima Shore, "Starting Early, Starting Strong," *Trust* (Pew Charitable Trusts) 5, no. 4 (fall 2002): 7.

25. Urahn and Watson, "Trusts' Advancing Quality Pre-K for All Initiative."

26. Pre-K Now, "Talking Points in Response to *20/20* Segment on Pre-K Movement," forwarded in email from Pre-K Now, March 13, 2009.

27. Susan Urahn, interview.

28. Rimel and Doggett quoted in David Kirp, *The Sandbox Investment: The Preschool Movement and Kids-first Politics* (Cambridge, Mass.: Harvard University Press, 2007), 158, 162.

29. Trust for Early Education, "TEE State Activities" (2003), www.trustforearlyed.org/activities_state.aspx (accessed November 9, 2007).

30. Kirp, *Sandbox Investment*, 163–64; Roger Williams, "Riding the Roller Coaster at Packard," *Foundation News and Commentary* 44, no. 4 (July–August 2003), www.foundation-news.org/CME/article.cfm?ID=2554 (accessed on November 9, 2007; Packard Foundation, "Preschool for California's Children," www.packard.org (accessed November 9, 2007).

31. Quoted in Kirp, *Sandbox Investment*, 165.

32. Lisa Klein, "Private Foundations and the Move Toward Universal Preschool," *Evaluation Exchange* 10, no. 2 (2004): 20–21; "$90M to Fund Model Early Learning Centers," *Bellingham (WA) Herald* (December 19, 2005).

33. Linda Jacobson, "Foundation Gives $43 Million to Bolster Pre-K," *Education Week* (August 6, 2003), 14.

34. Bruce Fuller, *Standardized Childhood: The Political and Cultural Struggle over Early Education* (Stanford, Calif.: Stanford University Press, 2007), 5, 63.

35. Susan Urahn, correspondence with author, December 18, 2003.

36. Quoted in Kirp, *Sandbox Investment*, 161.

37. Council of Chief State School Officers, "Building a Cadre of Champions for Early Childhood Education" (2003), www.ccsso.org (accessed October 2, 2003); Pew Charitable Trusts, "Business Group Calls for Universal Pre-Kindergarten with Support of the Pew Charitable Trusts," press release (May 9, 2002), www.pewtrusts.org (accessed October 2, 2003); "Preschool Education," *Education Week* (January 7, 2004), 19; and Fight Crime/Invest in Kids, "Quality Pre-Kindergarten: Key to Crime Prevention and School Success," www.fightcrime.org (accessed February 16, 2006).

38. Margaret Blood and Melissa Ludtke, "Business Leaders as Legislative Advocates for Children," Foundation for Child Development (1999), www.ffcd.org (accessed September 17, 2003). Blood and Ludtke, among others, use the phrase "unlikely messengers" to refer to business leaders who support public spending on preschool.

39. Janice Gruendel, Harry Orlick, and Abby Kantor, "Business and Early Care and Education: A Review of Engagement Strategies and a Connecticut Case Example," Connecticut Voices for Children (2003), www.ctkidslink.org (accessed June 4, 2003); Communications Consortium Media Center, "Early Childhood and Economic Development" (conference call, August 4, 2004); Trust for Early Education, "Engaging Business Leaders" (conference call, December 15, 2004).

40. "George Kaiser Speech on Childhood Education," *New York Times* (February 7, 2007).

41. Business Roundtable and Corporate Voices for Working Families, "Early Childhood Education: A Call to Action from the Business Community" (2003), www. businessroundtable.org (accessed May 28, 2003).

42. National Association of Manufacturers, "Public Policy Positions" (2008), www. nam.org/policypositions/ (accessed December 9, 2008).

43. "PNC Spending $100M on Education Program," *Philadelphia Business Journal* (September 8, 2003); Shelly Kalson, "PNC Kicks Off Kids Initiative," *Pittsburgh Post-Gazette* (March 24, 2004); John Krupa, "Rogers: Wal-Mart Grant Aids Pre-kindergarten Plan," *Little Rock Democrat-Gazette* (February 22, 2006); Maria Glod, "Group Offers $300,000 for Preschool Education," *Washington Post* (February 3, 2006), B6.

44. Art Rolnick and Rob Grunewald, "Early Childhood Development: Economic Development with a High Public Return," *Federal Gazette* (March 2003), 6–12.

45. Dan Haar, "Spending on Kids: A Business Argument," *Hartford Courant* (January 25, 2004), D1–2; Kevin Featherly, "Of Human Capital," *Minnesota Monthly* (January 2006), www.minnesotamonthly.com (accessed March 3, 2006).

46. Comments of Gov. Jodi Rell, "Effective Advocacy in the Pre-K Movement," Pre-K Now Satellite Conference (September 30, 2006), www.preknow.org/advocate/conference2006.effectiveadvocacy.com (accessed September 26, 2006).

47. Tamar Lewin, "The Need to Invest in Young Children," *New York Times* (January 11, 2006), www.nytimes.com (accessed January 12, 2006); Zogby International, "American Business Leaders' Views on Publicly Funded Pre-Kindergarten," Committee on Economic Development (2005), www.ced.org (accessed February 14, 2006).

48. Scott Jagow and Christopher Farrell, "Investing in the Kids," *Marketplace*, National Public Radio, October 30, 2006, http://marketplace.publicradio.org/shows/2006/10/30/AM200610301.html (accessed November 1, 2006).

49. Clive Belfield, "Early Childhood Education: How Important Are the Cost-savings to the School System?" Winning Beginning New York (2004), www.winningbeginningny.org (accessed March 15, 2004).

50. The Trusts supported a new initiative, along with several other foundations, to assess how different types of supports for children contribute to the nation's economy, and then to advance the "most effective investments in children." Susan Urahn and Sara Watson, "The Pew Charitable Trusts Advancing Quality Pre-K for All: Five Years Later" (2006), www.pewtrusts.org (accessed December 21, 2006), 7.

51. Greg Duncan, Jens Ludwig, and Katherine Magnuson, "Reducing Poverty Through Preschool Interventions," *Future of Children* 17, no. 2 (fall 2007): 143–60.

52. Fuller, *Standardized Childhood*, 284.

53. W. Steven Barnett, Kirsty Brown, and Rima Shore, "The Universal vs. Targeted Debate: Should the United States Have Preschool for All?" *Preschool Policy Matters* (National Institute for Early Education Research), iss. 6 (April 2004): 4.

54. Edward Zigler, Walter Gilliam, and Stephanie Jones, *A Vision for Universal Preschool Education* (Cambridge: Cambridge University Press, 2006), 247.

55. Merrow, "'Failure' of Head Start," 38.

56. David Kirp and Deborah Stipek, "On Proposition 82's Call for Universal Preschool," *San Francisco Chronicle* (June 1, 2006), B-9.

57. Karen Schimke, interview with author, January 9, 2004.

58. *Education Week* web chat with Marc Tucker of the New Commission on the American Workforce (March 17, 2007), www.edweek.org (accessed March 25, 2007).

59. Richard Kahlenberg, "Universal Preschool in California: Why David Brooks Is Wrong," Century Foundation (June 5, 2006), www.tcf.org (accessed October 20, 2006).

60. Barnett et al., "Universal vs. Targeted Debate," 8.

61. Ernest Boyer, *Ready to Learn: A Mandate for the Nation* (Princeton, N.J.: Carnegie Foundation for the Advancement of Teaching, 1991).

62. "School Readiness Gap Hits Children of Privilege, Too," *Winning Beginning*, no. 3 (2004): 4.

63. Fuller, *Standardized Childhood*, 207.

64. William Gormley, Ted Gayer, Deborah Phillips, and Brittany Dawson, "The Effects of Universal Pre-K on Cognitive Development," *Developmental Psychology* 41, no. 6 (2005): 882.

65. William Gormley and Deborah Phillips, "The Effects of Universal Pre-K in Oklahoma: Research Highlights and Policy Implications," Georgetown University Center for Research on Children in the United States (2003), 22, www.crocus.georgetown.edu/publications.html (accessed October 27, 2003); William Gormley, Deborah Phillips, and Ted Gayer, "The Early Years: Preschool Can Boost School Readiness," *Science* 320 (June 27, 2008): 1723–24.

66. Oran Smith, "Important Questions on Pre-K Initiative," *Columbia, SC, State* (January 24, 2006), A9.

67. Darcy Ann Olsen, "The Advancing Nanny State: Why the Government Should Stay out of Child Care," *Cato Institute Policy Analysis* 285 (1997): 1–33; see also Darcy Ann Olsen, "Universal Preschool Is No Golden Ticket: Why Government Should Not Enter the Preschool Business," *Cato Institute Policy Analysis* 333 (1999): 1–31.

68. Laura Schlessinger, "Orwell Tale Rings Alarm for Parents," *Oklahoma City Oklahoman* (November 8, 1999), 14.

69. "Stopping Kaine's Pre-school Scheme," Virginia Family Foundation (December 12, 2006), http://media.pfaw.org/Right/vaff-121206.htm (accessed January 23, 2007).

70. "Mixed Blessings," *Jacksonville (FL) Times-Union* (April 6, 2002),.

71. Matthew Brouillette, "Waiting at the Cradle," *Pittsburgh Post-Gazette* (October 16, 2002), A15.

72. David Salisbury, "Preschool Is No Answer," *USA Today* (January 10, 2002), www.usatoday.com (accessed Nov. 17, 2003); Darcy Olsen, "Assessing Proposals for Preschool and Kindergarten: Essential Information for Parents, Taxpayers and Policymakers," Goldwater Institute Policy Report (2005), http://goldwater.design44.com/aboutus/ArticleView.aspx?id=920 (accessed January 23, 2007).

73. See Center for Public Education, "More Than a Horse Race: A Guide to International Tests of Student Achievement" (2007), www.centerforpubliceducation.org (accessed March 20, 2009).

Chapter 6

1. Anne Mitchell, interview with author, Climax, N.Y., February 12, 2004.

2. Edward Zigler, Walter Gilliam, and Stephanie Jones, *A Vision for Universal Preschool Education* (Cambridge: Cambridge University Press, 2006), 247; Carolyn Goossen, "Preschool in L.A. County: A Multilingual Universal Approach," Pacific News Service (March 9, 2006), http://news.pacificnews.org (accessed March 10, 2006).

3. Zigler et al., *Vision for Universal Preschool Education*, 247.

4. Harold Meyerson, "The Reiner Riddle," *LA Weekly* (March 15, 2006).

5. Laura Mecoy, "New Boss for Prop. 82 Drive," *Sacramento* Bee (March 8, 2006); Jill Tucker, "Cops Back Preschool Initiative," *Oakland Tribune* (April 5, 2006).

6. Dan Morain, "Reiner Takes a Leave from Panel on Children," *Los Angeles Times* (February 25, 2006), B1; Dan Morain, "Reiner Quits First 5 Panel," *Los Angeles Times* (March 30, 2006), A1. A legislative audit later showed while that there were some improper contracting practices, the advertisements themselves were legitimate. Dan Morain, "State Audit of Reiner Panel Finds Flaws," *Los Angeles Times* (November 1, 2006), B1.

7. Greg Lucas, "Perata Withdraws Support for Reiner's Preschool Initiative," San Francisco Chronicle (March 1, 2006), B1.

8. Jill Tucker, "Reiner Initiative Qualifies for Ballot," *Oakland Tribune* (January 14, 2006), www.atlantadailyworld.com/ (accessed Jan. 17, 2006).

9. Policy Analysis for California Education, "Proposition 82—California's 'Preschool for All' Initiative," University of California, Berkeley (2006), http://pace.berkeley.edu/prop82brief.pdf (accessed April 10, 2006); Bruce Fuller, "The Preschool 'Spin'," *Los Angeles Times* (April 4, 2006), B13; Bruce Fuller, "Preschool Reform Measure Won't Close Learning Gap for Poor," *San Jose Mercury News* (February 28, 2006), OP1; Bruce Fuller, "Universal Preschool: Democrats' New Embrace of Big Government," *San Francisco Chronicle* (January 29, 2006), D7.

10. Dana Hull, "Should California Pay for Preschool?" *San Jose Mercury News* (February 12, 2006).

11. "Times Endorsements," editorial, *Los Angeles Times* (June 4, 2006), quoted in David Kirp, *The Sandbox Investment: The Preschool Movement and Kids-first Politics* (Cambridge, Mass.: Harvard University Press, 2007), 215.

12. Quoted in Kirp, *Sandbox Investment*, 217.

13. Dana Hull, "Voters Reject Prop. 82," *San Jose Mercury News* (June 7, 2006), www.mercurynews.com (accessed July 6, 2006).

14. Hull, "Voters Reject Prop. 82."

15. Laurel Rosenthal, "For Preschool Supporters, Time to Plot New Course," *Sacramento Bee* (June 8, 2006), A5.

16. Nina Rees, "The California Preschool Initiative: How to Turn Its Defeat into a Victory for Children," *Education Week* (July 12, 2006), 43.

17. E. J. Dionne, "Lessons for Liberals in California," *Washington Post* (June 9, 2006), A23.

18. Office of the Governor, "Gov. Schwarzenegger Signs Legislation to Expand Preschool," press release (September 7, 2006), http://gov.ca.gov/index.php?/press-release/3793/ (accessed December 4, 2008); Linda Jacobson, "Gov. Schwarzenegger Signs Legislation Expanding Pre-K," *Education Week* (September 13, 2006), 27.

19. Debra Williams, "Demand, but No Money, for Universal Preschool," *Catalyst: Voices of Chicago School Reform* 14, no. 7 (April 2003), http://catalyst-chicago.org (accessed November 17, 2003), 4.

20. "Preschool for Some," editorial, *Chicago Tribune* (February 16, 2006), 16.

21. Donna Leff and David Kirp, "Sandbox cum Laude," *Chicago Tribune* (July 16, 2006), 12.

22. Diane Rado, "Preschool Plan Not for All," *Chicago Tribune* (May 5, 2006), 1; Crystal Yednak, "10,000 More Let in Preschool Door," *Chicago Tribune* (July 26, 2006), 3.

23. Comments of Lana Seivers, "Effective Advocacy in the Pre-K Movement," Pre-K Now satellite conference (September 20, 2006), www.preknow.org/advocate/conference2006.effectiveadvocacy.com (accessed September 26, 2006).

24. Comments of Francie Hunt, "Winning Legislative Strategies" (Pre-K Now conference call, October 12, 2005); David Gleason, "The Road to Universal, High Quality Pre-Kindergarten for Tennessee's Four Year Olds," presentation for "Diverse Delivery Systems" (Pre-K Now conference call, November 16, 2005), www.preknow.org/advocate/confcalls/diversesettings.cfm (accessed November 28, 2005).

25. Beverly Carroll, "Tennessee Pre-K Sets Example, Group Says," *Chattanooga Times Free Press* (October 25, 2006), 9; "Bredesen: State Better Off Without Federal Pre-K Funding," Associated Press (September 20, 2006).

26. "Bredesen Announces Grant Awards for 227 New Pre-K Classrooms," *Chattanoogan* (July 13, 2006).

27. Comments of Libby Doggett, "Effective Advocacy in the Pre-K Movement."

28. Lucas Johnson, "Pilot Preschool Program's Success Justifies Governor's Initiative," Associated Press (September 4, 2005).

29. "Tennessee's Voluntary Pre-Kindergarten Program," www.tennessee.gov/governor/prek/govsplan.htm (accessed November 2, 2006); Duncan Mansfield, "Bredesen Signs Law Funding Pre-Kindergarten in Tennessee," Associated Press (June 16, 2005).

30. Erik Schelzig, "Bredesen to Stress Pre-K, Urban School Funding," *Knoxville News Sentinel* (November 29, 2006), www.knoxnews.com (accessed Dec. 1, 2006).

31. Jaime Sarrio, "Pre-K Program Grows and Grows," *Nashville Tennessean* (July 24, 2007).

32. Maria Glod, "Virginia Plans Pilot Program for Universal Preschool Next Fall," *Washington Post* (December 7, 2006), B6; Lindsay Kastner, "Kaine Embraces Early Education Suggestions," *Richmond (VA) Times-Dispatch* (December 7, 2006), www2.timesdispatch.com (accessed Dec. 7, 2006).

33. Scott Lingamfelter, "More Big Government Is Not the Answer," *Gainesville (VA) Times* (December 20, 2006), www.gainesville-times.com (accessed Dec. 22, 2006).

34. Matt Deegan, "Kaine Officials Tout Benefits of Pre-K Plan," *Charlottesville Daily Progress* (December 19, 2006).

35. Warren Fiske and Christina Nuckols, "Senate and House Panels Release Competing Budgets," *Hampton Roads Virginian-Pilot* (February 2, 2007); Tim Craig, "Kaine Trims Pre-K Proposal," *Washington Post* (August 17, 2007), B1.

36. Jacqueline Reis, "Pre-K Backers Plan Bill's Revival in 2007," *Worcester (MA) Telegram and Gazette* (August 8, 2006).

37. Jim Hampton, "How Florida's Voters Enacted UPK When Their Legislature Wouldn't," Foundation for Child Development (2003), 7, www.ffcd.org (accessed October 27, 2003).

38. Florida House of Representatives, H.B. 821 (2004), www.myfloridahouse.gov/bills_detail.aspx?Id=13908 (accessed November 2, 2004).

39. Anonymous subject, interview with author, Washington, D.C., February 19, 2004; Gene Maeroff, *Building Blocks: Making Children Successful in the Early Years of School* (New York: Palgrave Macmillan, 2006), 39.

40. Gov. Jeb Bush, veto message (July 9, 2004), www.upkflorida.org/index.cfm?Section=GovLeg&Page=GovVeto (accessed July 28, 2004).

41. In the state's poorer counties, enrollment was lower than this statewide average; Rachel Simmonsen, "Schools to Seek Money to Bus Poor Pre-K Students," *Palm Beach Post* (August 22, 2006), 3B. Note that a different newspaper reported a higher percentage of statewide enrollment: 48.9 percent of four-year-olds. Leslie Postal, "Pre-K Program Slights State's Poor, Many Say," *Orlando Sentinel* (April 18, 2006), A1.

42. Comments of Libby Doggett, "Effective Advocacy in the Pre-K Movement."

43. Kastner, "Kaine Embraces Early Education Suggestions."

44. Jeff Solochek, "State Pre-K Program Under Fire," *St. Petersburg Times* (October 25, 2006), 1B.

45. W. Steven Barnett, Jason Hustedt, Allison Friedman, Judi Stevenson Boyd, and Pat Ainsworth, *The State of Preschool 2007: State Preschool Yearbook* (New Brunswick, N.J.: National Institute of Early Education Research, Rutgers University, 2008), 19–20.

46. W. Steven Barnett, Jason Hustedt, Kenneth Robin, and Karen Schulman, *The State of Preschool: 2005 State Preschool Yearbook* (New Brunswick, N.J.: National Institute for Early Education Research, Rutgers University, 2006), 23.

47. Southern Regional Education Board, "Ready to Start: Ensuring High-quality Pre-kindergarten in SREB States" (2007), www.sreb.org (accessed November 1, 2007).

48. Pre-K Now, *Votes Count: Legislative Action on Pre-K Fiscal Year 2008* (Washington, D.C.: Pre-K Now, 2007), and Pre-K Now, *Votes Count: Legislative Action on Pre-K Fiscal Year 2007* (Washington, D.C.: Pre-K Now, 2006).

49. Pre-K Now, *Votes Count: Legislative Action on Pre-K, Fiscal Year 2006* (Washington, D.C.: Pre-K Now, 2006), 6; Pre-K Now, *Votes Count: Legislative Action on Pre-K, Fiscal Year 2008*, 6; Heather Wecsler, "Pre-Kindergarten Listed with Best in Nation," *Little Rock (AK) Democrat-Gazette* (March 14, 2007).

50. Julia Silverman, "Universal Preschool Trend Has Critics," *Seattle Times* (December 19, 2005), http://community.seattletimes.nwsource.com/archive/?date=20051219&slug =preschool19m (accessed Dec. 19, 2005).

51. Comments of State Senator Leticia Van de Putte, "Effective Advocacy in the Pre-K Movement," Pre-K Now, *Pre-K Post* (June 7, 2006).

52. Susan Urahn and Sara Watson, "The Pew Charitable Trusts Advancing Quality Pre-K for All: Five Years Later," Pew Charitable Trusts (2006), 5, www.pewtrusts.org (accessed December 21, 2006).

53. Education Sector, "Eight for 2008: Education Ideas for the Next President" (2007), www.educationsector.org (accessed February 26, 2007).

54. Pre-K Now, *Pre-K Post* (February 26, 2007).

55. Theda Skocpol, *Social Policy in the United States: Future Possibilities in Historical Perspective* (Princeton, N.J.: Princeton University Press, 1995), 260.

56. Theda Skocpol, "The Narrow Vision of Today's Experts on Social Policy," Chronicle of Higher Education (April 15, 1992), B1. See also Jerry Cates, *Insuring Inequality: Administrative Leadership in Social Security, 1935–54* (Ann Arbor: University of Michigan Press, 1983).

57. Edward Berkowitz, *America's Welfare State: From Roosevelt to Reagan* (Baltimore: Johns Hopkins University Press, 1991), 82.

58. Carl Kaestle, "Common Schools Before the 'Common School Revival': New York Schooling in the 1790s," *History of Education Quarterly* 12, no. 4 (winter 1972): 465.

59. William Reese, *America's Public Schools: From the Common School to "No Child Left Behind"* (Baltimore: Johns Hopkins University Press, 2005), 11, 28.

60. Tina Sheller, "The Origins of Public Education in Baltimore, 1825–1829," *History of Education Quarterly* 22, no. 1 (1982): 23–44; quotation, 34.

61. Carl Kaestle, *Pillars of the Republic: Common Schools and American Society, 1780–1860* (New York: Hill and Wang, 1983), 150.

62. Quoted in Sheller, "Origins of Public Education in Baltimore," 26.

63. Quoted in Reese, *America's Public Schools*, 23.

64. Sheller, "Origins of Public Education in Baltimore," 25.

65. Quoted in Chris Lubienski, "Redefining 'Public' Education: Charter Schools, Common Schools, and the Rhetoric of Reform," *Teachers College Record* 103 (2001): 649.

66. Reese, *America's Public Schools*, 62.

67. Alice Kessler-Harris, "In the Nation's Image: The Gendered Limits of Social Citizenship in the Depression Era," *Journal of American History* 86, no. 3 (1999): 1252, 1263.

Chapter 7

1. Ed Zigler, interview with author, New Haven, December 11, 2000.

2. Carrie Smith, "Public Preschool Would Be Costly," *Charleston Daily Mail* (March 5, 2002), 1A; Pre-K Now, "State Profile: West Virginia" (2007), www.preknow.org/resource/profiles/westvirginia.cfm (accessed July 29, 2007).

3. Ruby Takanishi, interview with author, New York City, October 23, 2003; Edward Zigler, interview with author, New Haven, January 6, 2004; Edward Zigler, "School Should Begin at Age Three Years for American Children," *Developmental and Behavioral Pediatrics* 19, no. 1 (1998): 39.

4. New Commission on the Skills of the American Workforce, *Tough Choices or Tough Times* (2006), www.skillscommission.org (accessed February 21, 2007); Comments of Marc Tucker and Sharon Lynn Kagan, "Moving Forward: The Role of Pre-K in Education Reform," Pre-K Now national conference call (February 21, 2007), www.preknow.org/advocate/confcalls/index.cfm (accessed on February 21, 2007).

5. National Association of Elementary School Principals, *Leading Early Childhood Learning Communities: What Principals Should Know and Be Able to Do* (2005), www.naesp.org (accessed May 26, 2005); Gene Maeroff, *Building Blocks: Making Children Successful in the Early Years of School* (New York: Palgrave Macmillan, 2006).

6. Donna Bryant, Dick Clifford, Diane Early, and Lloyd Little, "NCEDL Pre-kindergarten Study," *Early Developments: FPG Child Development Institute* 9, no. 1 (2005: 4, 19, www.fpg.unc.edu/~firstschool/index.cfm (accessed April 25, 2005).

7. Comments of Sara Watson, "Restructuring Early Childhood Education: Fifth Annual Symposium of the Foundation for Child Development," Foundation for Child Development (2002), 54, www.ffcd.org (accessed September 18, 2003).

8. Matthew Brouillette, "Waiting at the Cradle," *Pittsburgh Post-Gazette* (October 16, 2002), A15.

9. Maeroff, *Building Blocks*, 40.

10. Edward Zigler, interview, January 6, 2004.

11. Bruce Fuller, *Standardized Childhood: The Political and Cultural Struggle over Early Education* (Stanford, Calif.: Stanford University Press: 2007), 276.

12. Comments of Karen Hill-Scott, "Restructuring Early Childhood Education," 23.

13. Comments of Margaret Blood, "Restructuring Early Childhood Education," 54–55.

14. Anthony Raden, *Universal Pre-kindergarten in Georgia: A Case Study of Georgia's Lottery-funded Pre-K Program,* Foundation for Child Development (1999), 30–32, www. ffcd.org (accessed April 18, 2000).

15. Early Childhood Strategic Group, *Planning for Community-based Early Childhood Education: A Guide for New York City's Universal Pre-K Advisory Boards* (New York: Child Care, Inc. (1998), 30; New York City Independent Budget Office, *Implementing Universal Pre-kindergarten in New York City* (1999), www.ibo.nyc.ny.us/iboreports/ PreKind.pdf (accessed October 30, 2003).

16. Betty Holcomb, "A Diverse System Delivers for Pre-K: Lessons Learned in New York State," Pre-K Now (2006), www.preknow.org (accessed July 14, 2006).

17. Rachel Schumacher, Katie Hamm, and Danielle Ewen, "Making Pre-kindergarten Work for Low-income Working Families," Center for Law and Social Policy (2007), www.clasp.org (accessed September 10, 2007).

18. Gregory Potts, "Schools Add Pre-kindergarten Programs," *Oklahoma City Oklahoman* (February 10, 2003), 35; Carla Hinton, "School Programs for Four-year-olds Remain Popular," *Oklahoma City Oklahoman* (April 28, 2002); "Something Old, Something New," *Gallery,* Oklahoma Educational Television Authority (aired February 2, 2004).

19. Jason Embry, "Public-Private Preschool Gaining Steam in Texas," *Austin American-Statesman* (March 5, 2007), A1; Beverly Carroll, "Demand for Pre-K Outpacing Supply," *Chattanooga Times Free Press* (February 15, 2007).

20. Maeroff, *Building Blocks,* 39.

21. Raden, *Universal Pre-kindergarten in Georgia,* 28, 32.

22. Comments of Kathy Jones, "School Funding Formula" (Trust for Early Education conference call, September 15, 2004).

23. Anne Mitchell, *Implementing Universal Pre-kindergarten in New York: Blended Funding and Other Financial Considerations,* Families and Work Institute (1998), 1, www.ecsgnyc.org/docs/blendedfunding.pdf (accessed October 30, 2003).

24. Holcomb, " Diverse System Delivers for Pre-K."

25. Fuller, *Standardized Childhood,* 158–64, 187.

26. Janet Hansen, telephone interview with author, September 9, 2003.

27. Karen Schimke, telephone interview with author, January 9, 2004.

28. Comments of Kathy Jones, "School Funding Formula."

29. Kristi Lekies, Taryn Morrisey, and Mon Cochran, "Raising All Boats: Community-based Programs as Partners in Universal Pre-kindergarten," Cornell Early Childhood Program (2004), www.human.cornell.edu/che/HD/CECP (accessed November 29, 2005).

30. Kristi Lekies, Emma Heitzman, and Mon Cochran, "Early Care for Infants and Toddlers: Examining the Broader Impacts of Universal Pre-kindergarten," Cornell Early

Childhood Program (2001), www.human.cornell.edu/hd/cecp (accessed November 24, 2002); Karen Schimke, interview. The phrase "lift all boats" is also found in Pamela Emanoil, "Early Education for New York Children," *Human Ecology* 29, no. 1 (2001): 9–11.

31. Comments of Jim Robertson, background material for Roger Neugebauer, "Update on Child Care in the Public Schools," *Child Care Information Exchange* (March 2003), www.childcareexchange.com (accessed October 1, 200). For similar comments, see Charles Paprocki and Nancy Kolben, *The Universal Pre-kindergarten Program in Community School District Eleven, New York City* (New York: Early Childhood Strategic Group, 2002), 14.

32. Dan Bellm, Alice Burton, Marcy Whitebook, Linda Broatch, and Marci Young, "Inside the Pre-K Classroom: A Study of Staffing and Stability in State-funded Pre-kindergarten Programs," Center for the Child Care Workforce (2002), 25, www.ccw.org/pubs/ccw_prek_10.4.02.pdf (accessed January 19, 2005).

33. Jason Sabo, "Schoolhouses or Warehouses?" *Austin Business Journal* (October 5, 2007).

34. Anonymous, interview with author, Washington, D.C., February 19, 2004.

35. Joan Lombardi, Julie Cohen, and Helene Stebbins, "Building Bridges from Pre-kindergarten to Infants and Toddlers: A Preliminary Look at Issues in Four States," Zero To Three (2004), www.zerotothree.org/policy (accessed July 28, 2004).

36. Raden, *Universal Pre-kindergarten in Georgia,* 33, 48.

37. Comments of Cynthia Rice, "Mixed Systems" (Trust for Early Education conference call, July 14, 2004).

38. Gordon MacInnes, *In Plain Sight: Simple, Difficult Lessons from New Jersey's Expensive Effort to Close the Achievement Gap* (New York: Century Foundation Press, 2009), 49–51.

39. Comments of Cynthia Rice, "Mixed Systems"; Voices for America's Children, "The Movement Towards Universal Pre-K" (November 2004), www.voicesforamericaschildren.org (accessed November 12, 2004).

40. Early Childhood Strategic Group, *New Partnerships for Universal Pre-kindergarten: Implementation Survey, Year One* (New York: Child Care, Inc., 1999), 1; Karen Schimke, interview.

41. Lekies et al., "Early Care for Infants and Toddlers."

42. Holcomb, "Diverse System Delivers for Pre-K," 6–8; Anthea McLaughlin, *New York City UPK Advisory Boards: Making a Difference in Early Care and Education* (New York: Early Childhood Strategic Group, 2001).

43. Anne Mitchell, interview with author, Climax, N.Y., February 12, 2004.

44. Karen Schulman, Helen Blank, and Danielle Ewen, *Seeds of Success: State Pre-kindergarten Initiatives, 1998–1999* (Washington, D.C.: Children's Defense Fund, 1999), 160.

45. Rachel Christina and JoVictoria Nicholson-Goodman, "Going to Scale with High-quality Early Education: Choices and Consequences in Universal Pre-Kindergarten Efforts," RAND Corporation (2005), 64, www.rand.org (accessed March 1, 2006).

46. Nancy Kolben and Charles Paprocki, *Next Steps in Blended Funding: A Policy Recommendation* (New York: Early Childhood Strategic Group, 2001), 12, 21.

47. Larry Hanover, "Preschools Still in Financial Daze," *Trenton (NJ) Times* (July 17, 2005), www.nj.com/times (accessed July 21, 2005).

48. Holcomb, "Diverse System Delivers for Pre-K," 13; comments of Cynthia Rice, "Mixed Systems."

49. Holcomb, "Diverse System Delivers for Pre-K," 9.

50. Bertha Campbell, interview by Anne Mitchell, March 10, 2004; Anne Mitchell, interview.

51. Marilyn Brown, "State May Give Pre-K Star Treatment," *Tampa Tribune* (September 17, 2006), 1.

52. Comments of Libby Doggett, "Effective Advocacy in the Pre-K Movement," Pre-K Now satellite conference (September 23, 2006), www.preknow.org/advocate/conference2006.effectiveadvocacy.com (accessed September 26, 2006).

53. Anonymous official, telephone interview with author, April 19, 2004.

54. MacInnes, *In Plain Sight*, 46–47; W. Steven Barnett, Jason Hustedt, Kenneth Robin, and Karen Schulman, *The State of Preschool: 2004 State Preschool Yearbook* (New Brunswick, N.J.: National Institute for Early Education Research, Rutgers University, 2004), 49.

Chapter 8

1. Gordon MacInnes, *In Plain Sight: Simple, Difficult Lessons from New Jersey's Expensive Effort to Close the Achievement Gap* (New York: Century Foundation Press, 2009), 44.

2. Edward Zigler, Walter Gilliam, and Stephanie Jones, *A Vision for Universal Preschool Education* (Cambridge: Cambridge University Press, 2006), 111.

3. Stacie Goffin and Valora Washington, *Ready or Not: Leadership Choices in Early Care and Education* (New York: Teachers College Press, 2007), 39.

4. Stephen Herzenberg, Mark Price, and David Bradley, "Losing Ground in Early Childhood Education: Declining Workforce Qualifications in an Expanding Industry, 1979–2004," Economic Policy Institute (2005), www.earlychildhoodworkforce.com (accessed September 16, 2005); Dan Bellm and Marcy Whitebook, "Roots of Decline: How Government Policy Has De-educated Teachers of Young Children," University of California, Berkeley, Center for the Study of Child Care Employment (2006), www.ilr.berkeley.edu/cscce (accessed March 9, 2007); National Research Council, *Eager to Learn: Educating Our Preschoolers* (Washington, D.C.: National Academy Press, 2000); Kelly Maxwell and Richard Clifford, "Professional Development Issues in Universal Pre-kindergarten," in Zigler et al., *Vision for Universal Preschool Education*, 174, 180.

5. Deborah Chalfie, Helen Blank, and Joan Entmacher, "Getting Organized: Unionizing Home-based Child Care Providers," National Women's Law Center (2007), 6, www.nwlc.org (accessed March 9, 2007).

6. Marcy Whitebook, *Working for Worthy Wages: The Child Care Compensation Movement, 1970–2001* (New York: Foundation for Child Development, 2001).

7. National Head Start Association, "Issue Brief: Head Start Teacher Qualifications" (2007), www.nhsa.org/download/advocacy/fact/HSTeacher.pdf (accessed September 24, 2007).

8. Quoted in Michael Sadowski, "Degrees of Improvement: States Push to Reverse the Decline in Preschool Teachers' Qualifications," *Harvard Education Letter* 22, no. 1 (January/February 2006): 4.

9. Lola Alapo, "Bredesen Sees Hitch to Tax Hike," *Knoxville News-Sentinel* (March 23, 2007).

10. Maxwell and Clifford, "Professional Development Issues in Universal Pre-kindergarten," 180; comments of Margaret Blood, in "Focus on Early Childhood Education: Voices from the Field," *Harvard Education Letter* 23, no. 1 (January/February 2007), www.hepg.org/hel (accessed Jan. 17. 2007).

11. Comments of Marcy Whitebook, "Why BA Teachers?" (Trust for Early Education conference call, October 13, 2004); California Tomorrow, "Getting Ready for Quality: The Critical Importance of Developing and Supporting a Skilled, Ethnically and Linguistically Diverse Early Childhood Work Force" (2006), 13, www.californiatomorrow.org (accessed April 4, 2006).

12. Marcy Whitebrook, "Bachelor's Degrees Are Best: Higher Qualifications for Pre-kindergarten Teachers Lead to Better Learning Environments for Children," Trust for Early Education (2003), www.tee.org (accessed September 29, 2003). See also Marcy Whitebook, *Early Education Quality: Higher Teacher Qualifications for Better Learning*, www.iir.berkeley.edu/cscce (accessed February 15, 2005).

13. Bruce Fuller, *Standardized Childhood: the Political and Cultural Struggle over Early Education* (Stanford, Calif.: Stanford University Press, 2007), 219; Donna Bryant, Dick Clifford, Diane Early, and Lloyd Little, "NCEDL Pre-kindergarten Study," *Early Developments: FPG Child Development Institute* 9, no. 1 (2005): 19; Diane Early et al., "Are Teachers' Education, Major, and Credentials Related to Classroom Quality and Children's Academic Gains in Pre-Kindergarten?" *Early Childhood Research Quarterly* 21, no. 2 (2006): 174–95.

14. Bryant et al., "NCEDL Pre-kindergarten Study," 25–27.

15. Robert Pianta, "Preschool is School, Sometimes," *Education Next* 7, no. 1 (Winter 2007): 44–49.

16. Linda Jacobson, "Scholars Split on Pre-K Teachers with B.A.s," *Education Week* (March 28, 2007), 1, 13.

17. Matthew Pinzur, "Pre-K Plan at Risk of Veto," *Miami Herald* (March 23, 2004), 1B; Joe Follick. "State Pre-K Program May Begin Next Fall," *Lakeland (FL) Ledger* (December 1, 2004), B1.

18. Florida House of Representatives (Education Council) Staff Analysis of HB 1A, www.myfloridahouse.gov (accessed January 3, 2005); U.S. Government Accountability Office, *Pre-kindergarten: Four Selected States Expanded Access by Relying on Schools and Existing Providers of Early Education and Care to Provide Services* (2004), 18, www.gao.gov (accessed September 20, 2004).

19. Cynthia Rice, presentation at the annual meeting of the National Association for the Education of Young Children, New York City, November 20, 2002.

20. Rachel Schumacher, Kate Irish, and Joan Lombardi, *Meeting Great Expectations: Integrating Early Childhood Program Standards in Child Care,* Center for Law and Social Policy (2003), 21, www.clasp.org (accessed October 28, 2003); Rachel Christina and JoVictoria Nicholson-Goodman, "Going to Scale with High-quality Early Education: Choices and Consequences in Universal Pre-kindergarten Efforts," RAND Corporation (2005), 13, www.rand.org (accessed March 1, 2006); Emily Bazelon, "Sharing at the Sand Table 101," *Slate* (October 16, 2006), www.slate.com/id/2151416/ (accessed October 18, 2006).

21. Zigler et al., *Vision for Universal Preschool Education,* 113.

22. Walter Gilliam and Crista Marchesseault, "Who's Teaching Our Youngest Students?" National Institute for Early Education Research (2005), http://nieer.org (accessed September 19, 2005).

23. Comments of Marcy Whitebook, "Why BA Teachers?"

24. For example, in the New York City districts in 1999–2000, the percent of classrooms with certified teachers was 91 percent in district sites, 68 percent in community-based sites, and 44 percent in Head Start sites. Kristi Lekies, Emma Heitzman, and Mon Cochran, *Early Care for Infants and Toddlers: Examining the Broader Impacts of Universal Pre-kindergarten* (Ithaca, N.Y.: Cornell Early Childhood Program, 2001), 29.

25. Dan Bellm, Alice Burton, Marcy Whitebook, Linda Broatch, and Marci Young, "Inside the Pre-K Classroom: A Study of Staffing and Stability in State-funded Pre-kindergarten Programs," Center for the Child Care Workforce (2002), 7–8, 23, www.ccw.org/pubs/ccw_prek_10.4.02.pdf (accessed January 19, 2005).

26. Nancy Kolben and Charles Paprocki, *Next Steps in Blended Funding: A Policy Recommendation* (New York: Early Childhood Strategic Group, 2001), 12, 21.

27. Betty Holcomb, "A Diverse System Delivers for Pre-K: Lessons Learned in New York State," Pre-K Now (2006), 12, www.preknow.org (accessed July 14, 2006).

28. Comments of Cynthia Rice, "Mixed Systems" (Trust for Early Education conference call, July 14, 2004); Debra Ackerman, "Getting Teachers from Here to There: Examining Issues Related to an Early Care and Education Teacher Policy," *Early Childhood Research and Practice* 7, no. 1 (Spring 2005) http://ecrp.uiuc.edu/v7n1/ackerman.html (accessed April 28, 2006).

29. Sharon Ryan and Debra Ackerman, "Using Pressure and Support to Create a Qualified Workforce," *Education Policy Analysis Archives* 13, no. 23 (March 30, 2005), 11.

30. Christina and Nicholson-Goodman, "Going to Scale with High-quality Early Education," 66.

31. Deborah Stipek, "Head Start: Can't We Have Our Cake and Eat It Too?" *Education Week* (May 5, 2004), 43.

32. National Research Council, *Eager to Learn.*

33. Fuller, *Standardized Childhood,* 119–22, 159.

34. Fuller, *Standardized Childhood,* 84–89.

35. National Association for the Education of Young Children and National Association of Early Childhood Specialists in State Departments of Education, "Where We Stand on Curriculum, Assessment, and Program Evaluation" (2003), http://naecs.crc.uiuc.edu/position/standlcurrass.pdf (accessed August 10, 2007). See also Ann Epstein et al., "Preschool

Assessment: A Guide to Developing a Balanced Approach," *Preschool Policy Matters* (National Institute for Early Education Research) 7 (July 2004): 1–12.

36. Valerie Strauss, "Preschoolers' Test May Be Suspended," *Washington Post* (March 18, 2007), A9; Committee on Developmental Outcomes and Assessments for Young Children, "Early Childhood Assessment: Why, What, and How" (National Academies, 2008), www.bocyf.org/head_start.html (accessed May 21, 2008).

37. Catherine Scott-Little, Sharon Lynn Kagan, and Victoria Stebbins Frelow, "Standards for Preschool Children's Learning and Development: Who Has Standards, How Were They Developed, and How Are They Used?" SERVE Center (2003), www.serve.org/ELO/research.html (accessed July 9, 2003); Elena Bodrova, Deborah Leong, and Rima Shore, "Child Outcome Standards in Pre-K Programs," *Preschool Policy Matters* (National Institute for Early Education Research) 5 (March 2004): 1–10; National Association for the Education of Young Children and National Association of Early Childhood Specialists in State Departments of Education, *Early Learning Standards: Creating the Conditions for Success* (2002), http://naecs.crc.uiuc.edu/position/creating_conditions.html (accessed March 22, 2004).

38. Deborah Stipek, "Early Childhood Education at a Crossroads," *Harvard Education Letter* 21, no. 4 (July/August 2005), www.hepg.org/hel/article/288 (accessed July 8, 2005).

39. Christopher Henrich and Ramona Blackman-Jones, "Parent Involvement in Preschool," in Zigler et al., *Vision for Universal Preschool Education*, 156.

40. Lynda Ames and Jeanne Ellsworth, *Women Reformed, Women Empowered: Poor Mothers and the Endangered Promise of Head Start* (Philadelphia: Temple University Press, 1997), and Peggy Sissel, *Staff, Parents, and Politics in Head Start* (New York: Falmer Press, 2000), both find that parent involvement in program governance is more symbolic than substantive.

41. Arthur Reynolds, Judy Temple, Dylan Robertson, and Emily Mann, "Age 21 Cost-benefit Analysis of the Title I Chicago Child-parent Centers," *Educational Evaluation and Policy Analysis* 24, no. 4 (2002): 267–303; Arthur Reynolds, Judy Temple, Suh-Ruu Ou, Dylan Roberton, Joshua Mersky, James Topitzes, and Michael Niles, "Effects of a School-based, Early Childhood Intervention on Adult Health and Well-Being," *Archives of Pediatric and Adolescent Medicine* 161, no. 8 (2007 August): 730–39.

42. Fuller, *Standardized Childhood*, 198.

43. National Association for the Education of Young Children, "NAEYC Early Childhood Program Standards" (2007), www.naeyc.org/academy/standards/ (accessed August 14, 2007).

44. William Cutler, *Parents and Schools: The 150-Year Struggle for Control in American Education* (Chicago: University of Chicago Press, 2000), 2.

45. Annette Lareau, "Social Class Differences in Family School Relationships: The Importance of Cultural Capital," *Sociology of Education* 60 (April 1987): 73–85; Elizabeth Graue, *Ready for What? Constructing Meanings of Readiness for Kindergarten* (Albany: State University of New York Press, 1993).

46. Fuller, *Standardized Childhood*, 274.

47. Quoted in Barbara Beatty, *Preschool Education in America: The Culture of Young Children from the Colonial Era to the Present* (New Haven, Conn.: Yale University Press, 1995), 124.

48. Pre-K Now, "Tour a Preschool Classroom," www.preknow.org/resource (accessed February 25, 2008).

49. Pre-K Now has developed a list of suggestions on engaging parents that does incorporate some of these concerns, but it is not highlighted in the sections of its website aimed at policymakers and advocates.

Conclusion

1. Sam Dillon, "Obama Pledge Stirs Hope in Early Education," *New York Times* (December 17, 2008), A1.

2. James Oliphant, "Senators Praise Education Pick Duncan," *Chicago Tribune* (January 13, 2009).

3. Sara Mead, "Early Education Is First Pillar in President's Education Plan," *Early Ed Watch Blog* (March 10, 2009), www.newamerica.net/blog/earlyed-watch/2009/early education-first-pillar-presidents-education-plan-10551 (accessed March 10, 2009); Christina Samuels, "Stimulus Providing Big Funding Boost for Early Childhood," *Education Week* (April 1, 2009), 8.

4. Comments of Lana Seivers, "Effective Advocacy in the Pre-K Movement," Pre-K Now satellite conference (September 23, 2006) www.preknow.org/advocate/conference2006/ effectiveadvocacy.cfm (accessed September 30, 2006).

5. Ron Barnett, "Furman Study: Three Steps Would Help Education," *Greenville (SC) News* (September 21, 2007), A2.

6. Comments of Marc Tucker, "Moving Forward: The Role of Pre-K in Education Reform," Pre-K Now national conference call (February 21, 2007) www.preknow.org/ advocate/confcalls/index.cfm (accessed February 21, 2007); New Commission on the Skills of the American Workforce, *Tough Choices or Tough Times* (2006), www.skillscommission.org/report.htm (accessed December 17, 2008).

7. Richard Rothstein, *Class and Schools: Using Social, Economic, and Educational Reform to Close the Black-white Achievement Gap* (New York: Teachers College Press, 2004), 139–42; Jonathan Kozol, "Segregation and Its Calamitous Effects on America's 'Apartheid' Schools," *Voices in Urban Education* (Annenberg Institute for School Reform), no. 10 (winter 2006): 27; see also Kozol, *Shame of the Nation: The Restoration of Apartheid Schooling in America* (New York: Crown, 2005).

8. David Leonhardt, "Economix: What $1.2 Trillion Can Buy," *New York Times* (January 17, 2007), C1.

9. Deborah Solomon, "As States Tackle Poverty, Preschool Gets High Marks," *Wall Street Journal* (August 9, 2007), A1.

10. E. J. Dionne, "Rob Reiner: Ceaseless in California," *Washington Post* (March 3, 2006), A17.

11. Janet Hansen, telephone interview with author, September 9, 2003.

12. Benton Foundation, "Effective Language for Discussing Early Childhood Education and Policy" (Washington, D.C.: 1998), www.benton.org (accessed February 23, 2004).

13. Pre-K Now, "The ABCs of Pre-K," http://pre-know.org/resource/abc/prekvspreschool.cfm (accessed August 12, 2007).

14. Quoted in David Kirp, *The Sandbox Investment: The Preschool Movement and Kids-first Politics* (Cambridge, Mass.: Harvard University Press, 2007), 174.

15. Quoted in Kirp, *Sandbox Investment*, 152.

16. Leroy Dangeau, "An Early Years Strategy: Start Where We Can Win," *Education Week* (March 1, 2006), 32.

17. Ounce of Prevention Fund, *Ready for School: The Case for Including Babies and Toddlers as We Expand Preschool Opportunities* (2003), www.ounceofprevention.org (accessed September 12, 2005).

18. Nancy Kolben, presentation at the annual meeting of the National Association for the Education of Young Children, New York City, November 20, 2002; Center for Early Care and Education, *New York's Action Plan for Young Children and Families* (2005), www.winningbeginningny.org (accessed September 1, 2005).

19. Carolyn Goossen, "Preschool in L.A. County: A Multilingual Universal Approach," Pacific News Service (March 9, 2006), http://news.pacificnews.org (accessed March 10, 2006); Edward Zigler, Walter Gilliam, and Stephanie Jones, *A Vision for Universal Preschool Education* (Cambridge: Cambridge University Press, 2006), 247; Susan Urahn, telephone interview with author, October 2, 2003.

20. Greg Duncan, Jens Ludwig, and Katherine Magnuson, "Reducing Poverty through Preschool Interventions," *Future of Children* 17, no. 2 (fall 2007): 143–60.

21. Jack Shonkoff and Deborah Phillips, *From Neurons to Neighborhoods: The Science of Early Child Development* (Washington, D.C: National Academy Press, 2000), 372.

22. Edith Grotberg, "A Tribute to the Consortium," in *As the Twig Is Bent... Lasting Effects of Preschool Programs*, ed. Consortium for Longitudinal Studies (Hillsdale, N.J.: Erlbaum, 1983), xii.

23. Edward Zigler, Sally Styfco, and Elizabeth Gilman, "The National Head Start Program for Disadvantaged Preschoolers," in *Head Start and Beyond: A National Plan for Extended Childhood Intervention*, ed. Edward Zigler and Sally Styfco (New Haven: Yale University Press, 1993), 26; Ramey quoted in Constance Holden, "Head Start Enters Adulthood," *Science* 247, no. 4949 (1990): 1402.

24. Janet Currie, *Early Childhood Intervention Programs: What Do We Know?* (Chicago: Joint Center for Poverty Research, 2000), 24.

25. Jeanne Brooks-Gunn, "Do You Believe in Magic? What We Can Expect from Early Childhood Intervention Programs," *Social Policy Report: A Publication of the Society for Research in Child Development* 17, no. 1 (2003): 9.

26. Ruby Takanishi, interview with author, New York City, October 23, 2003.

27. Larry Cuban, "Why Some Reforms Last: The Case of the Kindergarten," *American Journal of Education* 100, no. 2 (1992): 175–76; Barbara Beatty, *Preschool Education in*

America: The Culture of Young Children from the Colonial Era to the Present (New Haven, Conn.: Yale University Press, 1995), 74, 88.

28. Cuban, "Why Some Reforms Last," 191; Beatty, *Preschool Education*, 127–30.

29. Gareth Davies, *See Government Grow: Education Politics from Johnson to Reagan* (Lawrence: University Press of Kansas, 2007), 280.

30. Zigler et al., " National Head Start Program," 18.

31. Delaine Eastin, quoted in Fuller, *Standardized Childhood*, 153; Cary Clack, "Pre-K Cuts Will Cost Us in the Long Run," *San Antonio Express-News* (February 5, 2007), 1C; Comments of Rob Reiner, "Effective Advocacy in the Pre-K Movement."

32. Tennessee Department of Education, "Pre-K in Tennessee," presentation to Senate Education Committee (March 2006), www.prekfortn.com/documents/SenateEdPresentation3–28–06.pdf (accessed November 2, 2006).

33. Kirp, *Sandbox Investment*, 172.

34. Harvard University Center on the Developing Child, "A Science-based Framework for Early Childhood Policy" (2007), www.developingchild.harvard.edu/ (accessed February 22, 2008).

35. Kirp, *Sandbox Investment*, 268.

36. Cynthia Rice, "Building Strong Rungs to Build Sturdy Ladders: The Status of Preschool–Third Grade Systems in New Jersey," Association for Children of New Jersey (2007), www.fcd-us.org/usr_doc/BuildingStrongRungs.pdf (accessed May 3, 2007).

37. Quoted in Betty Holcomb, *A Diverse System Delivers for Pre-K: Lessons Learned in New York State*, Pre-K Now (2006), 8, www.preknow.org (accessed July 14, 2006).

INDEX